Sky Trails & Pie Tales

An autobiographical memoir

Trev Turley

© Trev Turley 2022

All rights reserved. No part of this publication may be reproduced, stored in a retrieval system, or transmitted in any form, or by any means (electronic, mechanical, photocopying, recording or otherwise), without the prior permission of the publisher. Any person who does so may be liable to criminal prosecution and civil claims for damages.

The right of Trev Turley to be identified as author of this work has been asserted.

First published in 2022 by The Cherished Synapse

Printed and bound by 4edge Limited

Cover painting © PJ Crook

Cover design by Trev Turley

ISBN Number 978-1-3999-2654-6

This book is sold subject to the condition that it shall not be lent, resold, hired out or otherwise circulated without the publisher's express prior consent in any form of binding or cover, other than the original as herein published and without a similar condition being imposed on any subsequent purchaser, or bona-fide possessor.

Buy this online, or in person, as stocked at any reputable bookshop, or contact the author via contactbasstrev@aol.com

Salvo's & Say-So's:

'It is always interesting for one musician to read of the journey of another musician. Trev has delivered an entertaining and approachable insight into his experiences within the music industry and those he has met along the way. I'm sure this will be an enjoyable read for many.'
Dame Evelyn Glennie

'Musicians are never boring. Those blessed with the ability to do magical things with their voices and hands, who are accustomed to communicating inspiration and ideas, tend to be gifted raconteurs. Trev Turley is no exception. The veteran Midlands-born bass player has shared his talent with a wide range of artists and bands. The blues run blue in his veins. Now, he is sharing the stories. He turned up, played, saw, and kept the memories, stoking the top shelf of his mind until the time was right. Now here we are. He recounts a past thrillingly lived, letting slip a sharp wit. He infuses those memories with subtle humour and wisdom. He learned more than a thing or two along the way. We must never, they say, take a bassist for granted? Here is why.'
Lesley-Ann Jones – Author ('The Stone Age')

'In this era characterised by selfishness, laziness and a 'can't be bothered' mentality, Trev brings a passion and commitment to his music as he does to living his life. For those of us who feel the same way, we recognise a kindred spirit.'
John Altman - Composer

'Trev, for all the years of Crimsonising, thanks.'
Robert Fripp

'When I first met Trev at one of my 'private viewings' it was a case of mistaken identity. He was not, as I had thought, Trev the road manager for King Crimson, but Trev the bass player. Over time we've forged a touching friendship, entwined with a mutual appreciation for each other's creative talents. Thanks Trev.'
PJ Crook MBE

'Trev is a wonderfully collaborative musician, you instantly feel part of the team. He brings commitment and expertise to his wide variety of musical enterprises. A pleasure to work with.'
Amanda Lehmann

'Banded by a Birmingham and a Black Country heritage, we both simultaneously started our parallel musical journeys. We followed the path of gold. We burned bright, we got snuffed out, we smouldered. Still doing it.'
Tony Kelsey – 'Saving Grace'

'He knows what's what. A Machiavellian ambassador for the Bass, he was there when it all kicked off in the '70s and has been immersed in the throbbing underbelly of homegrown British blues and Prog Rock bands ever since. Without a doubt, it's a fractured musical colony that often devours the very talent it seeks to sustain but Trev's undying passion has never faltered and unlike so many musicians of the era, he is still standing. Over the years, it would have been impossible for a man of such ability and experience to avoid casting his penetrating gaze into corners both murky and pristine. Either way, what a tale he has to tell!'
Rod McRiven

Finally, relevant to pages twelve & fifteen:

'Hungry man, reach for the book: it is a weapon.'
Bertolt Brecht

About the author:

Born in the Midlands (West Bromwich) and a London resident since 1979, Trev Turley has been a musician on and off for over fifty years. Semi-professional for most and since 2015, professional. As with most semi-pro's a day job was essential and made the financial ends meet. His choice of instrument has been bass, the electric bass guitar and only the bass. A 'pure' bass player, influenced by many.

His other trade, call it a 'skill-set', is in design, ever the creative person from school days to current. He qualified as a Mechanical Designer/Engineer, designing products that no one will ever know about, all very 'Top Secret'. As for music, a complete and utter self-taught musician, with not one music lesson to his credit. (This didn't seem to stop him though.)

His love of drama, being a performer, was instilled in him at an early age at school 'Theatre Workshop'. As for art itself, this has been very much a subdued force. He can attribute a slow growing interest in art due to his wife Jill, but he has been known to produce the occasional pen and ink piece of artwork. Despite being encouraged, "You could paint/draw something like that" his brushes and pens have remained in the drawer. As for now, as it always has done, music in his life takes pride of place, precedence, whether it's performing it, recording it, composing it, or just plain listening to it.

Contents:

	Introduction	I
1	Prologue: A beginning	1
2	Ginger	25
3	Labyrinthus	39
4	Ferret	53
5	Still	65
6	Autumn	95
7	Nick and the Dogs	101
8	The Years In-Between	109
9	3am	123
10	Bare Bones Boogie Band (BBBB)	149
11	Malaya Blue & Band	171
12	Joe Anderton Band	189
13	Trev Turley & Friends (TT&F)	199
14	Fleeting Combinations & Odd Bob's	207
15	MoJo Preachers	213
16	Cherish Ever	233
17	Random Earth Project	267
18	Epilogue: What's Left/Next?	273
	Acknowledgements	285

Introduction

It was a Wednesday, the second of October 2013 about 5:45pm and I'd just pulled up and parked at Survival Studios in Acton, London. Wednesdays were band rehearsal night and as usual I was the first one there having driven the furthest from the East to the West. Survival was, as now closed and probably returned to its original function of a warehouse unit, a collection of ramshackle rehearsal studios, never finished, all plasterboard and acoustic insulation. They were cheap. I unloaded my gear, my guitar, exchanged brief words with Rob on the desk, nice bloke, and proceeded to meander down the tight and winding corridors to match the room number with the booking. I sat and waited for the others to arrive. They did. All at once, which I thought strange as it didn't match habit. I'm a great believer in a sixth sense, and I got that, that evening, you know when somethings up. Stilted unnatural conversation bore the bringer of something, of some announcement, something planned and obviously colluded, as this was. For the next two hours plus I pretty much said nothing, just absorbed the words, reflecting the incoming. As the evening wore on, I put my guitar back into its bed and left, but not without being forced into this ultimatum.

"A choice. I'm either no longer part of this band (that I sowed the first seed to form & create), so either sack me, or replace me, or find an acceptable solution, or I leave."

I walked out, drove home, and made a decision. This is just one of many stories atypical to the music business no matter at what level you play, not related to ability, your fame, or your standing; it comes with the territory. When I started to write this book I was advised by an old

Sky Trails & Pie Tales . . .

friend, a writer himself, amongst his many other talents; fine art painter, musician etc that 'Kiss & Tell' in a story, especially like this one here, sells. I could fill this book with many other stories like this, some that are funny, some that are libellous, some that cast dispersion over deluded reputations, some that make truths out of other folks lies. With this mantle hanging in its shadowy form throughout you'll just have to read the rest to see what unfolds. Depends very much on the day I write, the side of the bed I got out of and how much coffee has been consumed. There's a very famous quote about the music business by Hunter S. Thompson; "The music business is a cruel and shallow money trench, a long plastic hallway where thieves and pimps run free, and good men die like dogs. There's also a negative side." Over the fifty odd years I've seen and heard a fair share and can add my own to this, however, music has played a big part in my life and continues to do so, I just adapt, move on, but still enjoy. This is what 'Sky Trails & Pie Tales' is about; the joy, the hope, plus a living document to fifty odd years of my music making.

So why write this? My current age, as I write, dictates I'm no longer immortal. It all started back in the noughties. I thought I better write some of this down before the mind and the memories fade. It kind of was driven by family members receding from this world of ours as their memories disappeared. One, or two had 'living folders' which contained images and stories of their past to serve as memory joggers, or to rekindle those parts of the mind that needed it. I started mine earlier! As time has gone by, these facts have been embellished by my stories and events since 1968, with a few dim memories that precede added. Then I started to add in my take, my commentary, on subjects and technology of past times, we're talking from 1968 onwards here, pre internet, pre mobile phone, pre only a couple of channels on the TV, only four weekly papers to inform you of your music fix. Yes, I could put the record

Sky Trails & Pie Tales . . .

straight too, the dreaded 'Kiss & Tell' but I've tried desperately to remain on the moral high ground, that untouchable hill, avoid the 'naming and shaming', especially in my later years.

However, the content of a few notes, a few facts and dates became something more tangible, many more pages but never completed, until now. Back in late 2019 I had the (bright?) idea; wouldn't it be great to have a CD to accompany this book with a collection of songs that represent the bands I write about, a bit like 'Read & Hear', not 'Look & Learn', which was the so-called comic my parents bought me thinking it would be more in keeping with my 'education'. All I wanted was the Beano and be like the rest of the kids at school. The idea of the aural CD, with this book, soon manifested itself into what became my Legacy Album, 'Cherish Ever'. More of that later in the chapters that follow, but what I'd written up to 2019 served its purpose and was used as the primary source for the notes, background and stories for the 24-page booklet that accompanied 'Cherish Ever', the CD.

I've mentioned this so called 'Music Business'. It's changed drastically over the years. I'm of the view that at any point, from the first time you pick up, or play an instrument, or compose a piece and thus earn a crust, no matter how big, no matter how small, you are in the business, regardless; until then it remains a hobby, an expensive hobby at times too. Many go on and make successful careers, some become household names, some achieve 'Legendary Status', but most, like this author, was never going to achieve this; our dreams were 'Pie in the Sky' and we remained anonymous. I prefer it that way these days. For those that started in the era that I did the draw was mostly fame, notoriety, a confidence boost, to be in band, OK, maybe Sex & Drugs & Rock n' Roll too, but what a chosen grail, don't deny it! Throughout this book the words 'Pie' and 'Sky' can be used in many other connotations, and I do. Also,

Sky Trails & Pie Tales . . .

probably like many, I even had my own bible; first published in May 1974, Ian Hunter's (Lead singer for Mott the Hoople) 'Dairy of a Rock 'n' Roll Star'. My first edition was overly read into disintegration, smelt strongly of creosote and fell apart in the glove compartment of my van. (Creosote? Well, the old van I owned had leather seats and the driver's seat stitching came apart between the seat and the back support. With no money to replace the seat I found an empty creosote can in my dad's shed which was the size of an old oil can. This fitted perfectly under the driver's seat and the drivers rear end support was reinstated. Job done, or so I thought, until, after much sitting on it, it cracked, not badly, but enough for the inside of the van, me, and any contents to reek of newly coated garden fencing. Ian Hunter's book took on this odour like a sponge. Thankfully, as did Ian's paperback, the van fell apart, stopped working completely and I had to replace with a new one. I found it strange that my girlfriend quota fared better after I had cast the old van, with its creosote can, to that great scrap yard in the sky.)

What follows here, in hopefully and the best chronological order I can muster, is a documented history and associated stories of the bands I've played in, or those that I've had a fleeting association with and are indelibly linked to my story. As I've mentioned, I was never going to be radically famous, or well-known, but each step along the way might resonate with some of you who read this. Being in a band brings a bond that all musicians will understand, from the early days of 'all for one and one for all' to disintegration due to the dreaded blight of 'musical difference' and 'ego'. I've had a few of these over the years, but always try to learn to not make the same mistake twice; but must admit it's hard at times. Some mistakes I can attribute to as being mine! This book is also about growing up, having a dream, searching for the musical grail and just missing out, but making a lot of great music along the way all the same.

Sky Trails & Pie Tales . . .

The intention with 'Sky Trails & Pie Tales' is not to make it all about 'me', my story, however it is and hopefully can become a relatable vehicle with, by submission, yours too. I once worked with a colleague, in 'Day Job' mode, who was also a musician; more of that later; but he said that being a musician, no matter at what level, brings an experience, and stories, that are unique to this craft, very much a rollercoaster compared to the 'Flatline' that some others, or his best mate, in this instance, has/had; no names mentioned, bless. Most won't know the folks I write about, or mention, or have the same fondness as I do. Some are still long-time friends, some have come, and some have gone, but as Pete Brown and Piblokto's album title goes 'Things May Come and Things May Go but the Art School Dance Goes on Forever', so does my Art School Dance. For those of you who read this book and are involved in some way, either by name, named in here, or by proper association, then I hope it resonates even more with you. Some of this I couldn't have done without you, completely impossible and is still happening to this day, I thank you.

This book is about my musical heritage, plus with some observations along the way and maybe some 'kiss & tell', but you'll have to read it to find out. It's not about my life story, this is just the about the music, the creation of and of its influence in my life, all from the tips of my fingers, that's all, nothing more, nothing less. You won't find out about the day I was born, to whom and who my aunts and uncles were. My upbringing I've conveniently omitted, it was boring to me, and it'll be even more so to you, but woven in here you'll get a general idea, good or bad. All you read happened, is true, open and honest as the day I was born. The name dropping occurs as part of the story rather than the 'Big I Am' that I purport to be and is related purely by inclusion, as without I'd have to leave you all guessing. As regards names I have to mention that in one, or two instances I've omitted the name of the person to whom I refer, or at worst changed it, purely to save embarrassment on all fronts. Also, the stories, the real truths that have come to light over the years that can be deemed as 'Not Cricket' to either divulge, or regurgitate, I've left out. Those are mainly on libellous grounds and with insufficient evidence to stand its corner in court; I'm not either malicious, vindictive, or stupid. The rest are in here. Over the years there have been instances where I've been conned, a couple out of money, but I'm sure we all have, and I put it down to experience. Comes with the territory.

Hope you enjoy it, thanks for investing in a copy; it's made all the hours I've spent in typing it worthwhile. Big thanks to Jill, my wife, for the hours of silent support whilst I've tapped away. During the process of completing this and writing the new stuff, in 2022, I've also used and added in the pieces I started writing some ten years previous and some during this interim period. To me it's noticeable in style, the difference between new and old, you may not notice. In the end I decided to keep the bulk of the old writings as it was of the time and brought a certain panache, an innocent view maybe? I have edited some, amended the glaring mistakes, or removed the writing embarrassments, which is probably the major case. However, during these past ten years I feel I've developed, despite failing my English Language 'O' Level four times. I went from a complete failure to a sparkling Grade 2 at the fifth and final attempt; maybe I paid attention! In recent years writing for the Blues magazines has helped me no end. It was Paul Stiles, the now past, read retired, editor of Blues in Britain magazine that took me under his wing, gave me the opportunity, which helped to develop my confidence and style. Over these ten years I've written many an album review and gig review, plus the occasional feature length article cum interview. Most have been published, apart from a couple of reviews of past bands that I'd had association with, as after leaving either a member, or a manager, took offence to me reviewing their artiste's

Sky Trails & Pie Tales . . .

latest tome, especially, that for whatever reason, did not feature me. Two of these 'unpublished' reviews were quite glowing, probably more factual, but Paul's word was sacrosanct. One band missed out completely on a review in a worldwide publication and the associated PR it would have brought. One band didn't miss out as the request to cut, to pull the plug, was too late and slipped gracefully under the radar. Their manager has never spoken to me since. Each to their own, but as always, the Editor's word is final, I just wrote it and achieved the aim. It was a good review mind. As for 'Sky Trails and Pie Tales' I'm my own editor and can only read and re-read and get proof-read so many times such that I had to draw a line at some stage. As I pointed out to Ernie Sumner along the way (no relation to Sting, I don't think anyway) and following his fine advice, that no matter what, any author will be at the behest of those that like to find and point out errors, whether it's spelling, grammar, or content. I'll not be able to please everyone, but I'm pleased, so that will do. For those that do find any glaring errors I'll thank you in advance and my explanation is that it's 'Character', but the subconscious sin is lucid, deliberate and part of my so-called inner intended 'Character'.

When I first started to write this book, these were the first few words I wrote, the first paragraph. Look at it as an *alternative introduction* and I thought I'd include here as they go back some twelve to fifteen years and I've got quite attached to them since. I started with:

Before I lapse into the era of Saga holidays and my memory fades completely, I thought it's about time that I write all of this down, well at least the stuff I can remember. This is the story of my passion for music. A passion that has been with me for most of my life. A passion that has burned bright at times and almost fizzled out at others. A passion that grew up with me in the Midlands, during the late sixties and through the seventies. This is for me, my kids, Jill and anyone else brave enough to read it. Anyway, if it paints a picture of growing up, innocence and all the other stuff we think we are as a child, teenager etc, but now, in later life, look at it with a reverence, or relevance, or realisation of being, then at least it has served some purpose. This is a true story. A story about my single-minded attempt to break into the music business. No competitions here, where the final prize is fame and a record contract. A story of someone paying his dues along the way. A story where all the music played was live and real (no miming here) by real musicians, playing real instruments. A story where we learnt our craft, whether good or bad. It spans a generation where all the music is and was "Live". The records and songs taped were by original people. I had no record mogul interventions, no corporate image-makers, no people wishing to make a quick buck (some tried). A story of honesty, sweat, grief, pain, pleasure, highs, lows and above all passion.

With that succinctly out of the way, I can come to that point where I've sowed the seed, set the stage no less and chapter one beckons, where it all began for me, the how and the why. Read on and read number one.

1 Prologue: A beginning

Every musician has a beginning, a seed, a start. What was the first piece of music that each and every one of us ever heard? We all have them. Was it on the radio, on the television? Was it a live band, or an orchestra, or a solo singer? Was it from parents and family? Was it even an instrument, thrust into our hands? Then it develops, to cover influences; all of the above again. Some are by the individual's choice; some might be thrust on them. Music lessons? We all have the capacity to learn, but music is endless, from the cradle to the grave, never ending, always something new to learn, to develop, to play, to listen, to invent your own. We come into the world with the soft maternal sounds that birth brings. Some of us experience sounds in the womb with music played through the thin layer of skin and muscle, maybe giving those a head start, who knows? Then when we exit this world it's with the sound of music (not Julie Andrews, but one or two may choose this, not for me, please), these days often pre-chosen (pre-paid) before we enter our 'castle of care'. As those that file out, after our last curtain call, and parting shot, sombre thoughts are generally accompanied by a suitable piece of music to let the personal memories of the dead linger just that little bit longer. Music is all around us, all encompassing, but the musician is the one who chooses to create, rather than imbibe, a special mantle, a choosing no less. Over the years I've heard "You'll never give up, it's in your blood mate." so many times, it's become a musician's mantra. Music was there before our conception and it will remain long after our passing, some of us will even have our legacies played for time immemorial, with some of those, those that own our rights granted by death, will benefit long into their sunsets and their children's sunsets. So, what was my calling, my first piece of music? Frankly, I have no idea,

Sky Trails & Pie Tales . . .

no recollection. I know it was not one piece, one instant, but more of a slowly creeping pervasion.

I've left this chapter to write last, not chronological in process, in the vain hope that something might spark what kicked this all off as I've written the rest of the story. So far nothing has come to mind. The strains of music in the family unit were pretty non-existent. No radio, no record player; my parents had no record collection, but the car did have a radio. My dad used to play cricket for the company he worked for and I do recall having to listen to 'Sing Something Simple with Cliff Adams and the Cliff Adams Singers featuring Jack Emblow', on the way home most Sunday evenings. I can recall that bit with great ease, for some strange reason. Preceding this was 'Pick of the Pops' based on the current top twenty singles chart run down. The voice behind this was always Alan 'Fluff' Freeman. Sing Something Simple started in 1959 and 'Fluff' started broadcasting on the Top Twenty Show in 1961, so all of this ties in with my first musical exposures. For me there was no other voice on the radio other than Alan Freeman's, so 1961/62 was where it all started for me. As for which song, no recollection. It all depended on when the cricket finished as to how much of the Top Twenty I heard on the drive home. Bowled out early I'd get to hear most of it, long batting innings then less, if at all, but somehow it was always Sing Something Simple that never got missed, strange that. I formed a deep festering resentment on hearing Jack Emblow's accordion. The listening jewel in my crown became Alan Freeman; thanks 'Fluff', "not arf pop-pickers . . ." There was also the television, more of a piece of veneered furniture than a means of entertainment. Huge thing, small screen, black and white grainy picture, all terribly posh and Queen's English. Two large controls on the front were the way in, with a large amount of patience whilst the inner valves took an eon to warm up and cast their eerie glow and associated hum. For me, squeezing

Sky Trails & Pie Tales . . .

the memory bank, it was the 1962 Royal Variety Performance that became the defining moment. I'd been allowed to stay up and watch it. A Monday, a school night, no cricket, hurrah! The twenty-ninth of October became indelibly etched, somewhere. I was eight. This show featured Cliff Richard and the Shadows. My parents had seemed to have latched onto the Shadows as good, clean and wholesome people, well presented, with a modicum of talent and success, so were happy to let me listen and watch. By this point they'd had number one hits with Apache (1960), Kon Tiki (1961) and Wonderful Land (1962) which stayed at the top spot for a massive eight weeks. My cricket listening chances had improved and I was aware of 'The Shads'. Now I had the opportunity to match the music to the visuals, albeit in grainy black and white. It, and they, didn't disappoint. The big red Stratocaster of Hank Marvin and the boys duly impressed and sparked a lifelong interest and passion, for want of another word. Even in this world of black and white television, the greyness exuded red and bright colours, I was smitten. The music to which I was exposed was still sporadic, but I felt I had a voice and knew what I was missing. The following year the Royal Variety Show featured the Beatles and included Lennon's "rattle their jewellery" line. Rebellion too. That struck a chord with me too. I jumped ship from the 'The Shads' to the 'Fab Four'. I'm sure there were other TV musical opportunities, but these two are my most significant. My parents TV set was also very prone to failing regularly when either the horizontal, or the vertical hold valve failed. When both went all we got was a tiny white dot in the centre of the screen. This was regular occurrence in those days after the epilogue, accompanied by an annoying high-level pitch, just to make sure the slumbering woke up and turned the set off. Don't forget there were only two channels these days, BBC and ITV and only broadcast a few hours each day, from teatime to late evening and on special occasions. When the valves failed, good old Mr Wilson, the amateur TV repairman from the house on the corner was summoned. By a process of valve elimination and swapping he was successful on most occasions. I was always fascinated by his big black bag of electronic and glass trickery. Probably wrong to assume but this television seemed, to me, more out of action, than in action. Was this a ploy to avoid me watching certain unsavoury, in my parents' eyes, programmes and music? Seemed strange to me that I could hear it after bedtime. I was not daft, even way back then.

Why did I pick up a guitar, a bass guitar? Down to Hank Marvin, like many did at the time. Some learning from him, some emulating him better and going on to bigger and better things. However, even at this early stage my parents were never overly encouraging with my requests. "Dad, can I have a guitar?" "No son, you'll never make any money." "Mum, can I have a guitar?" "Ask your dad." . . . and so on. Was I thwarted, down hearted? Not me. They still took me to see the film Summer Holiday (1963) and a Hard Day's Night (1964). My insistence paid off. Summer Holiday was in colour and even more impressive. But still no guitar, so I made one, and not the first mind you. This one was out of cardboard. Here comes the really sad bit, rather embarrassing, but included in this story because it happened, I pull no punches. Shortly after the Shadows 1962 London Palladium gig, I made a cardboard guitar, yes folks, cardboard, silent as the day it was crafted from the biggest piece of corrugated cardboard I could find. I was that desperate and wanted to be like 'The Shads'. So, the cardboard guitar and VOX AC30 came into being. All complete with a string strap and a string lead. At this rather formative age I was there, with Hank and the boys. This was mostly a solitary bedroom activity, miming along to the music in my head. It didn't last long as I destroyed it in a fit of angry embarrassment after the final time, a onetime too many, that my parents thought it was hilarious to parade me in front of their friends, miming along to some imaginary music. We still never had a record player at this point. Why I duly complied with their request I have no idea. The sound of me hacking at the invisible, pencilled on, strings even now smacks of humour and desperation for this junior school kid. The final straw came when my dad insisted, I wear these oversized cardboard 'Hank Type' glasses he'd made. The thoughts of 'You're not taking this serious enough are you' pervaded. "Dad, can I have a real guitar?" "No son, you'll never make a career." The devil's music will always get its own back, won't it?

Both films, Summer Holiday and A Hard Day's Night were good to go for the interim. My mates and I acted out the odd scene on our way to and from home to school. Martin and I both went to see Summer Holiday a second time, just to correct the dialogue we'd invented. I know, sad . . . Mind, in 1963 the visual world and mostly television was to change its meaning forever one November day. It was a Friday, the twenty-second. Most of the world watched in horror as the thirty-fifth president of the United States of America was shot, right before our eyes. A day, of those that witnessed it first hand, on grey, black and white imagery, was a day that can be recalled with great clarity, for those of us now that still can. It played on my mind, a lot. It was one piece of world news that my parents were unable to shield me from, I couldn't miss it, it was right there, right before mine and their eyes. Despite the circumstances I felt this day was a day that there are other things, other news, other events going on in this world, in addition to the stuff I was shielded from. From this day on, I became inquisitive. I became aware of other things, especially in the world of music. I found out that the local paper shop used to stock a couple of weekly music papers. From early 1964 I bought every week, when I could, with my meagre pocket money, the Melody Maker without fail and the New Musical Express if funds stretched that far. These opened a world I had been totally unaware of, most of it was strange, but I was eager to learn. I read them with a newfound avarice. I also started to watch, when possible, this new BBC programme 'Top of the Pops', but not very often. 'Ready, Steady, Go', ITV's version, I never recall watching, probably banned in our household. RSG was the fore runner a full year before TotP's hit the airwaves, with the BBC playing catch up. All this time there was still the Sunday 'Cricket' evenings with 'Fluff' and the dreaded 'Sing Something Simple'.

Another momentous evening, nay event, was my very first experience of live music. Proper live music. Blues, Rock n' Roll; current and in the charts, everything. Every year my parents went to Bournemouth for a week during the end of May Spring Bank Holiday, schools had broken up, prior to the next term being exam time. Every year I got dragged along. Too young to be left on my own. Plus, maybe they thought it would be conducive for me to knuckle down and do some revising. At the beginning of each Bournemouth break the first evening there was spent on booking subsequent evening's entertainment, films, shows, end of pier quality stuff, nothing that really appealed to me. One year I'd been dragged to a concert with two so-called keyboard virtuosos of the day, Russ Conway and Mrs Mills. Bless them. Then one year, in the ads of the local paper it was advertised '16th May 1964 - One night only, Rock n' Roll Legend, Chuck Berry' apply to box office for tickets. My heart leapt. Imagine the joy when my dad reluctantly went to the Winter Gardens Box Office and came out with three rear row stalls tickets for the second house. A proper Rock n' Roll gig with proper stars of the day. This was to be a significant evening all round, for me mostly. My dad did try his best, but this was to be a massive failure, for all the wrong reasons, but drove my resolve in the wrong direction, according to my parents. The bill was made up of The Animals, The Big Three, The Swingin' Blues Jeans, Kingsize Taylor and the Dominoes who were also the backing band for Chuck Berry. I looked forward to The Swingin' Blues Jeans, but they failed to appear in the second show of the night, as having been booed and pelted off stage in the first house. All I wanted to hear was 'Hippy, Hippy, Shake'. The Animals opened. 'House of the Rising Sun' had just been released and was starting to make its way up the charts, then followed by sets from The Big Three and Kingsize. What surprised me was the volume, more so from the audience. Sure, these were all electric bands, but the Winter Gardens PA wasn't man enough to cope with all the solo and harmony vocals. The gathered were not that bothered, they had come for a good time and this good time got bigger and better until the point Chuck Berry came on, it then exploded. I just wanted to be carried along with the euphoria that surrounded me, bar my two parents. The gathered, me included, were on their feet at this point. My parents sat, quietly, with not very happy faces. I was loving it. This was the era of short but succinct sets, twenty minutes each, then off, ready for the next one. The Animals were the classic original line up, Eric Burdon on vocals, Alan Price on organ and Chas Chandler on bass. Chas later went to gain notoriety when he "found" and managed Jimi Hendrix, bringing him over to the UK from the States. The rest is history we should know. The guitarist with the Animals who occasionally played the guitar whilst lying down on the floor didn't take long to impress this nine-year-old, I can tell you. But it was Chuck Berry that people had come to see. He didn't disappoint. At this time, I was still pretty green around the gills as regards offensive language, my parents had done a pretty good job in casting the cloak, up until this point. Chuck being Chuck let loose a torrent of profanity, but to the assembled this was acceptable, they roared and encouraged the rebellious streak. Most meant nothing to me, but I was a quick learner. Of the whole crowd that night there were just two offended people: my mum and dad. My dad made his offence clear to those around us. Those around us voiced their offence of him. Fight? I was given one ultimatum. "One more swear word and we're leaving!" I held my breath, I offered up a prayer, but to no avail, it came in the introduction of the next song. Being grabbed by your collar, by your father, and unceremoniously dragged out of Bournemouth's Winter Gardens was no way I wanted to remember this evening. Sure, it was disappointing, but I'd experienced and been exposed enough to something that I found new, exciting and desperately wanted to be a part of. A nine-year-olds dream no less. The euphoria of that single evening was not too far from my thoughts over the following weeks and months. It festered. It wasn't on my parents' plan but remained on my plan.

One amusing image the following day has stuck with me all these years. If you can cast your mind back to those early 60's promotional clips, those that many used to feature the band, in full matching stage suits and ties 'frolicking', for want of a better and most ideal word, around, at various locations etc, then the one I witnessed the following day was a classic. Next to us on the beach were The Big Three, still in their full suited and booted stage attire just having a laugh and a joke on the beach, like three best mates on a stag night. Maybe alcohol was involved? I was star struck. Where are they now?

The next piece in the musical jigsaw also involved dear old Chuck Berry and his eighth album, released in April 1965. I had entered a competition in a kid's comic, I can't remember which one, but the prize was an album. To my great surprise, I won, and the postman came knocking with a rather large flat parcel. You can't write this stuff. On opening the album, it was by, would you believe it, Chuck Berry - "Chuck Berry in London". Only one drawback we didn't own a record player. So, it was with a great amount of pleading and cajoling that they eventually bought one of those all-in-one players. An Alba. Prior to this I had to go round to my uncles, who did have a record player and I'd attempt to listen despite the chatter in the room doing as much as possible to put me off. The record player that eventually found its way into our family home was one of those that you could stack up with a vast number of singles and set it going and it played one after the other. It wasn't subtle. Many times, this thing failed as about a dozen, or so precariously balanced 45's came crashing down, during play. Any of you ever tried to do the same with an LP? Take my word for it. It doesn't work. Anyway, at least I could now listen to Chuck Berry in peace. This was the beginning of my record collection, which grew at a very slow rate. Until I got a Saturday job my only source of income was the meagre pocket money allowance and any odd jobs that involved payment. My parents did a very good job in teaching me the value of money, I'll vouch for that, even with me today. If I wanted anything outside of the two normal events of the year i.e., Christmas and a Birthday, then I had to save, or sell off some of my old toys. I pity the poor souls whose birthday coincided with the arrival of Santa, luckily mine didn't. For a long time, I only had Chuck Berry to listen to, until the Beatles film 'Help'. After seeing the film, I did manage to scrape up enough money to buy the album, of the film. I wore it out, well, nearly. My very first ever single was '19th Nervous Breakdown' by the Rolling Stones. I got the distinct impression from my parents that this wasn't encouraged listening at the time, especially on their record player. I waited until they went out.

Roughly around this time I did get a musical instrument. I'd given up asking at this point, so was a mighty shock to be handed this antique mandolin. A family relation had died, and she had bequeathed this rather lovely, read expensive, family heirloom mandolin to me in her will. Aunty Lil, read Lillian, was very much aware of my interest in music. Most times we went round I'd ask to see the mandolin and sometimes she played it to me,

Sky Trails & Pie Tales . . .

but never let me touch it. A nice gesture to leave such a fine, highly crafted instrument to me. I could touch it as much as I liked now. Not exactly the stringed instrument I was hankering after, but it had to do I suppose. I spent hours trying to master this thing. The case even contained some sheet music. The day it dawned on me I ought to get this in tune was crucial. In the end my dad took it to someone who had a piano and they tuned it for me. A start. From that day on I was careful to the extreme in not trying to affect the tuning. It didn't last, but in the meantime, I'd worked out the rudiments to 'Camptown Races', with help from the sheet music and a self-taught mandolin right hand technique. Aunty Lil was musical and could play the piano too, or so I thought. In her house they also had a pianola. It looked like a piano, it played liked a piano and sounded like a piano but had one extra feature. Opening the secret door in the case above the keyboard revealed a mechanism of cogs and strange gears. It transpires that pre-cut cardboard sheets, complete with an odd array of holes, were fed into this mechanism. When coupled with vigorously pumping and peddling the two foot pedals this caused said cardboard sheets to enter and exit the mechanism, opening and refolding on themselves. This in turn operated the keys and lo and behold music came out. Then by moving your fingers over the keys, but not touching them, it looked like the person was actually playing. All these years old Aunty Lil had fooled us. Not a jot of music was ever actually played by her on this piano. The trick was to pedal and pump at a consistent rate such that the music played was at the correct pitch and tempo. Any variation in foot power either slowed down or sped up the music, at the expense of and with much jollity of those listening or trying to accompany.

I also bought myself a reel-to-reel tape recorder. For the ones taking notes, it was an Elizabethan LZ34 four track model, and mostly funded by selling my large Scalextric Racing Track and collection of cars. It was a sad day to

Sky Trails & Pie Tales . . .

see it go, but needs must. I now had the option to borrow my mate's music, singles and albums and record them (badly), when funds failed to stretch to buying my own real copies. Another bonus and step in the right direction, is that I found out that by cranking up the input volume, when on record, of the tape recorder, I could heavily distort the mandolin. A heavy metal wandering minstrel was not high on my agenda, probably not on my agenda at all. Bearing in mind this was 1965/66 and decades before Ritchie Blackmore's Black Knight but could have preceded. A school pal and I, he who lived round the corner from me used to, on occasions, (sad I know), think we were the Beatles. With the one album of theirs we happily mimed along, even to the point that the mandolin and a home-made drum kit came into play. The drum kit idea came from an old pair of wire brush drumsticks turning up on the scene. As for the donation of these, obviously military, we never did find out, but there they were one day. As with any budding, inventive, child of the day and age, the rest of the drum kit was assembled from borrowed cake tins and metal plates lurking deep within the kitchen larder. Cymbal stands were created from my dad's discarded plastic golf club tubes; was there no end to our creative source? We took it in turns. Being a 'Ringo' appealed to me no end. Maybe the start of a rhythmic seed in the musical make-up, who knows? I had no idea of what 9/8 meant until Genesis's 'Suppers Ready' came along. As for Dave Brubeck's 'Take Five' (in 5/4), no idea. We all start somewhere, don't we? So, my mate Martin (Parkes) and I ploughed on regardless. We even had a name. 'The Rovert Nitrams'. Work it out, childish schoolboy daftness ruled the day, while the rest of England went football crazy, with the national team closing down all the streets as they won the Jules Rimet Trophy one sunny day. They thought it was all over, but in my head, it was just the beginning. Nothing to do with music, but I'd watched all the 1966 England games on television, and my parents thought that it would be beneficial for me to spend the

Sky Trails & Pie Tales . . .

weekend of the final under the stars, camping with my buddies. I had no choice in the matter and was bundled off with sleeping bag and rucksack. I watched some of the final in a deserted street on a television in a TV Rental Shop window. No sound, no atmosphere. I'm sure my parents had a great time. To this day I've never watched the whole game, pointless really, I know who won. The greatest day in English football history and I'm under canvas and missed it. Bitter? Me?

As 1966 turned into the summers of 1967 and 1968, I was drawn to drama at school. Nothing musical about this, but all in the cause of the art of performing I suppose. As an only child I'd been fairly shy and chose my friends carefully, I suppose I still do. One year at school I was put in an English class with the most revered and most Bohemian English teacher available, all leather jackets and cigarettes. Mr Leach. "Sir", "no, call me Robert". We did and for me opened up a side of me that I was completely unaware of. His way of teaching made me grow to like a subject that I detested. He also ran the school drama club and often looked for 'victims', sorry, volunteers to join this after-hours, sometimes lunch times, club. I went to see one of the plays that Robert's Drama Group put on one evening, a bit of serious drama. Old Leachy had a penchant for the German modernist playwright Bertolt Brecht. The play was his 'Caucasian Chalk Circle'; no mean feat to perform by a bunch of third, fourth and fifth formers. I was smitten, bit like music but without the notes. Performing is probably the right word, but the actors can be other people, the inner personality remains hidden, but depends on the role cast I suppose. I pondered this, to the point I applied to join Drama Group. It wasn't a club that any old pupil could join, you had to apply, and was subject to an audition. I was granted an audition along with another handful. This was in front of Robert and a couple of other teachers, on the main school hall stage one lunch time and included a captive audience of

Sky Trails & Pie Tales . . .

many of the school inhabitants looking on with glee and amusement. Big leap of faith here, on my behalf, too late to back down, to retreat into the shell. Luckily, I had the benefit there were a couple of auditionees before me, so knew what was coming. Then it was my turn. I'd been given some good advice beforehand which was to look just above the audience, as near the back of the room as possible, avoid direct eye contact. Whatever I did, whatever my 'performance' was like, it impressed. I was accepted and the following week summoned to Robert's class one lunchtime. He put something to me that was either make, or break, for either of us. His next annual school play was Ben Jonson's 'Bartholomew Fair', another period drama. One of the prime characters was this bloke John Littlewit, a lawyer's agent. He was first on stage and set the scene for what followed. "Would you like the part?". Not knowing the play, the script, the story, the writer, I duly accepted. Stars in my eyes, or blind stupidity, but a challenge, nevertheless? I hesitated and accepted. By now drama club came under the new title 'Theatre Workshop'. Following my successful audition, weekly after school meetings brought something out in me that I was unaware I had, confidence. Mixing and meeting with fellow school mates of similar characters helped no end. In characters of other people, we understood that it was OK to be like this, with other views, with other accents and sometimes gender. Oh, how we sniggered at first, but these were Robert's little life lessons, taken seriously, or we're not accepted. Best I tell my parents of what I was doing on the late evenings home for tea. "I've joined Theatre Workshop". "Oh, that's nice dear, here's your tea, it's cold now, we've had ours." The script for 'Bartholomew Fair' was duly circulated amongst the cast after Christmas 1967 and offshoot sessions started. Lines were learnt, including the paragraph I had to regale as first, and solitary, actor on stage. Talk about pushing someone in at the deep end. These small sessions grew into full rehearsals and then dress rehearsals, over one full weekend. As regards dress, this was a period piece and costumes had to match the era. The school costume making department was commandeered, OK read needle-work class. Leading up to full dress rehearsals we'd all been measured, and outfits made. Bear in mind here that this play had first been performed in 1614 so the costumes reflected the era. I wore furry tights that itched and chaffed, knee length breeches, big, buckled shoes, a hat and baggy shirt to match, I drew the line at fake glasses, just the frames, no lenses, as I'd been mentally scarred by the cardboard Hank Marvin glasses episode, the ones my dad made. Now, for any thirteen-year-old something not to be encouraged to do in front of the rest of the assembled school, as one dress rehearsal was. I'd gone past the point of no return and was doing this for me, for the cast and Robert Leach. My confidence, strangely enough, had taken a boost in the first three months of 1968. I weathered the comments and the potential bullying in class the day after the dress rehearsal. Strangely I felt good, distanced, but good. Then came the run of performances. My very first ever stage appearance was on Wednesday 27th March 1968. The cast had assembled in the sixth form library above the main school hall to have make-up applied, by 'Make-Up Club', yes it existed and have costumes fine-tuned. Cues were sent up the stairs, "five minutes". I walked down the stairs and into the wings. The house lights went down, and I was pushed on. Stage fright was just about invade but I conquered. I was first on, on my own, with a large speech to regal. It was only a handful of sentences, but to me a page worth. Luckily, all the nights at home learning my lines had paid off. I'd learnt by now it's not important to just learn your own lines, having to be aware of those lines, the dialogue and the actions of others around you is also important. Like life, in general, the cues of others are also important, almost imperative in certain situations, this was one of them. I'd reached a euphoric and epiphanic moment.

Sky Trails & Pie Tales . . .

I'd become an A C T O R 'dah-lings'. This debut performance was nearly marred by me almost forgetting the advice I'd been given at the Theatre Workshop audition, of not making eye contact. Mid first few words in I spotted someone waving at me from the front row, I couldn't miss them, it nearly put me off my stride. My rule now would be not to get front row tickets for your parents, much further back would be better, not so obvious. I cracked on. Knowing by my second spoken line in I had to kiss my 'stage wife' in front of all assembled was coming, I'm sure this would generate commentary at home, it did. I cracked on. All the other performances got better as my confidence grew and I started to almost enjoy the experience and the attention it bought. Especially as subsequent performances were devoid of family members in the audience, I could relax. A couple of times, the lesson of knowing the play, other lines and cues paid off. A spot of unscripted ad libs and improvisations from me helped fool the audience with the odd missing or forgotten prop. (Could be applied musically perchance, for what was to come.) The reviews in the local papers and the odd picture were favourable. I'd finally found something I did that garnered a plaudit, a thank you, some interest, plus it made me feel good. In subsequent school terms and couple of years I was part of Theatre Workshop properly. In one play I ended up as one of Mother Courage's children, yet another play by Bertolt Brecht, I told you Robert had a fascination for this playwriter. I was Schweizerkas ("Swiss Cheese") in 'Mother Courage and her Children' and between my stage brother and I we had to pull this full-size cart back and forwards across the stage, along with acting and looking strong. Who needed PE lessons? Some of the other roles were in the lunchtime drama half hour plays. One of these short plays, just fifteen minutes long, was Edward Albee's 'The Sandbox', a play about life, death and involved audience interaction by the characters. This could have gone anywhere, and it did. Yet again I was cast with a stage wife. This version of the play only had four roles, I and grandma were the ones with previous acting experience, the other two were my wife and one other with just one line and were their stage debuts. The first performance we gave of this went off the rails completely, but probably most of the gathered never knew. At one point, my stage wife forgot her lines. I basically knew them, but no amount of my quiet prompting managed to spark her memory; she broke down in tears and left the stage. Completely not in the script. Now Grandma and I knew the story and basically ad-libbed the rest of the play, totally improvised. The final line of the play, given by the 'one-line-person', was prompted at some suitable point by both grandma and me. Like I say I don't think the assembled audience knew what was going on and I'd bet that most never knew, or had read the story, or script. We got away with murder. Here started my love, and the challenges that improvisation brings. I couldn't console my dear departed stage wife, but we did do another performance, without the improvisation section. I personally thought the improv' version was much better, but if Edward Albee was in witness of it, I'm sure he'd disapprove. The confidence of performing on stage over the previous terms and couple of years had helped me no end. All of this manifested itself in a school trip, for one summer recess, of which I'd been invited to take part. Theatre Workshop were on tour for three weeks in Germany, with a little-known play, the 'Royal Pardon' by John Arden and Margaretta D'Arcy. This was selected and performed at schools throughout Germany, during July and August of 1968. Selected because of it's simple to understand story line and enough visual clues for those children that were not as good as some of their peers in understanding English. In the end our German audience and families we stayed with had a better understanding of our own language then we did. We didn't perform this play in German as all told damage could have been wreaked on relations between both countries. It was still some twenty years after the end of hostilities and the whole crew that toured this play were under strict instructions to behave, including our glorious leader Robert Leach. There were a few incidents, which shall remain covert, but could have resulted, if the wrong person had seen it, being sent home disgraced, but by and large the touring party got away it. Two of these locations were at the location of the Nuremberg Rallies and atop one of the dam's breached by 617 Squadron. I'll leave it there, as part of a couple of free days on the tour and lessons in how not to entertain and educate a coach load of English school children. On return to the UK the whole tour and resulting stories was captured in a large multi-page booklet documenting the whole tour and performances. Yes, I still have a cherished copy, all complied from the written stories from all participants, some censored. Many memories still linger. For the full story, it's all in there. The very first performance we gave we were greeted by the whole hall chanting, in a slightly clipped German accent 'Albion'. It was the year the football club West Bromwich Albion had just won the FA Cup. We all felt welcome, and the home sickness miraculously disappeared. As for me, the whole experience gave me a taste of what playing in band was really like, as this performing bunch zigged and zagged their way across Germany and Belgium. All actors and associated crew, including the stage props, loaded and unloaded from the area of the removed rear seats, at every performance, occasionally becoming 'home' in this hired coach; 'On Tour'. As we progressed, the back windows of the coach gradually filled up with press cuttings and flyers announcing reviews and the impending itinerary. The coach was to break down on the home leg and we had to be rescued in the dark of night as a coach load of weary and worn-out troubadours went sleepily looking for familiar faces in the breaking dawn of another day. I was never the same after this.

I owe a lot to Robert Leach. It was he who gave me the support, the crutch, and the belief in myself that I never had at home. The confidence was always there but needed to be extracted. I owe you everything, "Thanks sir", "No, call me Robert . . . " This confidence spilled over onto and into my musical exploits. It still does. I'm not a great showman but can 'walk the boards' and concentrate more on the job in hand. I still get nerves, but without, any performance can be dulled, stilted and most audiences will know and feel this. Nerves gives an edge, to anything, not just music, but performance in general. Theatre Workshop, or more specifically Robert, gave me the ability to divide up, to separate, these two things: being on stage and not being on stage. I'm not the same person when it comes to 'Showtime'. Hopefully, some of those of you reading this will understand. When the two blur as one, then trouble occurs. A broad and possibly a dangerous statement, but when drugs are mostly involved the boundaries of on/off stage become blurred. Not that I have any experience in this, but just an observation. With the incidence of my own band, see later chapter, I felt no hardship in having to talk on mic between songs, all down to school drama club I suppose. I'm a firm believer that the better gigs are those that put on a 'show'. Just getting up on stage and playing the music is not always enough unless you're Eric Clapton, or (Sir) Van Morrison. BB King was a great in-between song orator, slick and polished, the music continued throughout all his shows, from start to finish, from first to last note goodbye. The audience like the performer to interact, give them something personal, something special not on a recorded piece of material.

After Robert Leach moved on, shortly after Germany, it was never the same. He'd written a book too about his view and experience of theatre in schools, in order to pass on and influence other educational institutions. The book was publicised on local BBC news with a select few from Theatre Workshop being chosen, myself included, to explain the virtues of his work, on camera. Somewhere, I still have a signed copy of his book, with the 'couldn't have done it without you' quote lurking. I'm still touched by this today. After Robert left for pastures new Theatre Workshop stumbled on, but it was never the same. Some of us got together with another English teacher and we wrote a play about the 1908 Hampstead Colliery mining disaster. Our play was called 'The Black, Black Coal' and ran for three nights at school, with a huge, assembled cast. It was the first and last play I've ever played a hand in writing. The writers were never cast in their own play as exams beckoned and were deemed more important. Maybe they were, but I felt something else gnawing at me. Music. I had no plan, less any knowledge of how to achieve. The careers officer was given the statutory answers he needed to hear, with of no help to me. I'd been given these tools, but with no idea in how to apply them, to use them. I went with the flow and let my dreams dictate, jumping from one day to the next, month by month. As part of the school subject options selection process our class were given a weekly single period music lesson for one term only. Most of the class took this as an opportunity to play up. I loved these short forays and did the best I could, given the classroom banter and general lack of control, and interest of the teacher. I would have liked to have continued over the following term/s, but both parents and career adviser had plotted again. The usual excuse of not making any money from music ploy. So why have a music department and curriculum? In a way they were both right, as over the years the monetary outgoings have far exceeded the incomings but put a financial value on the joy that music brings, both listening and making it. Now who wins? It was a nice summer though. I also hit the age that I had direct access to my Post Office account, which up until now had been put 'In Trust'. Without consultation, well it was mine, wasn't it, I emptied the account of cash and bought myself my very first, my very own, stereo record player, with separate speakers. "Where did you get this from?" It was too late. Rebel? With the event of a decent stereo system

Sky Trails & Pie Tales . . .

superseding my parents' single speaker Alba version it drove the need to buy, to obtain, more vinyl, in both the seven (45rpm) and the twelve (LP) inch versions. My record collection grew, albeit at a very slow rate, but I still was able record the odd 'borrowed platter' to the reel-to-reel.

As for radio, all during these years was spent listening to Radio Luxembourg on a toy crystal set under the pillow, as the signal appeared and disappeared on a regular basis, but I got the drift, until I heard, very loud and clear, at 7am one morning, on the thirtieth of September 1967 the voice of Tony Backburn say those immortal words "Welcome to the exciting new sound of Radio One." then proceed to play "Flowers in the Rain" by The Move. As we all now know most of the employees of this new Radio One had migrated from the now defunct, the now illegal pirate radio stations. John Peel became the 'go-to' DJ for me. Another late night under the pillow experience with his gone midnight 'Night Ride' programme. There was also his Sunday afternoon 'Top Gear', for a while.

As for television influences these were sporadically Top of the Pops and occasionally BBC2's 'Disco Two', which morphed into the 'Old Grey Whistle Test' in 1971, but it was the 'Whispering' Bob Harris 1972 era that finally struck a chord with me. As I got older, my parents' control of what the television divulged lessened. After leaving school and once I'd passed my driving test (November 1973) the OGWT was the weeks treat, mostly. Pub kicking out time on OGWT nights was much earlier. The show was discussed at length the following day at college. "You see the Test last night?" What are now legendary and seminal spots on the show were just absorbed and discussed at the time, now reminded by those that remained in the shows recorded archive. I won't list the ones that impressed the most, there were many. I did manage to watch the Beatles only showing

Sky Trails & Pie Tales . . .

of the 'Magical Mystery Tour' on television. First shown on Boxing Day in 1967, in black and white and repeated in colour five days into 1968. As my parents lagged behind the rest of the UK in upgrading to colour, I could have watched either broadcast. My dad got all fidgety during the strip club scenes and reached for the channel swap control, but it was over by the time he got there. Colour television had only reached the UK in 1967 and the sets were in demand, yet still expensive. BBC2 had started a limited service with a full colour service by 1968. Both BBC1 and ITV had caught up by 1969, but it was the event of the early 70's that most of the UK had invested in a colour set. My parents hired from Radio Rentals. The logic there was that if it broke down then a replacement would be supplied. It didn't breakdown as much as the old sets and my parents paid, over time, more than the price of a bought television. Good old Radio Rentals, good business acumen of the time. Yes, now a very dated high street shop, but every town had one. As solid-state electronics took over from valves the reliability of electronic equipment became much better and the price to buy tumbled to the point it was more cost effective to buy your own; Radio Rentals fell on its own sword, but it was good while it lasted. Prior to the colour television set my parents had replaced the old antique black and white set sideboard version with a much more modern version. The new one didn't required polishing and looked less Victorian.

So, these were all my very first musical influences. Some of it from radio, some of it from television, bits and pieces from the cinema, a fair bit from the music press, a growing collection of vinyl and taped music, but very minimal actual live music. If all considered it was the Summer of 1970 that music began to play a major part in my head, my thoughts and my dreams. This was the summer break that I started a Saturday job in West Bromwich and gave me some additional income complemented by the all-encompassing personal access

Sky Trails & Pie Tales . . .

to the Post Office Fund. I mostly bought LP's, possibly one a week. If they weren't available in the local record shops, I went further afield to the specialist vinyl shops who seemed to know more about the demand and culture. I fell in love with Prog Rock. I also started to venture out to proper 'Live Gigs' by proper 'Live Bands'. It was also the same summer that I made the transition from mainstream school to sixth form, O's to A's. The music though, both in genre and collected quantity grew exponentially. There's no right and real place in this book to mention the music and the musicians that influenced me, it's just an ongoing thing, a continual onslaught, it still is and there are still some utterly fantastic players out there, a lot of them very young. I could write about all the bass players I've listened to, and all the Prog Rock Virtuosity imbibed, but that could be another story, another book in its own right. One or two, and really only one or two, I actually got to meet, to share a few words, a hello and a handshake. These incidents were much later in my musical journey. To me they'd gone from idols to star struck icons and then to just nice folks in the same room as me. John Wetton (RiP) and Tony Levin are just two, both King Crimson bass players. Sure, my early exposure to King Crimson was a huge influence, not only the music in general but also Wetton's and Levin's virtuosity. I adored Yes's Chris Squire too, his sound and choice of guitar driving this young lad here in the mid-seventies. Same applies to Genesis's Mike Rutherford. I listened to as much Prog Rock as I possibly could afford. Not cheap this music lark. These current days, as I write, the LP is replaced by box sets of regurgitated and remixed and remastered versions of all those albums I bought way back when they were first issued. Some are willingly re-purchased just for one bonus (lost) track, or a signed postcard by all original members. The King Crimson collection is musically complete. I draw the line at releases of the same material and packaging just on a different label, or country, or print run, but some folks do. I'm not that a completist. Saying that, I do have some/most of the rarities. A couple are driven by myth and constant eBay searches, yes folks, they do exist, I have them. Over the years I have listened to most genres of music, depending upon your pigeonhole. The stuff I didn't listen to during the seventies that was deemed taboo, off the record, for your average Afghan coat wearing hippy, I've caught up somewhat in my later years. Most of this due to my wife being into Soul, Ska and reggae at the time I was sitting cross legged in a smoke-filled room with other long haired fine examples of mostly men. She liked other stuff too, a big Stones fan, but strangely enough I can't tempt her to jump ship. For her the Prog Boat sailed years ago, and her gang plank never materialised. Even today, as my current venture, the Random Earth Project, forges the Prog boundaries even further I can't seem to get her excited. It seems, for me, Prog Rock has been and always will be a solitary, only child, pastime. This Prog Joy is still strong with me and will never die. I will take it with me. Right back to my very beginning it was The Shadows and I probably can blame them for my listening quota to concentrate more on the instrumentation than the sung word, the lyrics. I still do today. The instrumental melody and accompaniment are the most important things to me. I have very few solo singer/songwriters on my shelves.

I also had a brief dabble, a brief love affair with the British Blues Boom players and bands, purely by a chance introduction by the brother of my school friend Colin, but that story follows. This era, peaking mid to late/end of the sixties, encouraged my playing confidence such that it was something I could relate to and play with a degree of success even from the start. I'm not saying the blues is easy. Sure, it can only have three root notes and only twelve bars on the bass. In its simplest form this could be even less. For me, it was an instant playing rate success, mostly. Then I found out that the blues is more than that, it's a feeling, it's a soul, it's a calling. I struggled. Some never achieved this. It can be about the notes you play in and around the structure and about the notes you don't play, the rests, the pauses, the slight hesitation, adding drama and feel and that, to me, it what the blues is all about. Again, I could write chapters about this subject. I could be mostly wrong in view, according to the flock, but will leave that subject from this book. However, ever since time immemorial musicians have listened to others, copied and borrowed and changed, putting their own personality, their own character and way of playing on the music. Over time some musicians have been unique in style, in a new personally developed style, thus becoming the source for others. My style of playing has changed over the years, nothing unique to make it identifiable, but of all the things I've listened to since The Shad's and onwards has had some bearing on what and how I play. Playing in different bands and scenarios are also hugely crucial. These events and listening opportunities all come into play and can spring into the consciousness at any point along the way. Those that I have now are still crucial. I can say that I'm unique as regards this, I don't think anyone else has listened to the music I have, in the order I have. I'm no technician in the virtuosity stakes. I can be wowed and appreciate a fast collection of notes, but too much over a length of time bores these ears. As for one very cleverly and well-placed note this will reap much (repeatable) pleasure, both secluded inner and visual external pleasure.

I feel I've given you enough in this chapter for you to be able to grasp the influences and opportunities I've had with music up until this point and which might explain some of the following things that happened in the next couple of chapters. I start the next chapter with my very first band and wind the clock back a couple of years to 1968.

2   Ginger

'Ginger' was my very first band. These following few paragraphs, writing them here now I find them, and the story, very embarrassing, very sad, very immature. What happens next in the story was very understandable to me at the time I suppose, I was very driven for want of another word, desperately wanting to be like my mate. His parents had bought him a guitar and mine were dead against anything musical, especially if it involved playing an instrument. What happened next was probably born out of frustration, of desperation. I just wanted to be like the others. I did think of leaving this section out of the story completely, but it happened and probably gives me and the reader an understanding of how deep these feelings were I had at the time. Not much was going to stop me. So, I've left this in, warts and all. My mates must have roared their heads off out of my ear shot, but it gave me a sense of purpose and direction at the time. Here goes then, head down, tin hat on. Do read this bit with the given circumstances and the musical emotions that had inflicted this young teenager in mind, thanks.

I didn't have a guitar at all, not what you could call a proper one, but, as mentioned, I had inherited my aunt's mandolin, many years ago, roughly about late 1965, so had been playing this instrument, or periodically attempting to play, ever since then. It was a proper one, probably would have been worth a lot of money now. Hand crafted with a bowl-shaped body, exquisite looking thing, but not to me at the time. It even came with a velvet lined leather case, proper! When I first acquired this, I did actually try to play it as proper mandolin, with a degree of success, following and slowly working out the sheet music that came with it. However, it wasn't a proper guitar, was it? These were desperate times. So,

Sky Trails & Pie Tales . . .

what did I do? I stripped the mandolin of all it's hardware, frets included, everything; and made my own. My parents were outraged, but too late. Maybe they should have bought me a proper guitar when I asked for one, rather than being dead against anything musical I happened to mention. It was never ever going to be in the same home-made craft circle of the guitar luthiers of the day. I had a bag of bits and that was all. I went looking for suitable bits of wood in my dad's shed. I found an old wooden clotheshorse, which became the neck. The body was a jigsaw of wood offcuts and hardboard and ended up shaped as per McCartney's Hohner bass. I found a small tin of black gloss paint and a roll of Fablon, read 'sticky backed plastic', and in true Blue Peter fashion this was what transpired as the 'here's one we made earlier'. I can tell you it was unique, a complete 'one off'. In my rush and enthusiasm, the frets were cut and hammered in any old position. I hadn't researched or even had the patience to find out the correct spacing, I just thought they looked about right; they weren't. It had four strings instead of the eight of a standard mandolin. As an acoustic instrument it sounded dire, mostly out of tune, unplayable, and an embarrassment. However, to me, at the time, it was better than the mandolin and I'm sure all my friends, behind my back, laughed, but were too kind not to burst my bubble. I took this 'thing' because it wasn't really a guitar, an instrument, one step further. With no pickup's installed, I cut a hole in the end of the body and pushed in the microphone that came with my reel-to-reel tape. I had found that by setting the tape recorder to record the sound that the microphone picked up came out of the speaker was much louder, read distorted here, than the natural acoustic twanging. The final flaw in the design was the strength of the joint between the neck and the body, like there wasn't any. By the time the strings had been tightened to some of degree of tuning, the neck had decided that physics would rule the roost and bent in the direction of the forces applied to the strings.

Sky Trails & Pie Tales . . .

Failed. I hadn't had the sense, or probably not enough wood to make the neck as a one piece, through the body. Major failure, but I remained unphased, undaunted. This design did give me an instant whammy bar, as I could easily bend the neck back to get the right note. Most normal people would have given up by now, but all I wanted to do was play a guitar, any old guitar. I persisted. I practiced and, in the end, developed a technique that I could just about get some sort of tune out of this, with a combination of bending the neck back and fretting the strings at various points on a completely non-standard fretted neck. I was happy in my own little world, in my head, in my bedroom. Somewhere in this world embarrassment ran riot, but not mine. My left hand took on the appearance of a heavy smoker as I used four of the better original mandolin strings, but all were rusted after years of neglect, I just hoped I didn't break any. Still, the incredible and varying, high action and the laws of physics helped no end to lengthen their already long life.

It was a mate at school, Colin, that had an old Hofner electric guitar and practised in his bedroom, mostly the blues. I went round there as much as I could hoping that my lust for a real guitar might transfer itself to me and give my parents the big hint. Most nights at Colin's I never was allowed to 'have a go', so I persisted with the mandolin monstrosity, obvious that it was never going to be up to the job. With four strings and the odd fret position it was impossible to play chords of any variety, so probably it was at this point that I started to lean towards single notes and the bass clef. Like most, I started off wanting to be a guitarist, but maybe, if it wasn't for the four stringed mandolin creation I might have been, so a bass man I became. Fate? Colin had also written a couple of songs. Impressive to these ears of mine. He couldn't sing very well with the songs being very rhythmic, almost to the point that the guitar phrasing matched the vocal phrasing. Looking back now,

Sky Trails & Pie Tales . . .

they were really rubbish, but I hadn't written them. No solos for Colin either. He adored Cream and we both often listened with intent to his older brother's record collection. We even skipped school one afternoon to watch the film of Cream's last concert at the Royal Albert Hall. It was a fleapit of a cinema, in Dudley, opposite the zoo, and this film was a special one off showing, we had to go, it was calling to us. I believe this was in 1969 and ties in with the release of the film. It ran a little late but we both explained to our parents that we were in detention that afternoon. Gullible? We thought so, but maybe not. Phone calls to school as to our whereabouts were never relayed to Colin and me. I'm sure our parents had secret dossiers on us, we'll never know. After this excursion the seed, the germ had been sown and we both thought wouldn't it be great to be in a band, as you do. I blame Clapton, Bruce and Baker. How 'Ginger' was born out of Colin and me then this has disappeared to time, but the name is likely to have subliminally been suggested by reading the LP sleeve notes for 'Fresh Cream' repeatedly. His brother also had a copy of the Groundhogs album, 'Blues Obituary', released in 1969 too. This became a go to listen for us, as did their follow up 'Thank Christ For The Bomb', we both bought copies and listened incessantly, even seeing the band at Birmingham Town Hall, as support to Canned Heat. A Tuesday, 22nd September 1970. We both went to the 6:30 show, about ten stall rows from the front. I was sixteen and this was my very first full proper gig, call it a baptism. The volume was the most impressive thing to these young lads. We both lived this gig repeatedly, in our heads, at school, during lessons, it wouldn't go away. Like the Chuck Berry concert all those years ago it was this concert too that had a significant effect on me and was another push towards the inevitable. We always went to catch the Groundhogs at every available opportunity, and saw many other bands too. A very young UFO was another. Again, it was Colin that was put onto this band, by his brother. They had

Sky Trails & Pie Tales . . .

been booked to play at Henry's Blueshouse. Their first album (UFO1) had just come out and Colin and I went, it must have been late 1970 as Henry's closed down in 1970 after three very short and successful years. The club was held on a Tuesday night in the upstairs room of The Crown on Station Street in Birmingham city centre; very quickly becoming established and known as the first progressive music club in the UK outside of London. Promoter and artiste manager, Jim Simpson, of Big Bear Music ran the club, he still does. Colin and I sneaked in, underage and sat in the front row, and by not turning round we hoped no one would challenge our obvious youth. We'd paid to get in, so I suppose that didn't matter. UFO didn't disappoint. They were loud, energetic and singer Phil Mogg left his imprint on my shoe after one of the many off stage excursions. The band went onto to become rather well known; I believe. Over the years Henry's Blueshouse grew in folklore albeit we didn't know at the time. Both, a very young, Ozzy Osbourne and Tony Iommi were regular Henry's attendees and asked Jim Simpson for a gig, at Henry's. He auditioned them, only to oblige and booked their band 'Earth'. Their fee was four Henry's Blueshouse tee shirts and they supported Ten Years After. Following this, a much-impressed Jim Simpson booked 'Earth' regularly, eventually managing them on the condition that they change their name from 'Earth' to 'Black Sabbath', you might have heard of them. Ozzy has been heard to quote and often acknowledges this period of the band as "being made by Jim Simpson". Most of the material from their debut album was played in and arranged at their gigs at Henry's. Jim couldn't hang onto the band. As Sabbath's debut album hit the top of the album chart the band became a commodity and legal proceedings were put in place to extricate the band from Jim's grasp. As for who took over, not for this story; but legend has it that it could have been two former members of Don Arden's company. His daughter was to later marry Ozzy a bit further down the line. Small world.

Sky Trails & Pie Tales . . .

It was also the tail end of Jim's era and the transition into new management of Black Sabbath that I/we occasionally used to bump into at 'Holy Joes' rehearsal rooms during my tenure with the band 'Labyrinthus', more of that later. I've kept a loose gossamer contact with Jim. My last contact with him was negotiating the gigs and the contract for two 2015 Malaya Blue Band gigs at the Birmingham International Jazz & Blues Festival in which he organises annually.

1970 was also the year of my O-levels, I knuckled down, quickly followed by sixth form and A-levels. I grew up somewhat in these years, developing the musical thoughts and how I could get it into my life on a more permanent and prosperous basis. I did well with my results for O's, but not so for A's. I failed all three 'A' Levels but picked up a few more 'O' passes along the way, not a great success. My waking day would be spent discussing with Colin, even more so at school, in how we were going to form this band. During the night I dreamt. Reasons to fail the exams perchance? Around this time a seminal album had been released, 'In the Court of the Crimson King, an Observation by King Crimson'. I observed. A friend of mine had a copy which I duly borrowed and taped. I never did buy a first release of this, shame on me. It was a slow burn of a release for me. I bought the follow up albums and then everything else that preceded it, but the night that truly cemented my fascination and love of this band was one night at Birmingham's very own Town Hall. I had a Saturday job at 'Hall's' West Bromwich's High Street stationer. In those days I was paid one pound a day, but still I managed to scrape up enough money for a ticket. One of the other so-called employees was going to see King Crimson that night and encouraged me to get a ticket. I did and picked it up at the box office that night. You've worked it out, it was a Saturday, but the day was synonymous with other events that would unfold later in the day; it was the twenty-second of May 1971. My seat

Sky Trails & Pie Tales . . .

at the Town Hall in Birmingham was front row of the balcony, at the end, at the stage edge. I looked out across all before me. Robert Fripp was furthest away from me, with the remaining band members lined up in formation and closer. Sax player Mel Collins was closest. What played out that night hugely impressed and made a significant and lasting impression on me. This is music? If so, I'd just found the grail that I probably had been subconsciously searching for. A mixture of the structured, the improvised, the loud, the quiet, all with dual Mellotrons and just from four musicians. For those wondering as to what I refer to as a Mellotron and are unsure, then this was generally either a single, or a dual, thirty-five note keyboard instrument. Each note was an analogue recorded single note, come cartridge, of an instrument, mostly orchestral, on a conventional tape, but not looped. Press the keys and you had an instant orchestra. It was deemed as the first true sampler, and all manufactured in Birmingham as well. Each key press had a finite time before the tape ran out, stopped playing and had to rewind, so the use and musical arrangement had to take this into consideration; probably why King Crimson had two in order to compensate for long single notes. It lets the other one rewind while the other one is playing, who knows. These keyboards were first used on the Beatles 'Strawberry Fields' but came to prominence with the event of Prog Rock, used widely throughout, but initially the Moody Blues, King Crimson and Genesis were great exponents. In these days a band without one were not deemed as proper Prog. An expensive badge of honour. These Mellotrons, whilst being cutting edge at the time were fraught and subject to many surrounding influences, such as temperature, humidity, moisture, power fluctuations, age and use, but when they worked properly the effect was mesmerising, and the night I first saw King Crimson live was one such night. Most nights they ended their set with an interpretation of Holst's 'Mars, The Bringer of War', for two Mellotrons and percussion. This built from a quiet and gentle Bolero snare pattern to something overly demonic and discordant, it slayed the audience each night. I and the rest of the crowd left the Town Hall that night in stupefied shock attempting to assimilate what we'd all just seen and heard. These ears got on the bus from Birmingham Snow Hill station to West Bromwich completely forgetting that I had to call home, letting it ring just three times. This was the signal for my dad to come and pick me up from outside Snow Hill. I never rang and wasn't there! As the bus pulled into the terminus at West Bromwich I saw my interconnecting bus back home drive out. Never mind there'll be another one. There wasn't, this bus, getting smaller in my mind's eye, was the last bus home. What now? I know, I'll phone home, explain and made my way to the nearest telephone box. Don't forget, in these days mobile phone technology was non-existent. As I walked through the shopping centre the internal glass doors were lit up with a bright shimmering glow. I went through the doors only to find the building opposite ablaze, completely engulfed. This was the old West Bromwich Adelphi dance and ball room. The fire crews had just turned up and in no way were they able to save this place from complete collapse as charred rafter after charred rafter came crashing down. With it went all the memories of the bands that had played there. The local and the not so local, even the Beatles, the 'Before Epstein' days. The Adelphi featured in many of the post war evenings out of the local youngsters. Future partners were met, fights were had, much rumbustious going on's and stories were had at The Adelphi, now just all in flames. I stood, with a now growing crowd for a while, watching events unfold then best thought I ought to call my dad. Finding the nearest payphone and with a handful of lose change in my pocket I rang. It rang and rang and eventually picked up. I went to put the money in, to connect, and the slot was disabled. I shouted down the receiver to no avail. I couldn't tell them I wasn't at Snow Hill Station as

Sky Trails & Pie Tales . . .

per the prearranged signal. After this call my dad drove to Birmingham City Centre, but I was miles away in West Bromwich. In the ensuing panic I couldn't find another workable phone box and started to walk home. It was a half an hour walk. By the time I got home my dad had driven to Birmingham and back and on realising I wasn't there, panicked. I wasn't 'missing' in their eyes for long, the story ended well, but I was in some serious trouble. Rather than stick to the prearranged signal of three rings from Snow Hill, which I should have done, I thought I was saving him a longer journey by a pickup from West Bromwich but that relied on a connecting call and an explanation, easy, or so I thought. I was genuinely helping but British Telecom failed me that night and I got into some serious. As a parent, I can understand their anguish, but as a then sixteen-year-old I'd just had the best, and a great, exciting night out for some time. No pleasing some eh! This evening will always be indelibly linked with King Crimson and the Adelphi Fire.

With all of this going on both my resolve and Colin's to start a band grew exponentially. We both thought that 'Ginger' would benefit from another guitarist, one that could sing would be helpful too, and a drummer. There was a young chap, went by the name of Clive Morris and a couple of years below Colin and me at school. He lived round the corner from us and had been seen walking the streets with this solid body guitar. The obvious ask went out and Clive, much to our surprise said he was interested. The drummer came in the form of Chris Morson. I didn't know Chris but apparently, he went to the same school as the rest of us, Churchfields High. Chris had already left school and was working. Colin knew Chris had a set of drums because he sometimes heard him. Chris lived in the next road to Colin, and he'd occasionally heard him when he used to walk past his house and over the canal. We were all in awe of Chris. He had left school, had a job, drove and seemed to know what he was doing. So, by both Clive's and my reckoning it was going to be Colin that should go round and ask Chris. Eventually he did, with Clive and me hiding round the corner. Much to our surprise Chris agreed and we gathered around Clive's house for that first very rehearsal.

Picture this, four budding musicians all squeezed into a garden shed at the bottom of Clive's garden in Stone Cross, between a lawn mower, various spades and other bits of general garden rubbish. How Chris set up the drums of his I'll never know. A power lead ran from the kitchen and snaked its way down the garden. At that time, it was Clive who had the only amplifier, all six watts of it. As I didn't have a proper guitar at the time, and I didn't want to embarrass myself I didn't bring the Mandolin Monstrosity. So, it was Clive and Colin who plugged into Clive's little amp. I alternated on every other jam by using either Clive's, or Colin's guitar and concentrating on the lower four strings. In the end we gave up because the perennial complaint came to "Shut that diabolical racket up!" Mind you, just imagine that garden shed, with the door shut, pulsating to what must have been an infernal din! We all have to start somewhere. We only did this a couple of times more as the roof leaked and we were governed by the weather and Clive's parents only letting us do this for one evening a week. So, it was down to my parents' house on the days and nights they went out. They had no clue as to what went on, but their neighbours did and probably told them. This was the first time I used my homemade guitar in front of anyone other than Colin. Embarrassing. I must thank both Chris and Clive now, after all these years, for not laughing directly at me as regards my monstrosity. We either played in the front room, or the garage, only on the days, or evenings, my mum and dad went out. We all waited round the corner for their car to drive past and I made sure I knew what time they were due back, it worked like clockwork, some military operations were run less slickly. Eventually the

Sky Trails & Pie Tales . . .

garage became out of bounds, after one evening I had a phone call from what must have been an irate neighbour complaining about the noise and threatening to call the police. Even after all this time we must have still sounded dire, when we thought we were great. On the odd occasion, when my parents went away for the weekend we cleared the front room, putting all the furniture in the other room. To this day I don't think they realised what we did. To us, the front room became a studio. Chris, Clive and Colin staying overnight, sleeping on the floor. It was soon after these first rehearsals that I got my first proper bass guitar. I blame the next-door neighbours as they probably couldn't stand my racket and complained to my parents, putting in a request to buy me a proper bass guitar. The Mandolin Special was trashed á la Townshend style one afternoon and put in the bin. Shame that all the hardware never got reunited with its original wooden body and neck, it would have been worth a fortune now. My fault. For one small glimmer of hope my mum and dad relented and bought me a £5 Hohner bass. It was from Modern Music in Dudley, opposite the zoo. My dad reluctantly drove me there and bought the cheapest one they had. I kind of felt they hoped that by buying this, showing a bit of interest, that my interest might fizzle out, hoping it was a five-minute wonder and we could all move on. Wrong on all counts and sides. It was not in bad condition, one pickup, plus with a bridge not permanently fixed to the main body. The tension in the strings held it in place. A couple of times, in those early days, the guitar strap broke, and the bass fell to the floor with a crash and the bridge moved under the shock. Even this event was captured on reel-to-reel tape all those years ago. Over the time I had this bass I was constantly adjusting, fiddling with the bridge. It was never perfect, but one has to be grateful for small mercies. Modern Music also supplied a free guitar case. I think they were glad to see the back of it, it was never fit for purpose, but I didn't care. Why? The main feature of this case was that it was

Sky Trails & Pie Tales . . .

an ex-Slade one and rather broken. It still had the sprayed on "Slade" logo. Suited me down to the ground. I got down and got with it, no pun intended. Modern Music would feature again at some point later in this story, but not in a most pleasurable way.

Colin, Clive, Chris and I became "Ginger" properly. We continued to practice at my parents' house on the vacant days, working up about six to eight songs. A couple of them ours. One Colin's, one Clive's and, yes folks, one of them mine. The rest were covers. At this point I had a proper bass guitar, but still used the tape recorder as an amp, so when Colin had sweet talked us into being offered a gig at our old school end of term dance then it focused the mind somewhat. We played Churchfields School Hall, shortly before I left in 1972. The actual date was, Tuesday 11th July 1972. Ours, and mine, very first gig. 'Ginger's' short set was halfway in between the DJ's two sessions. For posterity's sake we cleared the dance floor, but still got a smattering of polite, semi interested applause. On the night of the gig I borrowed an old Park 70W rig, conveniently blowing a valve and just about struggling to get myself heard on the remaining power. Colin and Clive had made their own gear. Colin's was finished bright gloss yellow as likely the only spare can of paint he could find in his dad's shed. Clive's single speaker blew up shortly before the end as was overpowered by his amp. Coupled with this, we had no vocal PA and relied on the goodwill of the DJ to accept our solitary microphone. He did, but the volume was woeful. What a rag-tag bunch we must have looked, but the gig 'duck' was broken. The lesson learnt here, as in the right location, our old school, was that we must get some better material and gear, reliable gear, and be a little bit tighter. Five out of ten for effort, must try harder. Failing that we did make the local papers. Basically, on the merit that we all went to the same school at some time or another and that two of the band had just left school that day. It made a loose story link to the band. The following night, after the gig, we reconvened at Clive's for the associated press picture that accompanied the brief article.

Where next? Well, I can tell you I never wrote another complete song, music and lyrics, ever again after this band. I pretty much sang and played it as a solo ballad on the night of this first ever gig. I borrowed Clive's guitar on the night. Exclusive and never, ever, repeated.

Sky Trails & Pie Tales . . .

3   Labyrinthus

We stumbled on during the Summer of 1972, but during August the other members of Ginger (Chris, Clive and myself) agreed and came to the unfortunate decision we felt we had to ask Colin to leave. What we were unaware at the time was that his illness was starting to manifest itself. His inability to listen and accept any other person's suggestions were frustrating to us and in hindsight it was a cruel decision. Before we decided we carried on practising without him, and it quickly became apparent that even at our age he was not maturing musically as quickly as the rest of us. After Ginger's demise I saw Colin only once and then never again. He became Labyrinthus' roadie for our first, and only gig. He was becoming more and more withdrawn. If I knew then what I know now then perhaps we would have been a bit more tolerant. He was diagnosed with Schizophrenia. Colin was not a well chap at all.

As 1972 drew to a close the three remaining members of Ginger decided that a name and a musical direction change was required. It was thus that "Labyrinthus" was formed. This was now Clive Morris on rhythm and lead guitar, Chris Morson on drums and me on bass. Clive and I even shared vocals. Yes, dear reader, I used to sing. All the old lasting recordings are evidence that I couldn't and shouldn't have sung. I've never done so since this era and only with this band, not me at all, I just concentrated on the bass from here on. It was also around this time that I bought a brand-new amp. A FAL50. FAL stood for Futuristic Aids Limited. Now was that a prediction for the future or what? Wouldn't have been very PC in this day and age. You couldn't call it a proper amp, but it worked, and I was happy. I made my own speaker cabinet using the biggest 100W eighteen-inch speaker I could buy. At least those woodworking

Sky Trails & Pie Tales . . .

classes at school had taught me something. At a distance, you couldn't tell the difference between a professionally built one and mine, most pleasing, even with proper speaker grill cloth and black Tolex cabinet covering, but boy, was it heavy. One thing I did forget. Handles, a lesson for next time. Getting some reliable gear was also the first step on the ladder, plus a much-needed PA. Finally, I was earning some real money to help fund the band. After leaving school, sixth form, and failing all my 'A' levels, my options jobwise were a bit limited. In the end I got a job and started real work during September 1972 as an apprentice at W&T Avery's, in Smethwick. The first year was spent at Warley College of Technology, which in later years would boast of one such student being Chris Collins (aka Frank Skinner). He studied English but was younger and a couple of years below us. Being an apprentice helped two-fold, one was to get some money and the other was to get some sort of trade behind me, if all else failed. Plus, I made some good friends, some of which were instrumental as to what happened next in this story. One such meeting of like minds was to happen shortly after I had started college. I met Peter Hill the week before Christmas 1972. Prior to that, unknowing to Chris, Clive and myself we went to see a local band 'Open Hands' at a church hall, just to investigate the competition, as you do. Pete was the drummer, and the band were mostly ex-pupils from the local Grammar School, Menzies. This band were quite impressive on many fronts, their brand new WEM PA was one thing, and they even had a light show. Sadly, the obviously homemade light show caught fire and was doused quickly with a couple of drinks, dangerous, and obviously were outside the current safety rules. I made a subliminal note of the drummer, very expressive. Their drummer was studying for a qualification in Engineering, and I was surprised to see him at college one day. Being this much surprised I went over and introduced myself and recalled the night we went to see his band and the combustible light show. We

Sky Trails & Pie Tales . . .

had a laugh about the fragility of tissue paper and hot bulbs don't always go well together. Pete said he runs a regular jam night at his father's old factory and suggested I ought to come over. Well, I did. It was local to me, in West Bromwich. The first floor of this old workshop was set up with everything that was needed, all very permanently looking and there was this WEM PA, the one we'd seen at the gig! That night I took my bass and borrowed an old mate of mine's six string guitar. At this point I was still very inexperienced with playing a normal guitar, bass I kind of knew my way around. There was already a bass player there that night, so I hacked around wildly on this six string, until there was an opportunity to step up on bass. I felt more relaxed and pretty much musically hit it off straight away with Pete. Our style of playing, even given our teenage years dovetailed in an instant. It was obvious straightaway. Pete said he'd like me to join his band. "What, Open Hands?" "Yes, why not?". So, I did, without a thought of my friends in Labyrinthus. In my youthful head, there was this band with a wonderful PA, a permanent place to rehearse and a rather better guitarist. I was convinced that this was the right decision, plus they had done a few gigs, which was more than Labyrinthus had done. I told Chris and Clive, which was received with a mixed reaction, sorry guys. In the New Year Open Hands became a three piece and practised regularly at the old factory. It didn't last long as the guitarist, whose name deserts me, left. The factory was dim, dark, dank and downright cold, but at least I could set up my gear and leave it there, and Pete and I could play at full volume, which was great to our ears. The sound reverberated off the walls. There were also those famed lights, the ones which caught fire, but had now been modified to something a little safer. Despite them being on most of the time, on cold, dark January nights I still froze. By now, I had also acquired Colin Jesson's old gear from his days in 'Ginger'. Colin had regressed even more into his mental issues and had stopped playing the guitar completely. I suppose I didn't help in his slide into schizophrenia by relieving him of his gear with an offer he couldn't refuse, persuading him to part with his gear. I feel awful now that I abandoned him when he needed me most. I'm afraid this was "The Music" talking now and not me, a feeble excuse, I know, sorry Colin. His amplifier worked a treat with mine and I bought two new fifteen-inch speakers which just about squeezed into the cabinet made for two twelve-inch ones. Pete and I got on like a house on fire, both musically and personally. The musical interaction often astounded us sometimes. It was one of those partnerships that fitted like a jigsaw. Many a time we gelled together, playing the same rhythmic fill without even looking at one another. Unbeknown to us this was the start of what I can only describe as an inbuilt mental telepathy. I have never experienced this degree of instant integrity with any other drummer, but I have come close on a few occasions. I really thought that I had made the right decision to leave Labyrinthus. Clive was almost driven to tears when I left, and he begged me to stay. It was Chris that pulled him away and I suppose Chris never forgave me for what I did. However, I was only with Open Hands a couple of months, over the Christmas period and into the New Year, when it all went pear shaped. I collected my gear from the first-floor factory warehouse, bade farewell, but kept in touch with Pete. My parents wondered where all this additional gear came from!

Shortly after this, it was that I found myself sitting on my own, in Birmingham Town Hall. I was a bit glum and in need of some cheer. What I was about to witness that night, Sunday 18th February 1973, was an incredible piece of theatrics, music, and showmanship. I'd seen Genesis before on the 'Six-Bob Tour', but nothing like this. The 'Six-Bob Tour' was put on by the Charisma Label with its own bands on the bill; Van Der Graaf Generator, Lindisfarne, and Genesis, all for the princely sum of 6 Bob, or 72p in today's currency. A bargain, no

Sky Trails & Pie Tales . . .

less. I've seen every Genesis tour since, even to the bitter end. I nearly missed out on 'The Lamb Lies Down on Broadway' tour as the initial batch of tickets went in a trice. However, on the night of the Birmingham concert, I was offered a spare ticket at work, but I really needed two. A quick phone call lunchtime gave me the conundrum and the choice. "If you go to see the Lamb, then you can forget about us." I went to see Genesis that night, on my own, and lost a girlfriend in the process. Wise decision? A musical choice. Back to the Town Hall gig and Genesis were headlining having just launched into their "Foxtrot" tour. For those of you who remember, the stage was completely draped in white cloth, floor to ceiling, stage side to stage side. No amplification equipment was visible, just guitars, percussion, and keyboards. They came onto the stage lit only by Ultraviolet tubes, thus picking out the luminous make up around Peter Gabriel's eyes. The whole Town Hall remained quiet, what next? As the sweeping mellotron chords to "Watcher of the Skies" hit the air it was apparent to us all that this was a major step in your normal gig theatrics, something never heard, or seen, before. Welcome to the 70's. Welcome to the first time I ever heard 'Suppers Ready'. For the next ninety minutes we all sat there stunned, enthralled, completely swept along with the euphoria and the ethereal magic. One of those pivotal concerts that would change the view of many, forever. I was only 18 and at the time didn't appreciate the visual and aural impact that a rainy Sunday Birmingham evening had made. Only in later years was this to become clear. This, I believe, was the measure of how far advanced that Genesis were at the time. Wouldn't it be wonderful to be in a band like that? In the coming weeks I relived this gig in my head, over and over again. Shortly after, I bumped into Clive, by coincidence and after mentioning the Open Hands failure and that incredible Genesis concert to him, it was he who suggested that we all get back together again. At this point I was desperate to get back into a working

Sky Trails & Pie Tales . . .

group, albeit it was Pete that I kind of abandoned, but I still saw him at college, and we continued with our friendship that way. I was very much up for re-joining Labyrinthus, but with hindsight I felt Chris was a bit reluctant, as regards my return, I don't blame him. I think what swayed him was my decision and commitment to the band to fund the missing PA. This came in the form of a loan of which I'd cover the regular monthly payments. In the end this was to be known to me as the 'Loan From Hell', more of that later. I re-joined Labyrinthus and during the Summer of 1973 I spent the entire six weeks school holiday period, at Clive's house making speaker cabinets. All the material being funded from the pot fed by the loan. Chris had been able to secure a loan with a friend of his (I think it was in the region of £250, nothing in today's terms but a fortune back in 1973, in current inflation rate about £3000) on the understanding that I kept up the repayments and I did, regular as clockwork. My parents had no clues whatsoever and was probably the best under the circumstances. With this money we bought a WEM 100watt PA amplifier (what else!), loads of mikes and stands, speakers, wood/materials etc. Clive's garden and fabled shed, where it all started, resembled a factory at times as we, mainly me, built what was to become our PA. For the technical amongst you reading this, we had an eight-speaker cabinet PA, four each side, all professionally finished, Tolex and covers included, with a mixture of twelve and fifteen-inch speakers. Chris was over six foot and even he couldn't see over the top. Colin's old amp supplemented the PA and I bought for Clive, as he was still at school, a second hand 60W valve amp. Being a valve amp this, for those of you technically minded, gave Clive's guitar the attack and sustain he was sorely lacking. Using my, or Colin's old 2 x 15" speaker cabinet finished him off. I remember the first time we set up this newly acquired gear and turned it on, words cannot describe our euphoria. Everything was miked-up, guitar, bass and drums. So here ended the

Sky Trails & Pie Tales . . .

first lesson, we'd got some reliable (and loud) gear. All we had to do now is get some decent material and to tighten up as a band, minor points. I'd just turned nineteen and a few of my dreams had manifested.

As mentioned, my commitment to Labyrinthus was in the form of the loan and PA. Chris's was via 'The Van'. In the end he got the bands ideal vehicle, a Ford Transit, in green, and we went about transforming it, complete with a rear partition for the gear and a bench seat behind the driver and passenger seats. Our intention was to spend a few hours in this van, up and down the motorways. Bands' vans: if they could talk, would give up untold riches of many stories, some that were covert and secret, of all manner of things. Where bonds were forged, where arguments spilled over into fights, break ups, 'sorry's' and "I love you MAN!", where gigs were planned and dissected, where sleep, meals and many other 'on-the-road' activities were acceptable. We all had them, didn't we? Most of all, the secular fun and laughs of being on the road, in a van, in a band, became ingrained in a musician's psyche, regardless of level, of talent and standing in the business. Rock and Roll broke the interminable hours travelling. Genesis, in the very early days, used to take a picnic hamper, that's education for you. In the end Chris agreed to fund the running of this van if I paid for the rehearsal rooms, as well as the loan. Was I made of money? Not really, but the dream was tangible and strong. Clive was financially strapped, he was still at school, so Chris and I funded the band together, no going back now, or jumping ship. It was Chris, via the local music grapevine, who found the ideal rehearsal room. It was in Wednesbury, St James's Street, next to the church. The half a dozen rooms were the remnants of an old school and run by the vicar of the church. I can't remember his proper name, but he was this round, jolly, rather overweight person who came round to collect the money and was quite happy to go under the acronym of 'Holy Joe'. If you

Sky Trails & Pie Tales . . .

didn't cough up, he wasn't so jolly! Over time and in the odd latent Brum Beat Scene biography you can read about these rooms that referred to them as 'Holy Joe's', and those that used them, or in the know, can recall them quite vividly. Looking on Internet map sites it's still there, as is the church. Many of the local musicians first starting out, like we were, rehearsed there, passing through these rooms, went on to greater notoriety and earnt much more than we ever did, but it's not about the money, is it? Many a time, after rehearsing all night we piled into the small pub on the corner of the road only to find "Holy Joe" propped up in the corner with a beer in his hand. No wonder he got upset when you didn't pay. He relied so much on us and all the other bands funding his after-hours activities. Many a time this became a 'lock-in' session not only for the few regulars but the odd band member. Members of Black Sabbath and Judas Priest were occasionally seen to be rubbing shoulders with those from Labyrinthus! Our guitarist Clive was young, underage and looked young and often we were turned out for the cheek of trying. "He's not eighteen, is he?" with good old Tony (Iommi) and Geezer (Butler) buying drinks for us. The air thick with Black Country accent. At one point Ozzy gave one of his satin purple shirts to a friend of mine, generous. I wonder where this is now. As mentioned, within the close-knit scene using 'Holy Joes' there used to be a fledgling Black Sabbath and an early Judas Priest. When Sabbath turned up, we all knew, mainly due to the volume they played at. They rehearsed at roughly the same volume they gigged at. The rehearsal rooms were mostly brick built, with no sound insulation. Open the windows and the whole street could hear. The sound reverberated all night, with all seven, or eight bands playing their very best, but never the same tune, or at exactly the same time. You'd get the picture if you stood outside in the road. However, there was one room that was slightly better than all the others. You had to get there early to reserve this room, as room availability was on a first come, first bagged

Sky Trails & Pie Tales . . .

basis. Once they'd all been reserved then that was it. Reserving was solely down to a personal presence. I've known rooms lost when no one was in there after the original 'reservee' had gone to the bathroom. Having a bottle of something to drink helped, when thirsty, and I've known the same bottle be used for bathroom relief, in order to avoid losing the room. Rock n' Roll eh. The power of physical presence was strong, respected and an un-written rule. Both Clive and I took it in turns to leave school/work as early as we could and get to 'Holy Joes' as quick as the bus would allow. Sometimes this had to be mid-afternoon in order the get the best room. This was a downstairs room, on the corner of the building, next to the pub, with the added bonus that whoever occupied this room didn't have to carry all the gear up and down the stairs, which we invariably had to do. This corner room was more wooden and tended to absorb the sound, as all the other ones were just masses of brick and glass, built pre-war, and very solid. Apart from all the local bands rehearsing in these rooms, the inner sanctum, or middle rooms, were reserved exclusively for the judo and karate fraternity. On warm nights the smell of body odour, clothes and lots of expressive shouting filtered through the air. If you were local to Wednesbury, then passing this establishment must have been an experience. Us musicians kept our distance from and gave these oriental sportsters much respect. I'm sure they had a lot to put up with us.

It was here, at these Wednesbury rooms, that we built our set list. We started to do our own versions of other bands material, OK covers, such as Trapeze's "Black Cloud", Stray's "All In Your Mind" and the Cactus version of "Long Tall Sally". These songs were interspersed with our own stuff. The way we use to write was basically to improvise a jam, as you do. If we started on something that the rest of the band picked up on, we stopped, wrote down the chords, or riff, or recorded these sections onto my reel-to-reel tape, but I didn't always bring it with me. I've kept some of the initial sparks of inspiration for posterity, but the rest has been lost. Never to be found again. One particular song, written this way, I would rate as a classic out and out rockin', Labyrinthus piece, entitled "Run Down". Very much upbeat, we liked it, but would anybody else? Over the months we had complied enough to start thinking about getting on the road. Over the months we were rehearsing 2 nights a week and on Saturday, either in the afternoon or evening. Sometimes we put in a Saturday double shift with the music and the band getting much tighter. We also started to develop more as musicians, learning our craft as we went. As we spent a fair amount of time down in Wednesbury, we became quite well known. Some evenings we even heard people outside calling for particular songs! Was this the start of our fan base? With all this time spent rehearsing girlfriends were non-existent or fell by the wayside, comes with the territory. The band was very much a priority. As 1973 petered out Clive by then had left school and had got himself a job. As Chris and I were still funding this band I thought, at last, Clive can now bring his financial contribution and we can only forge ahead. How wrong was I? The job he had only lasted for two weeks. Clive was a technician, work this one out yourself, at the local sewage farm! Whilst he worked there, the nights we picked him up to go to rehearsal we made sure that he'd had a bath. Even so, some nights he still smelt of raw sewerage. In the end he couldn't stomach it and gave up the job and Chris and myself reluctantly went back to paying and covering for Clive. He had over the months of intense rehearsals developed into quite a good guitarist and singer. I don't blame Clive for giving up the job. I wouldn't want to do it, especially as it was coming to autumn time. Despite the lack of Clive's financial input, the band had pretty much had mission accomplished. We had got some decent, reliable gear, enough material to keep the punters happy and we'd rehearsed beyond belief. Time to gig. Labyrinthus'

Sky Trails & Pie Tales . . .

first, and only gig, was at a pub, whose name deserts. We only managed a couple of numbers when the manager, who didn't like the volume we played at, came in and pulled the plug. I suppose stadium sized PA and back line in a leafy, quiet Birmingham suburb didn't mix very well. I remember him coming up to me and holding the frets of my bass guitar between my fingers and the main body to try to stop me playing. It must have sounded awful. In order to be different, novel perhaps, we always started the set with a bass guitar solo. Between the manager and I we did a real good job. I think it was the first time he had organised a Rock Night. The assembled booed, I stood up and apologised for what had just happened, they cheered. If we had got another gig straight away, then I think Labyrinthus would have gone from strength to strength and made a real go of it. I know we were a little raw around the edges, but we certainly didn't lack enthusiasm, energy, power and we were all very young.

Chris had a friend, Neil Lewis, very much a poseur, looked the part, big on ego, and Chris thought that it would be good for the bands image to get him in on vocals. At the time both Clive and myself shared vocal duty. Clive had the better voice, I must admit. I was more of a full tilt shouter, often not in key, no accounting for taste then. During my time with this band, I even managed to break a tooth whilst singing. Nothing volume related. I bit the mike whilst I had my eyes closed, not paying attention, lost in the moment. My excuse anyway and still have the witness 'chip'. Chris convinced Clive that Neil was the going to be our saviour, our star of the show, but I wasn't fooled, probably not convinced are the right words, even today. Neil only came to a couple of rehearsals. He would put in a late appearance, after we'd struggled up those stairs and set up the gear. He flew into the room, with long mane flowing, throw the mike stand around, invariably breaking it. I was always the one that had to mend it,

Sky Trails & Pie Tales . . .

reinforce it, and pay for it post damage. As the evening wore on Neil continued to pose around, waggle his backside, put both hands on his hips and make some attempt at singing, then cleared off down to the pub as we dutifully packed the gear away. I wasn't impressed. What Neil wasn't was a singer. I wasn't perfect, by no means, but Neil's phrasing and sense of rhythm was all out of kilter. Sure, he looked like the next Robert Plant, but best mute. Neil also suggested that we write some more up to date material, Please do suggest Mr Lewis. He again convinced Chris that this was the way forward. Chris was listening to a lot of Genesis and Jethro Tull at the time. Jethro Tull were new to me, but I absorbed all the Tull music Chris had, or had borrowed off his brother. We spent an afternoon at Neil's flat listening to 'Home', a good place to start. In the overpowering glow of Neil's persona, a keyboard player was introduced, and we set about writing new material. It didn't come easily, if at all. What most people had forgotten, me included, was that Labyrinthus was an out and out rocking band. No great airs and graces. Also, we had not matured enough as musicians to be able to compose such grandiose music. This was the start of the fracture. Within a few weeks of that first gig the void and impetus that was being generated by Neil, his introduced ideas, and musical muse drove the band apart like some wedge. I wanted to carry on in the original vein, but with Chris being constantly "Neil-ed" and Clive being dragged along with the flow it was not to be. Around this time, I fell foul of the demon bug which developed into bronchitis. I was bed ridden for two weeks, during which time I missed a few practice sessions. While I was out of action, Chris and Clive took this opportunity and tried out another bass guitarist, whom they both liked. He was in another band, and we'd all often see him rehearse at 'Holy Joes'. He also had an Orange 100watt stack which seemingly impressed both Chris and Clive. Eventually, they both came to see me, at home, and basically told me that this was the end of Labyrinthus. It was time for some of my own medicine. After the initial shock I thought it was for the best. As I said before I think Chris never forgave me for leaving in the first place, to join Open Hands, so that was the end of that. The split was a little acrimonious, as I demanded that I have back all the gear that I had paid for and was legally mine. That included the complete PA and Clive's favourite valve amplifier and speaker cab. It left them with very little in the way of gear, but they had Chris's van. As I had spoken to Peter Hill about the split, it was he who suggested that I store the gear at his father's old factory, where Opens Hands used to rehearse. Seemed like a very good idea at the time. I suppose that was the reason that Pete and I drifted back to playing together. I was looking for another band to join, but I spent the evenings down at Pete's place developing the 'Rhythm Buddies'.

What ever happened to Chris, Clive and Labyrinthus after the split? I never saw them at 'Holy Joe's again and the Birmingham music grape vine was mightily quiet.

Sky Trails & Pie Tales . . .

4   **Ferret**

Back to those 'Rhythm Buddies'. If you remember, Pete and I hit it off musically and rhythmically in an instant. We had, I can only describe it as, a mental oneness. It must have been during these evenings, during late 1973 and into 1974, that we honed this ability to a fine art. As there were only the two of us, with Pete laying down a varying and sometimes sonic rhythm, I developed the ability to improvise over the top. Some nights we played for hours, like this, in the dark, with only the glow of the valves in those amplifiers for company. My quest for another band became somewhat dimmed, mainly due to these most enjoyable evenings. Pete had left college by now. He didn't want to do Engineering and opted for a Philosophy Degree at Birmingham University. Just for the timeline, it was during October 1973 that he started the course. Some evenings, a Uni' mate of his, who was also doing the same degree, came over. This was Ian Ellis. He played the saxophone. Ian was a quiet character, with very long straight hair and small glasses. Very archetypal University Graduate. Ian wasn't too good at holding a melody, so we moved into free form jazz. We all developed this confidence to what is commonly known as "Blowing". I think that wasn't all we were blowing too! But hey, man, this was the Seventies. I can only describe it as the "Canterbury Scene", but in West Bromwich. The music, if you could call it that, was very Van der Graff Generator archetypal. Pete was a great fan of VDGG and we had both listened to their seminal album 'Pawn Hearts' repeatedly. I think it was around this time that he also introduced me to the intricacies and the bizarre musical world that belonged to Gentle Giant. I still find them compelling and enthralling. It was also during this time I was introduced to Pete Gregory, by Pete Hill, and unbeknown to both Peter and I, it was going to be Peter Gregory who was to play a significant

Sky Trails & Pie Tales . . .

part in not only my career, but also that of Still. The two Pete's went to Menzies Grammar School and had met there. Only now I realise what a part that school played in many people's heritage, some directly, some passively. Mine was just a passing through phase.

I thought that I'd better mention the meeting with Terry Luckett. It was around this time that Terry worked at Avery's. After leaving school, sixth form, W&T Avery's had employed me as an apprentice. It was part of every apprentice's duty to do the tour of the factory spending a few weeks in each department, over their four-year period to full qualification. Cheap labour. I also used this as a vehicle for furthering my contacts within the local musical fraternity. I knew, via the grapevine, that Avery's had spawned many musos. So, one day, I was introduced to Terry and spent a week 'working' with him. I say 'working', I was supposed to learn about the job he was doing. In the end both Terry and I educated each other. We spent the entire week talking about bands and music in general. I don't think he was on piece-rate, but if he was, then, at the end of the week his pay packet would have been empty. Terry played guitar and was in a band. I still have his business card; 'Saloon' The Band. Terry was to prove crucial. He introduced me to his circle of friends and drinking haunts that, over time, without this, this story here would have been very different. There are quite a few instances in my life that can be associated to Terry, many times, I've said, "If it wasn't for meeting him." The bass player in 'Saloon' was Brian Roberts. Brian, as did Terry, eventually became close friends and still are today. Anyway, Terry invited me to the "Shed" for a drink one evening. This night was the start of an introduction to a great crowd of mates. Brian was there that first night. I did go and see Terry's band, can't remember where though. It was a cross between Classic Rock and The Eagles. Terry was only a little guy and the Gibson Flying Vee he played dwarfed him, but what a fabulous player. He invited me round to his house

Sky Trails & Pie Tales . . .

one evening. I think this was basically to show off his collection of guitars. Working at Avery's had enabled Terry to create a rather fine collection. I remember he had a black Les Paul, a burgundy Gibson 335 and the Flying Vee. He probably had some others stashed away somewhere else too. He now lives in Spain as does his guitar collection and still plays live music regularly.

For those of you who don't know Birmingham 'The Shed' wasn't as you might expect. Not like the one that 'Ginger' started off in, at the bottom of Clive's Garden. 'The Shed' was long and straight and resided at the bottom of a beer garden of a pub and if scaled down you could have stored your mower and hoe, but to Terry, Brian and now me it was to be my home from home, on and off, from now until the end of the 70's. If 'The Shed' could talk it would have many stories to tell. There are some evenings I spent there I can't recall anything about them, mainly due to the demon drink. The proliferation of pubs around that area housed the same sort of sad Brummies', all trying to drink their way to the future and dim the way of life that was about growing up and living in Britain's second city. The late seventies were all about trying to keep your job, avoid redundancy, avoid the coming recession and drinking helped to blot things out. I still had the music to raise my spirits though.

Despite being band-less for a few months, this was about to change. On odd days, rather than play at Pete's dads old factory, we packed the gear up into my van and drove to Birmingham University, where Pete had started his course and was circulating with all and sundry. How we got everything in the van I don't know, but we did. Pete had blagged his way round and was able to use this empty room on campus. To us it was like doing a gig! It was at the University that Ferret was born. Ferret eventually consisted of James Goodwin on guitar, Ian Ellis on saxophone, Pete on drums and me. We debuted at Birmingham University, where else, supporting the

Sky Trails & Pie Tales . . .

jazz/rock outfit Poliphony, on Sunday 10th March 1974. This was one of the many gigs we played there and in and around the surrounding area. As mentioned, Ferret came about after one evening Pete and I had quaffed a few beers at the Union bar. There was an impromptu "Session" which alternated various musicians. Luckily, I had my bass with me in the van, so, Pete used somebody else's drum kit, and I borrowed an amp. The other fellow on guitar was James. Somehow, it was just one of those magical moments. All three of us just gelled and we took over the evening from then on. Pete got hold of James's phone number and we started to practise around at James house in Edgbaston, in his front room. A good old cassette tape was produced featuring just the three of us from one of these first sessions. Ian was a rather reluctant addition to Ferret. Musically, he wasn't the most confident person in the world, but as he'd been "blowing" with both Pete and myself we convinced him to join as he sure looked the part if nothing else. Ian hid behind that long, straight mane of his when the confidence was lacking. I thought he was great to have in the band. At this point it was the first time that I'd ever played alongside a saxophonist in a proper band format, it didn't disappoint. All the songs/tunes in Ferret were instrumentals, mainly from the pen of James, but a couple were derived from the melting pot of both Pete and I. All the songs were similarly structured. There were 'written' beginnings and endings, but the middle section was always improvised. Depending upon the reaction of the audience Ferret could take any song to a place it had never been before. The middle section could be as short or as long as, Pete and I would make it. Those nights that Pete and I spent together, alone, in the cold, learning the noble art of improvisation were finally paying off. I always remember one particular night. It was again another one of those 'special' nights in James's front room. Pete and I drove home, from Edgbaston, in the early hours, after packing my van up with the drums and bass equipment; we felt we could do no wrong. We were on top of the world. We were a four-wheeled rhythm section on a 'mission'. Not exactly the Blues Brothers, but youthful exuberance coursing through our veins and probably something else to help this along.

One particular gig I recall was, again, at Birmingham University. We were on this huge stage, miles above the audience. James was on one side of the stage, and I was on the other. When we started, I couldn't hear James at all. In the end I had to look at his fingering to guess where we were in the song. We must have sounded awful that night, with the songs drifting in and out of time, like some electronic phased effect, but we didn't really care at the time. The audience seemed to enjoy the cacophony, drink, or drugs? As for effect pedals, in Ferret, this was my introduction to them as I was finally able to introduce a Wah-Wah pedal. I had bought one and had been tinkering around with it for a long time, on bass. The tonal qualities I could achieve were quite staggering. Unbeknown to me, the bass player with 'Yes', Chris Squire, used to use one too, but I'm sure he thought of it first. He was just one of my influences. One Christmas I spent the entire time at home listening to and attempting to dissect his bass lines on 'Fragile'. They still outstand me. After the seasonal period I returned to Ferreting finding out that by using a combination of the Wah-Wah pedal and hitting and slapping the strings I was able to add, complement and occasionally add an offbeat to Pete's rhythmic patterns. In these early days I was always more of a rhythmic player, than a melodic one, always using a plectrum, rather than the 'normal' bass players technique of fingers only. With a plectrum I was able to add attack and be louder than normal. I suppose this stems back to the really early days when I didn't have adequate amplification. I had to make the loudest noise possible, given what I'd got. There were certain patterns I played which I would argue are impossible to play without a plectrum, but then I was just a kid with the technique to learn. In many years to come the well-known King Crimson bassist, Tony Levin, would use these things called 'Funk Fingers'. To the uninitiated these were basically (no pun intended) long bits of thin wood secured to each finger of the right hand. OK if you were left-handed, or Paul McCartney, then they would fit your left hand. You then hit the strings with these 'Funk Fingers', like a drumstick. The rhythms produced were the next logical step from a plectrum, to me at least. I never got this far, stuck to the old plectrum. Old habits die hard.

Ferret continued, in equal amounts, to stutter and forge a bit of a growing reputation on the University Campus, until one day Pete Hill gave me a call, which was to prove disastrous. He'd had a break in at his father's factory. All of Peter's drums, some speaker cabinets of mine, an amplifier and many mikes and stands had been stolen. Luckily, I had taken my bass guitar home together with an amplifier and a couple of speaker cabinets. We spent the morning down at the local police station, but the items were never traced. Even back then the police were never going to take much notice of two longhaired, scruffy individuals. Peter was devastated. At least I still had the bass and enough gear at home to keep me fluid. The spark that fuelled 'The Passion' crackled, but the flame still burned brightly. Ferret bolted back to from whence it came. I tried to talk Pete into buying another kit. I seem to remember that he eventually got one. A student grant in those days was such a meagre subsistence. It was a mishmash of drums. It fitted easily into my van, and I stored it in the old coal shed, in the garage, at my parents' house. After this we never seemed to recreate that old Trev & Pete magic. That robbery also cut the musical umbilical cord that co-existed between us. To this day if I ever found out who was behind the break-in, well . . . enough said, here at least. At the time both Pete and I came to the same conclusion that it was somebody we knew. We had

Sky Trails & Pie Tales . . .

an idea, an inkling, but have left this locked into this time, this era and event. Whoever it was knew what was stored there and only took what belonged to us. Other more valuable items were left behind. I can't turn back the clock, but it happened and that was that. Most of the gear that was taken were those items that the loan, the one I had agreed to cover, had paid for, and from here on all the outstanding payments became a financial millstone. Here I was paying off for the stolen gear that I didn't even own. In the end I honoured the agreement with Chris's friend and settled my debt. I wasn't going to do this again, and I never did, well, not formally, with added interest.

After this and with Ferret falling apart, Pete faded away and receded back to his university degree course and circle of friends. Ian went the same way as Pete, who was doing the same degree anyway. James finally linked up with this band he had been talking about for some time now. In the final weeks of what was to become Ferret's death knell, he was already practising with them in his days off from Ferreting. I occasionally saw Pete and went around the flat he was sharing, but it was apparent that he was being dragged into the life of a student, with all the associated culture and substances. However, Pete did get to playing the drums again, but not with me. He and a few other flat members had this part time gathering known as both Little Boys and also Geoff Wilton & Friends. Pete played with me once more, in this guise, on the same bill, more of that later. They supported Still, with whom I was to join, at the Junction, Harborne, Birmingham; a well-known, at the time, music venue and close enough to the university campus and even more local to the QE Hospital, with a view in dragging in the suspect punter and nurse. It worked and the gig did, being the first one that I'd booked the room, PR'd it, sold the tickets, covered the loss. A start to what was to come in later years. Even then I had become a musician, booker, ticket agency, promoter, PR and

Sky Trails & Pie Tales . . .

market-ier. After this night I lost track of Pete and he of me. It has only been recently that I have finally traced him to Sheffield, where he now lives and works, probably retired now, like me. He was able to fill in a few gaps and rekindle a few names for me at the time of compiling the 'Cherish Ever' booklet, but time and Pete have once again put distance between us. Once a ferret, always a ferret I suppose, more comfortable in someone else's dug tunnel, than one they can dig themselves, albeit badly.

After this Pete Gregory, Pete (Hill's) old acquaintance, and I started to spend more time together, going out for a few beers and talking music. Pete didn't play an instrument, but his musical and band knowledge was impressive. He lived close to me and as he didn't drive, I was more than happy to pick him up on the way and hopefully find our way back to his house at the end of the night. Most nights we used to end up at JB's Club in Dudley. More about JB's later. Despite paying back the loan from Labyrinthus days, which was coming to an end, I was desperate to get a better bass, something a bit more in keeping with the aim I had in mind, let's say more kudos and professional. I knew Pete had a good job and was always saying he didn't know what to spend his hard-earned cash on, so, with some front, I asked him to borrow some money in order to get this new bass. There was no way I could ask my parents; they'd flatly refuse and make things even more difficult than they were at the time. I had seen this bass hanging up in a music shop in the centre of Birmingham. It was a walnut finish, Gibson EBOL, long scale. Just like the one Jack Bruce of Cream used to play, but with one pick up. Whilst working I had saved some money, but it was not enough, so, good old Pete lent me the rest and I paid him back without interest. Was he a genie in disguise? Another great memorable day, when I traded in my old relic, my very first proper guitar, if you could call it that, for this brand-new Gibson, plus a new guitar case. I

Sky Trails & Pie Tales . . .

have to say Pete Gregory was to feature and play a key role in my next band Still, but his character, his affable nature, his kindness is always one I can recall in an instant. Pete liked his beer but was always clear minded with all the investments and decisions he made until his untimely death. I have no exact date, but the consensus with those of us left who knew him, and he didn't have a great circle of friends back then, feel it was shortly after I'd left the area, probably early 80's; Pete was fatally injured whilst staggering home alone one cold, dark night down West Bromwich's Expressway. He was hit by a car and probably knew very little about it. I can still conjure up his face, his long straight hair, his glasses, always seemingly wearing the same jumper, hands stuffed into his pockets, a slight dishevelment, but Pete to a tee. In a strange way I still miss him. He was good to me; he was good to everyone to be honest. Had a huge encyclopaedic knowledge of the music scene at that time. Taken too early.

So, armed with a new bass, off I went on the old audition trail. One audition was with Sorahan. I turned up at the audition and much to my surprise James's car was parked outside. Was this band the one I had heard him talk about? The band he was thinking of joining whilst 'Ferreting'? It certainly was. As I burst through the doors in the hall and clapped my eyes on James, was I ecstatic. I thought that, with a friend and an ally in James I was sure to get the job. Maybe he sensed my over exuberance as at some point, just before we started, James took me to one side and said, "Play it simple". Even then I was quite an overly, sometimes unnecessarily 'busy' player, I 'simpled' it up as much as the old fingers and mind would let me. In the end it was down to me and this other bass player. Needless to say, I didn't get the job. I think I was too 'Up' for their liking. The guy who got the job was quiet, laid back and didn't overshadow the main man of the band, Tom Sorahan. At least I took a crumb of consolation from this. Musically

Sky Trails & Pie Tales . . .

I felt I had improved enough to be able to compete with the best of the others, but lessons learnt. Hard at the time but I had to take these episodes in a positive light, I was young enough and still learning. I saw Sorahan a few times after this, namely at The Junction and JB's. I was still reasonably close to James. By now Sorahan had gone professional and were gigging across the country. If I had got the job, then, would I have had to relinquish my day job. I would have been only 20. Would my parents have accepted this? I shall never know, but the answer would have been a resounding 'NO'. I think if the offer was on the plate, then I would have enforced orphan-ism on myself. They released a single. A copy of which resides in my collection. One of the songs I recall playing at the audition. Sorahan eventually dissolved into obscurity. I was still hunting in the adverts, the wanteds.

Around this time, during various other auditions, none of which really appealed, I was at one of them when I first came across and met Nick Parry. Some auditions were a failure, others were more successful, but I was looking for a band with potential and similar musical interests. Something specific. I kept the bar high, limiting my choice by decision. One evening I was invited to an audition at the Midlands Arts Centre. It was pouring with rain and the drummer had failed to turn up. Despite wasting my time, I was soaked through and not in the best of moods; it didn't take much. However, something that was said must have sparked my imagination as a week or two later I was back there. Nick, the missing drummer, turned up, and looking back now the evening was memorable and forgettable all rolled into one. We all ended up back at Nick's house with a bit of an entourage in tow, girlfriends etc. Nick took centre stage. He knew his way round a drum kit and most impressive with it too. He was, then, a character, very confident, had an ego, but cool with it in a strange appealing kind of way. Many stories were regaled. Transpires he had worked as

Sky Trails & Pie Tales . . .

drum roadie for Irish band Fruupp and was well connected with their manager Paul Charles. Nick also had a cloak, a Dracula Cloak, which made an appearance as the evening wore on, along with much mirth and jollity. However, what impressed me at the time, apart from his drumming, was that he had a vision. A vision of the music business. We parted company after exchanging phone numbers, but with no concrete plans and nothing that would come to fruition. Little did I know that this evening was to become a fairly key event and contact as regards the future of Still. Nick was a pure showman and like a cat he always would seem to land on his feet no matter what was thrown at him.

There were many other auditions, most of which have faded completely from memory. All I can recall is that most of them were a darn sight younger than me, even then, and there was no way that I was going to retreat down this yellow brick road. I had arrived at this particular crossroads and was only going to go in one direction. There was no reverse gear on this bass player. What happened next was rather fortuitous, meant to be, and written in the annals of history. Fate can often play its own card sometimes and it sure was going to do that one night in Dudley, West Midlands.

Come in Pete Gregory, your time is up. "Fancy a few beers at JB's Pete?", "Yeah, why not", "Get in then", and off we went. I parked up at the building behind Pathfinders on Dudley's Ring Road.

Sky Trails & Pie Tales . . .

5   Still

Pete and I trundled into JB's, avoiding long direct eye contact with 'Jimmy the Con' on the door. Jimmy was what he was, the best security person you could ever have on the door of a club of this ilk. No messing with Jimmy. Beers were ordered, with conversation difficult over the loud music, so we just listened, absorbed, and took in the sights surrounding. It was likely a Thursday night as I'd driven there. Most Friday's and Saturday's I'd get the bus, or a taxi home as I couldn't be found driving after too much consumption. During the evening Pete came across and spotted an old school friend of his, Robert Lake. Rob was with a mate of his too, a young Larry Homer. At this moment in time, both Rob and Larry were singer and guitarist respectively in a local band called 'Still', transpires it was a Symphonic Progressive Rock Band; interesting. During Pete and Rob's shouted conversation Rob mentioned that the band were looking for a bass player. A point of star alignment if there was ever one! With that Pete turned round to me, pointing in my direction and also shouting in Rob's right ear "Here's your bass player". By the end of the evening, I'd had a short chat with Rob and an even shorter one with Larry and an invite to an audition at their next Sunday afternoon rehearsal. This meeting and gathering of musicians were key in many ways. As you read the story, these names from this era often crop up and one person in particular, rekindles the past some four decades later. It was a very important day. A few days later, as the Sunday lunchtime drinkers meandered home from Dudley's Hen and Chickens pub, back to their wives; their Sunday Roasts, another bunch of unruly people descended on the first-floor function room. This time it was a burgeoning bunch of talented local musicians. It was late 1974. In these days of no mobiles, no Internet, I had nothing to go on as regards preparation. This band 'Still' wrote all its own material, was a five-piece band, complete with a keyboard player and a newly acquired synthesiser. My attention went from interesting to impressive. Nerves that day played a big part, finding such a band, and one that was idly seeking a bass player too, from just an ad hoc social couple of drinks at a local music club is very much 'Roy of the Rovers' territory. You can't really write this sort of thing, but there I was standing in this function room, new bass in hand, with some very serious and talented people, on a Sunday afternoon. Could I cut the mustard? Some of my previous auditions had taught me a few things as regards playing and outward emotion control. Don't mess this one up Trev, played on a loop in my head, even more so as first notes rang out. These guys were good and knew what they were doing. The style of music was in the vein of Yes/Genesis/King Crimson. I finally had found the band that I was looking for, but had the band found its bass player they were looking for? Rather than flit from one song to another it was decided they work with me on one song and see how it develops. The song was called 'House on the Hill', written by Larry, with lyrics by Rob; remember this song, it features later on in the story. A fairly simple arrangement but had a huge building sonic structure and dynamics. I sensed this was key. It was almost a song in two sections, verse/choruses in the first section and a repeating, building guitar motif in the last part. I gingerly tiptoed through it a few times, but don't ask me from where it came, but I seemed to hit on something, a line, that fitted. I dared not seek visual approval. We worked on 'House on the Hill' for most of the afternoon and from a very distant memory, a couple of other pieces. Did I get the job? Classic let me know. I sat by the phone at home every evening after college. It rang. "We'd like you in the band, let's see how the next couple of rehearsals go." Even today I can sense the joy this brought me; such is this lasting tangible emotion. Maybe someone up there was smiling down, probably not my parents. Let's

Sky Trails & Pie Tales . . .

attribute this to local musician Johnny Bryant as it was his initials that were used for the club in Dudley, JB's, as without that club none of this would have happened. I could also say it goes back to Pete Hill introducing me to Pete Gregory at College. Fate does work in some strange and convoluted ways, never anything straight forward, or planned. This felt right and over the following few years it was right and is now rekindled in a future context.

JB's was key in the future lives of many of the people that frequented this notorious club. You had to be a member, so it was a proper club, I suppose. You paid your dues, even getting a membership card. Many lifelong relationships were forged there, both musical and personal. I've seen a few terminated as well and was probably party to one or two! This 250-capacity venue was situated in an old building behind the menswear shop Pathfinder on King Street, on the outskirts of Dudley, teetering on the cusp on the Black Country. In my days it was pretty rough, but well policed by Jimmy on the door. He kept out unwelcome guests and joined in with any fight going on in the club. You never messed with Jimmy. Best kept on his good side. Respect was a badge you had to earn. We were all kind of one big family, looked out for and supported each other. 'Big Dave' Hodgetts was another one, I liked Dave, down to earth, told you how things were, like it, or lump it. He used to work behind the bar and was Robert Plant's estate/housekeeper whilst he was away on musical duties, very much Robert's right-hand man. As Dave succumbed to illness later in life it was Robert who paid for his treatment, sending a taxi to bring him down to the O2 in London on the tenth of December 2007 for Led Zeppelin's reunion as part of the Ahmet Ertegun Tribute charity concert. Robert is heard to say at the end of the gig "How was that Dave?" It was Big Dave Hodgett that this was directed to, just one face in the crowd, but a longstanding friend, still part of the JB's family. That was Dave's last gig. Even after all those years the JB's bond is strong, long and binding. We'd all do the same, despite and regardless of our social standing, fame, and notoriety. Same applies to Roy Williams. Roy was there at the very beginning, as part of the formation of the club. He was a regular DJ and all manner of other things. Like Dave, he was part of Robert Plant's inner sanctum. Roy was his go to sound engineer and was on the mixing desk that night of the 2007 O2 reunion. For the rest of us, Robert was just another face in the club on those nights he was free: heady days! JB's can also own up to being the place that many forged their identity in this world after leaving school, gave them a purpose, a direction, a meaning in life. JB's probably did more for many that went there than the later school years we attended. Many times, I've heard people say JB's made them into what they are today. I can attribute a lot of that in my life, plus the beer was cheap and the music exemplary. I met a lot of people in there! To find out more and the full story behind this club read Geoff Tristram's book 'JB's: The story of Dudley's Legendary Live Music Venue'. This is now sadly out of print but the book is jam packed with memories that chronicled our youth, our identity, and the reason why we all became the people we are today, having passed through the doors, every Thursday, Friday and Saturday night. Even I get a mention in the book and supplied some of the stories and memorabilia. One story that doesn't is the night in the 'Gents', well, you couldn't call it a proper toilet, just a trough with a pipe through the wall. So, I'm standing there, as you do and next to me is the very well-known lead singer from Led Zeppelin. Nods are exchanged as well as a little bit of 'splash-back' on my shoes. His, or mine? The annals of history will explain. I know the answer. I didn't clean my stack heels for weeks after. Over the years we've occasionally crossed paths. Once he nearly ran me over when he drove into Molyneux as I stepped out in front of his car. He was pulling into the private car park at

Sky Trails & Pie Tales . . .

Wolves Football Club. I actually never saw him, and it was my lad James who pulled me back. Could have been nasty. My team, Leyton Orient, drew with Wolves that day. I'd call that a result. In later years I used to correspond more with his sister Alison. My wife spoke to him briefly when offering him a flyer at one of my old band gigs at his regular haunt in Wolverley, the Queens Head, a pleasant rebuff was accepted. The most recent 'could have been' was in 2022. I'd been invited to the 'After-Show' by one of his band, Tony Kelsey, when 'Saving Grace' played in London. This was Robert's offshoot project with most, as he said that night, musicians that all live within five miles of each other. The after show passes I needed had been placed at the venues box office. There were a couple of misplaced messages that night which ended up with me in not picking up them up. An opportunity missed, but nice to have been asked all the same.

JB's used to book bands on Friday, Saturday and sometimes Sunday. The bands were either local, up and coming, or sometimes reasonably well known. Some Saturdays, which was the night for reasonably well-known bands to appear, disappeared into an alcoholic haze. For a time, Saturdays was the night that a bunch of about twenty of us used to go, taxis home only. No driving. After each and every one of us had dutifully bought a round, "Twenty bottles of Pils mate", the evening usually ended up in a toxic, memory-less and usually, falling over throng. Many a following morning I used to wake up with no great recollection of being extremely close to Mark Knopfler of a pre-pubescent, pre-first album, Dire Straits; Sting when he played in the band before The Police; Annie Lennox and Dave Stewart as The Tourists before they formed the Eurthymics and so it goes on. Thursday nights at JB's was DJ night and usually was the night you went down to eye up the competition, but mostly ended up walking home alone. Those Saturdays and Thursdays were usually spent in the company of the crowd I had become embroiled in from 'The Shed'. Most Saturday nights were spent staggering away from the club attempting to find the taxis we'd booked earlier. On really cold evenings, especially after a frost, or when the ice and snow lay, we had to negotiate the slope from the club up to the main road. Even when sober this was a difficult task, but when drunk, wearing stack heeled boots, nearly impossible. Most attempts found yourself back at the bottom of the slope. Those that wore Afghan coats had one extra layer of protection from the cold, the ice, the snow that most of us hadn't. Much hilarity ensured as we grimly clung to the fence and scaled the heady heights to King Street. Most of the time these Afghan coat brigade wearers were viewed as a fashion statement of the time but was one that came with the tag of 'odour'. For the uninitiated, these coats were made from goat skin with the fleece on the inside and a soft suede leather exterior. The more expensive ones didn't smell as bad as the cheaper ones. I had one of the cheaper ones from the Oasis retail market outlet in Birmingham. Oasis was really a hippy emporium, a collection stalls selling most things that your regular burgeoning hippy needed in order to fit in, to be trendy. One stall did a good line in leather stack heel boots. Yes, I had a few pairs; one in nearly every colour. Saturday morning was the attraction for most in the area, especially to the record stalls. A piece of twelve-inch plastic was an almost necessary purchase needed to make the trip worthwhile. So, one cold Saturday morning my parents shoved me out of the door with the instructions to get yourself a coat, a raincoat. Not a great clothes shopper and with no girlfriend for advice I bought this cheap Afghan coat. Brand new it was great. My parents were horrified. Brownie points for me in upsetting them then. As the months and usage went on this coat grew into a life of its own. It started to smell. Being rained on, dried out, rained on, dried out, had given its own odour, coupled with the fact that every time I took it off much animal hair remained on the

Sky Trails & Pie Tales . . .

clothes I was wearing. I still thought it looked great, until the day I was ill on it. I'll spare you the details, but the damp patch on the middle of the back never returned to its original suede like finish and had shrunk, pulling the rest of the coat with it. This fashion statement then remained as an 'inside-out' rear seat cover in my van. Thankfully the odour was masked by the slow, ever pervading fumes of creosote. Creosote Gate is told elsewhere in this story. The Afghan coat, the creosote can, and the van all died a simultaneous death.

Having accepted the bass players seat in Still, after the Sunday lunchtime audition, I had arranged to go round to Rob Lake's flat the following night in order to start working on the songs. The feeling I had with this band was that, as time went on, that this was most promising, maybe the one, the right band? All the pointers seemed to be in the right direction; a path to fame and fortune? Now Rob was a character. All the time I knew him he was perpetually on the dole, scrimping, begging, borrowing, not paying back; but to me, over time, he became a lovable rogue. The flat he originally had was in Smethwick, quite near 'The Shed'. I dutifully turned up with my brand-new Gibson, but most of the evening was spent chatting and Rob getting rather 'oiled' on cider. In his out-of-work state, to relieve the daily boredom Rob had turned to cider as his shoulder to cry on. I didn't know then, but over the coming months I realised that this was the case. His wife turned up later, Jenny. She was in-work, extremely flamboyant, very 70's, lots of bangles, dark eye make-up, very big curly black 'afro' hair, long skirts, big on charisma and very grown up. Over the months, how she put up with Rob's and the band's antics, I'll never know. Not much time was spent on the songs this evening, but useful, nevertheless. It was at the next full rehearsal at the Hen & Chickens, that things were to start gelling. Those rehearsals at the pub were always Friday evenings and Saturday lunch times, well into the afternoon. On those first sessions it was then I was to come across Rob's novel playing style and guitar. Why Rob played the five-string guitar I don't know, but it was something he did and possibly something he gleaned from 'Keef' Richards who did the same. I borrowed it one night, to learn to play something else at home. Being the kind and generous person that I was, I put on the missing string on for him. When I gave the guitar back to Rob, the first thing he did was to remove this sixth string. I put it down to his fingering and couldn't cope with all the strings . . . I still firmly believe it was his voice, style of singing and phrasing that really was his instrument. I suppose that came from the many hours he spent at home listening to and mimicking the voice of Peter Gabriel, whilst the rest of us went to work. Listening back now to those archived Still recordings, his phrasing and occasionally sounds, were a dead ringer for the then Mr Gabriel of Genesis. It was also at those first rehearsals that I realised that my Gibson was too dull sounding for the music that we were playing. Too much Bruce than Squire. So, in order to brighten it up a bit I went to Woodroffe's and bought this effects pedal called 'The Screaming Tree'. This tended to increase the treble content of the output of my Gibson and made it sound more Rickenbacker like, but no replacement. "Use The Screaming Tree"! Larry called. In the end this was abbreviated to the "God Tray". With this pedal and in conjunction with the Wah-Wah and volume pedal I plucked and twiddled all night long, with my feet and fingers, until perfection was gained. We continued to rehearse and build the material into a usable set. I've mentioned Rob and Larry, the other two in the band were keyboard player Howard Rushton and drummer Arthur 'Art' Matthews. Howard was a quiet sort of chap and Art was the ultimate bohemian, always wanting to "Make the coast, man" with his then girlfriend in his VW camper van. The use of the rehearsal room at the pub came as part of Howard's connection with this hostelry. Even then everyone had other roles and uses.

Sky Trails & Pie Tales . . .

By now Rob had moved from Smethwick and was living with Jenny in Wolverhampton. This flat was barely big enough for the two of them, but when we all turned up to talk Still the place was packed. It was in this flat, that between Larry and Rob, that most of the early Still songs were spawned, born and refined. Many an evening was spent there, trying to play my bass quietly, working out the new and varied runs and riffs. Unfortunately, bass always carries the furthest and most evenings there was someone banging on the door, complaining. Back to the old days at my parents' house. What we didn't know, at the time, was that these evenings were keeping Rob sane. Something to break the daily, job-less days, the monotony. One night, at the end of October, Jenny and Rob had organised a Halloween fancy dress party. We all turned up in various disguises. I went as a gangster, with my mum's big fur coat on, a trilby pulled down tight over my eyes and a violin case. In the violin case wasn't the obligatory machine gun, but another highly charged, metal contained chemical. OK, cans of lager. For a laugh, as you do at that age, we all thought that it would be the right thing to do and go to the local pub. Now, as usual, Larry was the most outrageously dressed. His normally curly hair was pulled back tight, in a bun and had copious amounts of white make-up, applied to his olive skin. The final touch was dark eye makeup. He resembled an early form of Michael Jackson and frightened all and sundry. On his way to the flat that night he had to stop to get some petrol. He pulled into the garage and wound down the window. What greeted the pump attendant was this white and black apparition, with a high collared cloak, and an extremely deep voice, which said, "Four gallons of four star please". The reaction was as you would normally expect, he ran, but Larry still got his petrol. Anyway, back to the party. On our way to the pub, we all piled into my van, and I drove off into the wilds of Wolverhampton. As I turned the corner to the pub, I misjudged the severity of the bend and on a fairly cold, late October evening, my van and its contents careered across the road, bounced up the curb and into the park. Thankfully, there was no traffic coming the other way, no near pedestrians and no fence round the park! With the weight of nine to ten people in my van we came to a graceful halt in the park with a great scattering of autumnal leaves. We all piled out in a semi-alcoholic daze for those that had been drinking, followed by a deep blue cloud of cigarette smoke. The potential of our actions could have been plastered all over the next day's Wolverhampton local rag. "Up and coming rock band killed and eaten by ghouls and ghosts!" Anyway, after much merriment and waving at the old couple who had just walked by, we eventually had a more sedate journey to the pub. If you want to silence an entire room in one fell swoop, then just walk into a pub, all dressed like us and order some beers. Brilliant!

Whilst on van stories, same van, is this, yet another full load. It consisted of coming home, at about two in the morning, from Barbarella's nightclub in Birmingham. I'd been there all night and most of the people I was with had missed the last bus home and couldn't be bothered to wait for the night bus. So, their Good Samaritan (i.e., me, having remained below the legal limit all night) turned up trumps and went out of his way to drop them all off. I had six in the back and three in the front, including the driver, me. This was the time I had fixed a wooden panel behind the front seats and painted the rear windows black, effectively sealing the back of the van off. This was so I could store my bass gear in my van without people looking in. Even so, it still didn't stop someone from breaking in one night whilst I slept. Thankfully all my gear had been taken out the night before. Nothing else was stolen, so obviously they were looking for something specific. Maybe the same bunch who broke into Pete Hill's warehouse and stole his drums and a few items of mine; who knows? So, the six people in the back couldn't see out, but hey, they were getting

Sky Trails & Pie Tales . . .

a free lift. On the way back towards Dudley the police stopped me. I think it was down to my doubled up two passengers, sitting on top of each other. I was told to get out of the van and dutifully invited to sit in the back of their police car. I really thought that this was it, to be breathalysed and done for overloading. Whilst they checked out that the van wasn't stolen, I held my breath. It was much to my surprise that they let me out, no breath test, but with a severe telling off and I was allowed to continue my journey. Only after the police had driven off did I breathe a sigh of relief. So did the six people in the back of the van. Little did I know, at the time, that the two people in front had banged on the partition to tell them to keep quiet whilst I was in the Police car just in case they wanted to search the van. They didn't. But if they had, then I'm sure I would have been in trouble and all the others would have had to walk home. As the police car disappeared into the night, I opened the back doors of my van and was greeted with six, breathless red faces and billowing clouds of smoke. How we all laughed! How safely I drove back home too! Another good evening had come to an end.

One more good van tale involved transporting a whole bunch into the city centre for a night out. This time a few were secreted in the back, and I just had one passenger in the front, next to me, this time. Sadly, as to whom this passenger was, for this story, I've conveniently forgotten, probably best. On the journey in I pull up at some traffic lights and a motor bike squeezes in between me and the pavement. The biker then starts to take a keen interest in my van and the passenger. Stares are exchanged, going well so far. Unbeknown to me as the lights go green my passenger decides to wave goodbye to our motor cyclist friend, but with only two of their fingers used. A now slightly enraged Speedy Gonzales decides to follow me. He's weaving in and out of the traffic, attempting a passing manoeuvre at any suitable time. I ponder to my passenger "I wonder if they're following us?" The advice I'm given is to turn left at the next road, "We'll find out then." I turn left, the bike follows. Many other turns are made, I speed up, I slow down, the bike is still there. The folks in the back of my van are now wondering on what's going on. My passenger regales them the events. I carry on this insane chase through the suburbs and outer Birmingham City Limits (good subject for a song there?), until I take a wrong turn. The road is a cul-de-sac with an island at the end with no way out. Barry Sheen is still with us. At the tenth time of island circumnavigation, I stop. Cue: 'Yakety Sax', the music. I get out of the van as does my passenger who then proceeds to open the rear doors of my van and all those in there pile out. By now Barry Sheen has taken off his helmet and was just about to vent his anger, but his words never came as he was slightly outnumbered and pondered on his escape. We had no intention to cause a fight or spawn his anger. Someone then said, "Are you Benny Hill?" The whole situation diffused into howls of laughter, the biker joining in too. We all carried on our way and now this story is cast into posterity in this book.

By this time the band had started to gig. At the end of this chapter, I've listed all the gigs I did with Still, purely as a record for me, and for those remotely interested. History shouldn't be eradicated; I haven't. Looking back, it wasn't that many gigs, but the band were writing and refining material all the time and there were huge gaps in the gigs as the set was chopped and changed and improved. In order to help getting work the band decided it was time to get a decent studio recording in order to be able to send these to record companies and venues alike. The only local, reasonably cheap, studio we found was in the depths of the Black Country, down a long country lane. The studio was on the top floor of a converted barn. The cheapest rates we could negotiate were a late evening to early hours of the morning session. OK so this was it. We struggled up the stairs

Sky Trails & Pie Tales . . .

with the necessary gear, amps, drums and keyboards and set ourselves up as best we could, given the cramped space. The clock ticked. Our money went down. Tensions and arguments and egos pervaded the session. Problems beset the start, with me, as usual being too loud for the microphones. No matter where I set up, everybody else picked me up. In the end they wanted me to directly inject my bass into the mixing desk, which is a common practice these days, but I was having none of this. Stubborn? Me? I wanted to be able to hear me. In the end we agreed a compromise and my speaker cabinet was pointed at the wall, shrouded in cloth, with the microphone jammed in there somewhere. At the volume I was made to play I was near inaudible as it was. It did the trick and the sound on the recording came out true and warm, so I was glad that I stuck to my intuition. For the next few hours and into the night, were spent recording the backing tracks for three songs. In the end, we were all reasonably pleased, even with Howard's gurgling and churgling Hammond organ fills he had added. Luckily, we had found this old, battered Hammond organ and Leslie cabinet lurking in the darkest depths of the studio. On finding it still worked, Howard, was economic with his frills and embellishments. I believe Larry also put his guitar through this rotating Leslie cabinet too, a lovely effect. Rob took an age for his vocal takes, but it was eventually finished. A handful of 'Still' material had been committed to tape. We packed up, left, and went home. At what point as to what happened next, I'm unsure of the sequence of events, but after we left and the studio had been locked up, the barn caught fire. Most of the studio was gutted, but the tape and the recording survived. I still have a copy. Over time this has degraded due to time and transfer from 'reel to reel' to cassette and then digitised, but the essence of that night's work remains. Mixing, correction and editing never occurred as the means to do so were burnt to a cinder. Everyone involved were lucky to be able to tell this story. We'd all gone home and were blissfully unaware of what was happening behind the locked doors until it was too late, and the fire brigade were in touch. If the fire had started in effect at ground level, whilst we were all upstairs in the studio, then the likelihood of casualties and not escaping was strong. At worst we could have all perished. There was only one staircase, cum fire exit, from the studio, right into the source of the fire. Lucky boys?

It wasn't all plain sailing and musical treats. Despite the great and very unique voice that Rob had, he also had some serious demons and other issues; his lack of job, his drinking and the emotional pain from his personal life; much of it self-inflicted, some of this infliction physical pain as well. I did my bit when I could by going round to pick him up from his flat in Wolverhampton and take him to the Dudley rehearsals, keeping an eye on him otherwise. One particular evening, I was just going out for a beer with a few friends when I had this garbled message from Larry. "Rob's tried to do himself in". I knew Rob was pretty down at this time. Still out of work and drinking heavily during the day. To this day I don't know what prompted him to do it, but he'd self-harmed, again. His arms and wrists bore the brunt of these occasional low points. This was another call for help, another low point. The situation was dealt with by sound engineer Graham Ford and Larry. They'd dropped him off and it was Graham that said that they ought to go back and check on him, just to make sure; it was wise that they did. This saved Rob's life, for now. It was 1975. It's not my story, or for these pages, but sadly both Rob's and Jenny's relationship eventually crumbled, and Rob found himself on his own again. We had to keep an eye on him all the time. Many rehearsals after this were a struggle. Rob usually turned up half inebriated and it affected the band to the extent that Art, had had enough and calmly announced one evening at the end of the night that this was the last one. So, that was that then . . . or was it? A drummer was required.

Sky Trails & Pie Tales . . .

My suggestion was to put forward Nick Parry, as replacement drummer. I'd met Nick as part of the auditions I'd had, pre-Still, at the Midlands Arts Centre. Nothing had come of this, but Nick's style of playing, his character had stayed with me ever since. I called Nick asking if he'd be interested. An uncertain reply was forthcoming so I gave Nick's phone number to Larry to see if he could influence him. Whatever Larry said over the phone, or in person when they both met, must have worked. Nick was on board and Still Mk1 became Mk2. On the journey from mark one to two the band had also lost keyboard player Howard. As for the reasons? Lost to the mists of time, sorry reader. This new model of the band was Nick on drums, Larry on guitar, Rob on vocals and keys and me on bass. Rob's expertise on keys matched that of his guitar playing. He was able enough, playing chords mostly, but gave a colour to the band and was different to the hue that Howard brought. It also gave Rob something to physically hide behind, the stack of keyboards. We reconvened at the Cradley Heath warehouse of Larry's father's business having lost the room above the pub in Dudley and rehearsals for Mk2 commenced. On warm days it was too hot, on cold days I wore fingerless gloves. The warehouse was unheated and deemed not worthy to have air conditioning. It was during this time that Graham Ford came on board as permanent sound engineer, investing in his own custom-made multi-channel mixing desk and sundries. We were all getting a bit serious about this. Graham was another friend of mine, introduced to the band, from the days of Pete Gregory and Pete Hill. I also introduced Paul Andrews to the band. I'd met him at college. He had similar long hair to me, and we just started taking about music, as you do. Paul was a dab hand at electronics and became a lighting guru for the band. Drummer Nick got Paul to design and install a lighting rig in his kit, triggered by Nick, whilst playing. My commitment came in the shape and form of a new bass guitar, yes, I went looking for a Rickenbacker.

Sky Trails & Pie Tales . . .

I thought if I'm going to give this band, this opportunity, the best shot I need the best guitar. I stepped up, not telling the others, but Graham and I went looking for a Rickenbacker 4001. I found one in the good old wanted's of Melody Maker. The guy selling it lived in Stratford upon Avon, so off we went. We found the house in a posh part of Stratford, and I knocked on the door. Following a cup of tea and a chat he brought out this guitar, in black. If you believe in love at first sight, then this was a classic case. Rather than falling for the opposite sex I fell head over heels for this chunk of wood and metal. It was lovely and sounded just what I was looking for and in a very good condition, almost brand new. Not wishing to play my ace card I tried to play it cool, whilst inside my emotions were running full tilt. I tried to talk him down in price, but he didn't budge. We couldn't agree and, in the end, he gave me a week to raise the necessary, otherwise he was going to move it on elsewhere. Talk about burning a hole in your pocket. I couldn't sleep and eat and talked incessantly to Graham about it. The asking price was much over the odds of my budget and available funds as to what I wanted to spend. In the end this burning sensation in my head and my pocket eventually got the better of me and I coughed up, but there was a risk. In order to keep this deal and the financial out goings from my parents I had to sell my current bass, the Gibson, first. I then had enough money, coupled with what I'd saved to buy the Rickenbacker. I didn't have time to place an advert. What happened? I sold the Gibson bass back to the shop from where I bought it in the first place. I got a trade-in value and lost a fair sum if compared to its current market value and private equity, but this way gave me the full amount of cash I needed and was quick. The risk here was the few hours that I physically didn't have a bass. What if the guy in Stratford was out (he was, in the end), or at worst had reneged on the deal and sold it to someone else? Before I sold my Gibson on that morning, I phoned the Stratford man and told him I'm

Sky Trails & Pie Tales . . .

coming over later with the agreed cash, so don't sell it! It's now Saturday afternoon, another sunny day, and I find myself tearing over to Stratford, with Graham, listening to Yes's 'Close to the Edge' on repeat, on eight track, with a large wedge of money in my pocket. I was extremely close to that edge . . . too. I knocked on the door, a second time in a week. The guy was out but thankfully had left instructions. I handed over the money, opened the guitar case to make sure it was what it was; and it was, and drove home on 'Cloud Nine'. More Close to the Edge ensued on the return journey. All that I had to do was parade this bass at rehearsal the next day. There was a great amount of bowing and scraping and praying to that great Rickenbacker God in the sky, by the rest of the band. I think I'd proven, not only to the band, but to me too that I meant business and my commitment was with Still. Other than that, it was a lovely guitar, beautiful to play, well, it ought to be, at that price. Also, during all of this I wanted to put a couple things in place should my and the bands future dreams flounder, qualifications. Probably my parents would have been pleased but I needed to take a couple of weeks off, away from music and my thoughts from Still in order to concentrate and prepare for my end of year exams as they were creeping up and I needed to pass, with as good grades as I could muster. This, hopefully providing the career crutch, comfort and to lessen the musical risk, so to speak. Music had taken over in my head during 'A' levels and I failed miserably to achieve the grades, despite turning in a massive, good collection of results for my 'O's'. Not wishing to throw away four years of college progress, I knuckled down. However, I missed the band so much and one sunny Sunday afternoon I'd had enough of revising and popped down to the weekly Cradley Heath garage rehearsal. I stepped in to play for a bit. Bit of a light bulb moment, but realised how much I had missed it, these guys, this band, the music. Bit of a mistake in hindsight, but was it? I returned to full duties; welcomed back with

Sky Trails & Pie Tales . . .

open arms the afternoon following the last exam paper being sealed in the envelope. Results? Yes, I achieved the pass and the grades I needed, with this day being the very last day I ever took another formal exam in my life. Since then, I have concentrated on the music.

I mentioned eight track tapes earlier. I would assume there's a few reading this that have no idea of what I mention. For those of you who do, put your hands up. Weren't they great! How many of you never had a problem with them? See, no one. I bet you all had days when the continuous tape loop ended up in the machine rather than the chunky cassette and, like me, ended up spending many happy hours winding the tape back in. Mine never seemed to work properly after that happened. My parents bought me this eight-track machine for my van because the basic player was much cheaper than a normal cassette player at the time. No one had told them that the actual eight track tapes were twice the price of a cassette, and you couldn't record on them and they were due to be an obsolete format soon! Highly collectable now. Mine all went to that great plastic recycling eatery in the sky. Another obsolete format that bit the dust, in a very short time. How many of you bought into BetaMax rather than VHS? Those eight track tapes cost me a fortune and spent money I really didn't have, ending up with not a great collection. These tapes were just wonderful when just at a musical high point, the track faded, the machine clicked and graunched its way to continuation on what was left of the same track. The only time they came into their forte was that you got continuous musical entertainment, without stopping what you were doing. Change the subject . . . When I could afford it, I bought a cassette player for the van and taped from home, from my vinyl LP collection. The eight-track player died an untimely death.

With the change in drummers in the band and a rejigged line up came one piece of momentous music, a twenty-four-minute opus that came with the title 'The Garden'. 'Still' wrote all of its own music and lyrics, mostly coming from the mind of Larry and lyrics by Rob. However, 'The Garden' was to eclipse all that preceded. Most Prog Rock bands of this era only earnt their badge of honour with long pieces of music, this opus was a classic and memorable. 'The Garden' initially came about from roughly six individual parts and sections, some of which had a reoccurring theme and lent themselves to being tied together. Once this was realised, work over a few months took place to complete the structure with some ideas on how to musically stitch each section together. Homework sessions coupled with sporadically held full band rehearsals took place, until the day we had pencilled in to play this from start to finish, with no gaps. At this point only each section was playable, and a couple had their joining sections loosely rehearsed. The day dawned and we assembled. I'd brought my reel-to-reel, in order to capture 'The Garden' in its entirety, the only reason being so that we could listen to the whole piece afterwards, with the joints assessed, revised, and see if they were usable. I turned the tape on, set to record and pressed play. Count in and off we went. The plan was not to stop until we got to the very end, twenty-four minutes later. What transpired was a recording of the very first time we ever played 'The Garden' in its entirety. Sure, there were a few warts, sure there were a few momentarily glances of panic as we all wondered what was next, but in essence, not a bad first take. I still have this recording, now digitally captured, but time and transfer from tape to CD has dulled its edge. For those who created this recording it's priceless and within the inner sanctum has earned its own legacy. As a result, it's not the most musically polished piece of music, this only came after repeated listens, major tinkering and arrangement, plus a growing familiarity with playing this piece that rehearsals and gigging brought. It took up a major part of the bands set, until the demise of the Mk2 line-up. Even now, on the odd occasion when I listen to this recording it can vividly bring back the memories of playing it and the circumstances surrounding. This is what music can do. There was a great sense of relief and awe in all four musicians when the last note decayed into silence, and I had turned the tape off. These are what memories are made of, in this case, pre mobile phone technology, I still have the aural memory to serve as a reminder to this day. To you, meaningless, but to Larry, Nick, Rob and me and sound engineer Graham, priceless. These are moments of playing in a band that can dilute all the other unpalatable issues, words, egos and arguments. Bands have them all, don't they? In addition to 'The Garden' I still have a sketchy collection of tape to digital recordings that go back even further in time of the creative juice flow of this band and its members. A grainy and hard listen, but a great example of how this band matured very quickly and even then, the seeds of potential are very much in evidence. Given the technology of today compared to then, I'm convinced that this band would have gone on to bigger and better things and reaped the associated opportunities. There was a fair bit of talent in this band, and it showed. Fate? Déjà Vu?

As for the gigs they threw up one or two memorable moments and stories. There were many but only a few I can write about. The twentieth of January 1976 was one such booking. The band took the trip to London and headed for the UCL, the University College of London. Via Nick's affiliation with the manager of Fruupp, Paul Charles, 'Still' were booked for one evening. This was with a view to show case the band and potentially persuade Paul in taking us on, possibly signing the band. From what Paul had heard so far, he was suitably impressed. He was, but the final words were his, spoken in a broad Irish accent; he loved the band "a lot" but thought Rob the singer ". . . sounds awfully like Peter Gabriel." For that reason alone, he thought the world

Sky Trails & Pie Tales . . .

didn't need another PG at that point and it went no further. Come in number nine, Derek William Dick ('Fish'), singer of Marillion. History dictated that 'Still' were never to be signed. Paul was also the A&R person for a record company with links to Hansa. Close, but not close enough. We tried. I had a migraine on the way home back to the Midlands, a few hours in bed and then back to college the next morning. JB's also spawned some other good tales. One particular evening the band incurred the wrath of JB's doorman Jimmy The Con. 'Still' used a 'walk-on tape', a piece of music played as the band came on stage, as was de-rigueur in those days. We had a small section from Vangelis's Heaven & Earth. This one night we're ready in the dressing room waiting for the strains of the music. We wait, nothing. People are starting to get fidgety. The usual plan is that Graham, our sound engineer, has the tape and presses play, simple, or so we thought. This night it got to the point that Jimmy launches himself onto the stage, grabbed the nearest mike and bellowed "Put the [expletive deleted] tape on!". Within seconds the strains of the tape come floating over the PA. Jimmy had a certain way with words and minds usually became concentrated shortly after. His surname 'The Con', preceded by Jimmy, was relevant, apt and came with an unwritten warning of his presence. Once you got to know him, he was really quite a decent chap, honestly. The other story which features heavily in the annals of this band's history was the day we played at The Granary in Bristol. Larry's dad Les would regale this event, this story, on a weekly basis and did so, with unwavering accuracy, always starting with the words "Did I ever tell you of the rescue mission to Bristol?". We all used to cast our eyes skywards. The day had started well, with plenty of time to spare as the convoy snaked its way down the M5. How we ever managed to find the Granary in the first place was a miracle in itself. I was in my van, with the rest of the gear and the people that wouldn't fit in the main band van. Rob was in the van in front, and it

Sky Trails & Pie Tales . . .

was he who had the map. At one point on the M5 at seventy miles an hour I see a hand out of the window of the van in front, it was Rob's, waving. Nothing in particular, just waving. Then he's got the map too, also waving. Next second this map leaves his hand, hits the window of my van and disappears for ever. Like I say, how we ever found the venue is a wonder. The reason for why the map disappeared was that it had been used as a lap tray to roll a cigarette, as for what type, you can fill that bit of the story in and any residual tobacco was duly shaken off the map, out of the window. At this point, the grip on the map was less than the laws of physics and ultimately took over. No map in the van anymore! We all pulled over into the next motorway café to reconvene, for a necessary toilet break and refreshments. We never thought to buy another map, and just revelled in the fun of it, until it's time to continue with the journey. The van refuses to start. Nothing, a dead van. What now? No one was an AA/RAC member. Do we call the venue to say we've broken down, or do we call Larry's dad to come and find us and get us to Bristol? Plan B it is. We sat in the motorway café watching every lorry pull into the car park, until hallucination set in. After an hour, or so, Les turns up. Les had brought a flatbed truck with a view to getting the van on it and to transport us the rest of the journey by this means. This plan was abandoned pretty quickly with a tow rope haul the rest of the way to Bristol. Towing on Britain's motorways today is governed by current rules and regulations, but back in 1976 we got away with it, all the way to The Granary. I gingerly followed. Without a map it was purely by luck and chance that the venue was found. Given the flatbed-truck/band-van train it was impossible to reverse around the streets of Bristol, especially if lost, or the wrong turning taken. Eventually we turned up outside of the club, complete with all the gear. The Granary was already open and packed with people. What followed was a rapid and utter nightmare of a setup, up two big flights

Sky Trails & Pie Tales . . .

of stairs. No sooner had we set up it was show time, no sound check, just get on with it lads, with the guitarists hands still showing the oil and dirt from attempts at getting the van started. The whole day was a bit of blur, no down time, no mind focusing on the music. I recall we seemed to go down well. In fact, we went down extremely well, it transpires the best gig this band ever did. The place emptied after last orders time, we packed up and I drove home, as for the broken-down van . . . That had to be parked up, in Bristol, in a side street, complete with most of the band's gear in the back. A suitable, or so Larry thought, place to park was found and he and Les drove home with the intention to drive back to Bristol the following day and tow it home. Les was unable to tow the van home that night due to work commitments and transport logistics. Early the next day saw both him and Larry drive back down to Bristol. The van had been left close to a building with purported links to local government. The van was still there, not broken into, all good so far. The only drawback were the armed policemen surrounding it. Given the era, the issues with certain factions, the Midlands registration, pub bombings etc the police were taking no chances, especially with a vehicle parked in close proximity to government premises. The timing of Les and Larry's arrival this day were complicitly key, explaining the situation to the armed police; opening the rear doors showing them that all was as told. With the situation defused, no pun intended here, the band van was hitched up to Les's van and they retraced their tyre marks back up the M5 to relative safety. This was not the end of the 'Granary' story. Supertramp, the band, yes them, came calling.

In true Roy of the Rovers fashion and unbeknown to 'Still', the night the band played in Bristol, the Granary was also frequented by an A&R and record label person currently associated with Supertramp. In a little-known story, at this point, in January 1976, singer and songwriter Roger Hodgson had temporarily left

Sky Trails & Pie Tales . . .

Supertramp. The A&R person present on the night at our gig was suitably impressed with both guitarist Larry and singer Rob as a potential replacement for Roger Hodgson, both as songwriters and musicians. Supertramp's A&R link made enquiries with the venue and the booker, and eventually traced and found their prey. Subsequent mutual contacts were arranged to discuss the matters further, only to be scuppered by the decision and role reversal of Roger back to the Supertramp fold. Another close call came and went. If Larry and Rob were lured to join Supertramp, then this story would have taken on yet another different hue, with 'Still' calling it a day at this point. The band had many close dalliances, with possible fame and notoriety, but it was never to be like the close call of potentially being signed to Paul Charles and the infrastructure of Fruupp. Pie in the sky it is but can now be viewed with a perceived degree of quality, of talent and of the potential music and musicianship that these four unruly West Midlands boys had and together were 'Still'. Yet in just over another forty years musical threads were picked up, needles rethreaded, and a new weft and weave created for two of these band members.

After the Bristol escapade, the poor old band van was repaired and deemed roadworthy again, using, this time, the money earmarked for taxing it. The tax was 'in the post'. Luckily at one rehearsal we noticed that the local constabulary were quite interested in the sell by date of the van's tax disc but were unable to do anything about it as the van was parked on private property at the garage we used as our rehearsal space. With the van loaded up with the bands gear after rehearsal, the police were just around the corner ready to pounce once the van's wheels struck public roads. It didn't, as Rob slept in the van overnight, keeping one eye on the gear in the back and the other on the dalliances of the police. I'm sure there were other far worse crimes committed that night and missed. In the end an in-date tax disc was

Sky Trails & Pie Tales . . .

installed, and much waving was had as the legal van drove past the incumbent law enforcers.

As for the demise of the Mk2 line-up of this band, the how's and the why's have dulled with time. What did come out of Mk2 was Mk3. Mk3 was an amalgamation of three members of Mk2 and of three members of another local band 'Clear Days'. 'Still' had also shared a bill with this band in the past. The links were strong with this band as one of the guitarists brothers, Geoff Tristram, was instrumental in starting the very first band that eventually became 'Still'. Geoff played guitar in 'Clear Days', along with his brother, on bass, and Kenny Stephens, on keys. It was these three that, along with Larry and Nick from Mk2, formed Mk3. Rob Lake wasn't initially included but was invited after a suitable singer was required. Rob was under strict instructions and part of the conditions of his return was that he behaved and 'towed the line', doing more of what was asked of him. He seemed the obvious choice to me. In Mk2 Rob had made our lives weary and brought a lot of his private issues with him into the band, but he was still (sic) the ideal singer for Mk3. Are you still with me? As for me, the band didn't need two bass players and Dave was a far better trained musician than I was, at the time, he probably still is. This line-up survived to the end of the decade, like the band in the next chapter 'Autumn', falling foul of the Punk Movement and the change in the mood towards Symphonic Progressive music.

Going full circle and in order to completely top and tail this band, the 'Still Story' and the sequence of events, prior to that fateful night at JB's when I was introduced by Pete to Rob and Larry, this is how the band came about, off the drawing board no less. Initially it was guitarist Geoff Tristram and school friend Steve Webb who formed a band together (name unknown) with drummer John (surname unknown) and singer Robert Lake. As to how bass player Steve knew of Rob, no one

Sky Trails & Pie Tales . . .

knows, but it was he who sowed the seed. Rob used to bus it in from West Bromwich to John's Kingswinford home, where they rehearsed in his parents double garage. Always a good starting point. I used to use my parents garage as a practice room back in the days of 'Ginger', until the constant phone calls from the neighbours put a stop to that. We moved inside, only when my parents were out. So, Geoff, Rob, Steve and John practiced away but never played any gigs; familiar story there. We all must start at some point, this was theirs. One rehearsal nearly killed Geoff. Whilst waiting for Rob to turn up, his bus was late and missed a connection, Geoff went to test that the microphone was on and working. Next minute he finds himself on the floor, in shock, with a dislocated arm and a crushed guitar which had broken his fall. The full effect of the national grid had shot up his arm only stopping short of a complete circuit via the rubber soles of his footwear. He was hospitalised and suffered greatly from the aftereffects of shock and visionary hallucinations that came part and parcel of touching a live mike. The hospital said Geoff was lucky. Only a few weeks prior, 3rd May 1972, Les Harvey of 'Stone the Crows' was killed on stage when he completed the circuit by touching a badly earthed mike. He was twenty-seven, Geoff was much younger. This garage band then morphed into 'Fallen Angel'. The obligatory change in line up became Geoff and Rob, supplemented by Mike Spedding on drums, Trevor Gadd on bass and Geoff's lifetime friend Larry Homer on guitar. This band did a handful of gigs in the area. 'Fallen Angels' debut went something like this.

DIX Disco & Cabaret Club, Wolverhampton
TONIGHT! HEAVY SOUNDS Presents
The Introduction of the Incredible Band
FALLEN ANGEL plus STYLES and STOZ
Nice one! 9 PM TILL Late
Ain't it great to be alive!

Sky Trails & Pie Tales . . .

A very indicative, sign of the times, advert in the local press, with an overuse of the exclamation mark!! Notice no date. A few more gigs followed, including one in Nottingham, culminating in a support slot to 'Home' at Dudley Tech' College. 'Fallen Angel' drew very much on Geoff's love and inspiration of 'Free'. Maybe it was the 'Home' gig that inspired Rob and Larry to move on to form the band 'Still' and follow their dream of Prog Rock, who knows? This was likely around 1973 as 'Home' were due to release, or may have released, their eponymous album 'The Alchemist'. Homes' guitarist Laurie Wisefield went on to join 'Wishbone Ash. A first edition release of 'The Alchemist' went on to be a most sought-after trophy by the album collectors of the world. I have a copy, nearly mint. Rob Lake and Larry Homer went on to form the band and vision that I was to join shortly after this momentous decision. It was around this time that Larry wrote a lot of the music, with Rob chipping in with the lyrics. One song being 'House on the Hill' which eventually found its way onto my legacy album 'Cherish Ever', over forty years later. It needed to age over time, like a fine single malt. The full story of 'House' is in the 'Cherish Ever' chapter. As for the gigs that Mk1 and Mk2 Still did I attempted to keep a record and what follows is nearly complete and listed here purely for the record. The big date gaps were due to line-up changes, new material and set changes being worked in. We were always thinking we can do this better, always adapting, maturing, not only as musicians, but personally.

Sky Trails & Pie Tales . . .

4-3-75	Town Hall, Stourbridge
19-4-75	Bogarts, Birmingham
10-5-75	Railway, Birmingham
11-5-75	Silver Dollar, Wolverhampton
24-5-75	Railway, Birmingham
4-6-75	Railway, Birmingham
27-6-75	Junction, Birmingham
20-1-76	University College, London
27-1-76	JB's, Dudley
30-1-76	Arley, Bewdley
17-4-76	JB's, Dudley
6-8-76	JB's, Dudley
12-8-76	The Granary, Bristol
8-10-76	Kidderminster College
29-11-76	Bogarts, Birmingham
21-1-77	Town Hall, West Bromwich
18-2-77	Aston University, Birmingham

With most of these stories in this book I shy away from the 'what happened next' sections, as a). I'm not involved and b). it's not my story. However, I make an exception here. Larry Homer: I'm still making music with him almost fifty years after this band; see chapters 'Cherish Ever' and the 'Random Earth Project'. Nick Parry went on to play and record with Lol (City Boy) Mason's 'Maisonettes', with their one-hit single 'Heartache Avenue' reaching number seven in the UK charts of 1983. Geoff Tristram became a well-known professional fine artist and author. UB40's iconic album cover 'Signing Off' is one of his. His brother Dave is a well-known comedy writer. As for the others, Rob Lake and Howard Rushton are no longer with us, Kenny Stephen has disappeared completely, and 'Art' Matthews is likely to have 'made the coast . . . man'. What happened to generous Pete Gregory? He formed Blackruby Ltd, his own booking agency and promotions company. 'Still' were on his books. As Mk2 crumbled he had us booked as support to local heroes Trapeze at West Bromwich Town Hall. I still have one of the original A2 sized

Sky Trails & Pie Tales . . .

posters, mounted for posterity. It was Graham and I that fly postered these all-round West Bromwich and the surrounding suburbs one night, working from about 1am to 5am with a big brush and a never-ending pot of glue/paste. In the morning West Bromwich woke up to freshly pasted advertising hoardings. We never got caught either. With Mk3 Pete invested a lot more time and money, but never really reaped the rewards. As a slight digression, he made a fortune on one event, just one gig. He'd booked the Bay City Rollers, again at West Bromwich Town Hall, booking them when their fee was small and paltry, and matched their pre-fame obscurity. During signing the contract and their appearance The Rollers had hit the big time, but still honoured all existing contracts without renegotiation, or cancellation. That night West Bromwich heaved and Blackruby danced all the way home. The police bill had to be settled in the morning as the Town Hall was besieged with screaming fans. Pete then took a dip into the funds amassed and booked his favourite band, Mott the Hoople. That night wasn't as a comparable success to The Rollers but achieved the aim for Pete and something to cross off on his bucket list. Sound engineer Graham Ford went on to work with other bands and the bass player nursed a massive hangover the morning after the last 'Still' gig. His lesson there was never to play paralytically drunk again. I blame the free bar.

After the demise of Still Mk2 I went back to the papers and the auditions. I still bought all the latest Prog vinyl, reverentially taking it home and playing it repeatedly, trying work it out, a habit I had got from the days of being in this band. Musical influences were constant and almost a full-time job.

Sky Trails & Pie Tales . . .

6 Autumn

Absolutely nothing related to this band, but in July 1975 I went to see Pink Floyd at Knebworth Park. In 1976 it was the Rolling Stones. My parents thought I was camping on the south coast with some mates for the Floyd gig, in the end I'd got one ticket and the person I went with blagged their way into the site with no ticket; wouldn't happen these days. Then they took something 'on offer', I declined, but spent a couple of hours attempting to pacify their hallucinations that followed. For the Stones gig I got two legitimate tickets. That was the gig that Lynyrd Skynyrd won the day over the Stones on what was a blistering hot day. Much beer was quaffed in order to bring the temperature down. The Stones took to the stage rather later than their allotted slot. It was a tiring and long drive home, but the day is permanently ingrained in my memory. Around this time, I joined a Working Man's Club band based in Streetly; don't ask. We rehearsed in a Church which doubled as a meeting hall. I'm sure one person wouldn't have been very impressed with setting up on the altar. This band didn't last long, we never gigged, thankfully.

I started to spend a lot of time in Bogarts Club, in the city centre of Birmingham. This club is no longer there but occupied three floors of 68 New Street. It was a bar that doubled as a live music venue, with a very small stage on the first floor and a Bier Keller in the basement. The club upstairs featured many bands. Some well-known, most unknown. I did a couple of gigs there with 'Still'. In order to get the band gear into the club and onto the stage it was a struggle up the spiral staircase, just wide enough for two people to pass, made even worse when carrying up large speaker cabinets and drums. A logistical nightmare. One evening when we played, we, or rather I, had to park the Luton box van

Sky Trails & Pie Tales . . .

outside in the main road on double yellows. As I only had Graham, the sound engineer with me, we had to take it turns to take the equipment in whilst the other guarded the van. We couldn't lock the van, I'd hired it, and trusted no one. This van also came without a reverse gear! Try driving in and around Birmingham without getting into a place such that you don't have to use reverse. In the end I did it. Don't ask me how. I was glad to get rid of it the next day. We nearly didn't make this gig; it was fraught with problems. Prior to the gig, at the warehouse load in pick up point, we were unable to shut the van doors. The weight of our gear had loaded the vans suspension to a point that the now open doors were too low to clear the factory shelving nearby. We unloaded the van, moved the offending items and re loaded, plus it started to rain, in bucket loads. Tempers were beginning to become frayed. As for Bogarts, it was a good gig in the end, and you soon forget about all the other trials and tribulations along the way. The other nights that Bogart's didn't have on live music they usually played records. Friday night was the best night. No bands, packed to the rafters. Perspiration and beer and smoke and loud music, the good old days. However, towards the end of 1976, the 20th of October to be exact, a band under the name of 'Substitute' were booked. This was an acronym for the 'Sex Pistols'. Word went out prior and I went with a couple of mates (Brian, Colin and Paul) as curious on-lookers, it was packed, but no band. At this point the Sex Pistols were largely unknown in the general populous, unless, like the throng that turned up that night, had been tipped off. The band were the pre-Sid Vicious bass player version in the form of Glen Matlock. The small first floor, meandering room was packed beyond belief with a cross section of all people. Punks, people trying to be punks, the curious (me), the regular late 70's "Hairies" and those that just liked a drink. The band didn't turn up till late. It was hard enough in attempting to set up a band in this place when it was empty but tonight, with all those people, pushing, shoving, nigh on impossible. How they did it I don't know. Anyway, the Pistols came on. Johnny Rotten and the rest of them! We were mid-way back, between this tiny, cramped stage and the bar, far enough away from any human spittle being shared between band and audience and vice versa. This was inherent as part of the then Punk culture. The band were overly loud, distorted and thankfully only did a short set. At the time I thought they were most unimpressive. If I had the foresight I have today then I would have realised what an event this was for many people, especially after reading the biographies of both Toyah (Wilcox) and Chris Collins (aka Frank Skinner) as they were both there at Bogarts, on this infamous night. Toyah was so impressed that it was this evening that made her realise that this was the sort of music (!) and ideology that she wanted to follow. No accounting for taste then but has done pretty well since. Some redemption was granted later in life, as she married my lifelong hero, Robert Fripp. Guitarist Robert has always been the solitary and constant member of King Crimson, but my fascination with King Crimson is another story. Frank Skinner, allegedly, shook Johnny Rotten's hand! You'll have to read his book too, especially regarding the lemonade bottle incident!

It was around this time that this was the closest I got to becoming a professional musician, for now. Following an advert in the Melody Maker I applied for a job on Thursday 24th March 1977, from that week's edition. It was in the 'Legendary Melody Maker Wanteds'. Up to this point I'd placed my own adverts; 'Bass Player seeks Band etc'. I'd had a mixed response, but nothing that appealed. I'd added my home telephone number to the advert so maybe what I'm about to write may have had a bearing on response. Parental Interception Perchance? I tried the alternative approach; the apply to a band seeking a bass player advert approach. A week later I received a letter from Nick Magnus who had selected my name from 14 applicants and invited me down to

Sky Trails & Pie Tales . . .

Rowlands Castle, near Portsmouth, for an audition. I nearly missed out altogether. Prior to the letter from Nick, my dad had intercepted a phone call from him which resulted in my dad promptly declining Nick's invitation. My dad never told me about this phone call, so Nick then had to write a letter. I was amazed that my dad didn't intercept the letter as well. I'd never had any encouragement from either parent regarding any musical tendencies. There were other incidents, but too numerous to mention. I bet when he found out that I was going down to meet Nick he was most impressed! I'm afraid my resolve in those days was stronger than anything they dished up. The more they criticised and gave negative encouragement, the more I dug in my heels. So, who were the 'Ex-Names' contingent mentioned in the advert? A group of musicians had left a band called the "Enid" and were re-grouping. Ironically Robert John Godfrey's Enid are still going after all these years. It must have been the following weekend that I went down on the Saturday morning. I stayed all weekend rehearsing new material with them and came home late Sunday evening. This weekend and this experience in particular was just such a joy, and if I'm brutally honest, humbling to playing with musicians of such calibre. I went to Barbarella's, in Birmingham, later in the evening. I was back on a high/roll. However, it was not to last as sadly, it was me who decided not to take the plunge, leave my job and join them down there as a full-time professional musician. It was too tentative, too far, too risky and with the advent and the peak of Punk at the time I thought that being in an instrumental symphonic Prog band it might be slightly limiting. Musical times were hard. With good old hindsight, the band, who became 'Autumn', didn't last long thereafter. The drummer went back to the Enid and keyboard player, Nick Magnus, forged a solo career for himself with a divergence to playing with ex-Genesis guitarist, Steve Hackett, for a few years.

Sky Trails & Pie Tales . . .

Strangely enough a CD was released in 1999 entitled Oceanworld and featured this Rowlands Castle band. They eventually found a bass player and for a few months during 1977/78 toured, as "Autumn". The material recorded was their legacy. Unfortunately, the 4 track CD didn't feature me, but I do remember rehearsing all of them. One track in particular 'Little Finger Exercise' rings many bells when I listen to it now. Anyway, it was not to be. Done that. Tried that. Didn't buy the tee shirt. Nick and I have kept in touch over the years, following and generally supporting his solo career and his work with Steve Hackett. Most recently Nick has been heavily involved with contributions to Amanda Lehmann's album 'Innocence and Illusion'. Amanda has much involvement with another 2022 project I have association with, the Random Earth Project: a close-knit world. Amanda also plays in Hackett's band, when time permits. Given she's Steve's sister-in-law the bond is strong. As for drummer Robbie Dobson, he died in July 2021.

Sky Trails & Pie Tales . . .

7   Nick and the Dogs

1977: The year of the Queen's Silver Jubilee, I remember where I was for the celebrations. After the Autumn decision I was a bit of a lost soul, picking up the odd bit of work here and there, but nothing serious, nothing that tempted me. I did join a band, a rock covers band, but nothing memorable. Their name has completely been lost to the mists of time, but I recall we played a Silver Jubilee street party, mid to late afternoon. It was somewhere in the deepest suburbs of Birmingham, and we always started off with Deep Purple's 'Smoke on the Water'. It had rained most of the day. During our set the heavens opened again and the drummer and I played under a slowly filling up tent roof. The balloon above us got bigger and lower as we played on until the drummer couldn't play any longer, or even stand up. If the roof had burst, under the weight of the water, then we would have been soaked, electrocuted, and frazzled. Obviously, we'd have been generating our own "Smoke" at this point. We collected the fee, packed up and headed for town in order to celebrate what was left of Her Majesty's day on the back of a well-paid gig. This carried on to late evening as all the profits were duly quaffed, and just before 'falling over' time, found ourselves at The Railway in Digbeth. The Railway was synonymous with live music, having played there a few times in the past myself. A jolly time was had by all, and the general consensus was that we carried this on at the singer's flat. So, we did, complete with girlfriends and partners. Unbeknown to me my then girlfriend secretly chatted up the guitarist, meeting up a few days later at Bogarts in Birmingham in a secret tryst. I only found out as they arranged a night that she and I used go there regularly, bless her. She hadn't the sense to pick another night that she should have known I wasn't going to be there. The odds were pretty stacked from the outset for them. I didn't see much of her after this and the band even less so; pretty much never again. Thanks Liz. (That's Queen Elizabeth to you.)

After the Jubilee gig I then applied to an advert in Birmingham's Evening Mail for a bass player. Always a good source. Some days were better than most. I called. I was offered an audition. I got the job. This was with a semi-pro, Brummie, Funk (not Punk!) band, called 'Nick & the Dogs'. With a name like that they should have been a Punk band! So, I ended up being a 'Dog'. My first gig was at the Barrel Organ, Digbeth, on Friday 30th September 1977. A well-known venue on the local Brum Beat circuit. Over the years it had grown a reputation to host some decent bands, one or two had gone onto bigger and greater notoriety. I believe local lass, singer Ruby Turner cut her teeth here, so there always was a quality to be had at the Barrel Organ. This first gig of mine with the 'Dogs' was recorded. I still have a copy of the four-track cassette produced from this night. The intention was to circulate as PR to bolster the gig list. The cassette was very much a hand-crafted item. Each one copied from a so-called master, the single sided hand produced artwork photocopied, cut out and carefully glued, to the right side mind. As with most things tape made, the past forty plus years has not been kind to the audio quality. One microphone dangled above the band, probably from a lightshade, was the source. This captured on reel to reel, complete with audience chatter and the sound of an active bar it wasn't going to be of great quality in the first place. My third-generation cassette copy was digitally captured when the technology was available in order to stop the aural rot. Before the digital capture, time had dulled the tape's frequencies but not enough to make out the songs, the instruments and the band chatter. Even to the point I can hear singer Paul saying "Trev Turley, his first gig with Nick and the Dogs, come on, come on" after a scheduled bass solo. I've never been a fan of my own

Sky Trails & Pie Tales . . .

solo work; much prefer listening to others. Still, for me it's a record, a time capsule of the night, the moment of an autumnal debut. It will stay in the vault. Shortly after I find myself in the van with all of them travelling to Essex University as a support to Roogalator. During the gig, during the bass and drum solo, I stood back too far and trod on my guitar lead. It parted company with my amp and disintegrated on the floor. Panic ensued. As we had no roadies, I quickly reached over and ripped out one of the speaker leads and used that instead. I was much quieter too, running on just the one speaker cab. The drum solo also lasted a bit longer that night. We drove home late into the night. It was a never-ending journey back to civilisation. I tried to grab some sleep in the back of the van on top of the gear. My bass bin was an almost comfy place to sleep. We all got home late; I drove home from the bands HQ after having been dropped off. The sky was getting lighter. I was back in my own van very soon and on my way to work. The toilets at work were happy to accept my folded arms and sleepy head on the cistern, straddling the toilet itself. In the department I worked there was another musician (with a day job). He was much more active gig wise than me at the time. On odd occasions we all took it in turns to push his feet back in the cubicle when they had slid out from under the door during his deep slumber. Most times the feet still wore his glittered stack heel boots, all the rage in those days. We covered his absence in the department with all manner of excuses. In the end the bosses accepted this, the word tolerance is a good one. These days we'd have been disciplined, cautioned and served a P45, but we were happy, these were the 'Golden Days' of music. The musical bond was strong. For me, over these short few years in the mid to late 70's, the tiredness at the day job was just all part of living the dream, doing the slog that comes with that age old adage of 'paying your dues'. The late nights, the early morning drop off's, the sneaking in up the stairs taking care we don't wake up the parents, then the arguments that were followed by a tired expletive when all you wanted to do is lie down and go to sleep, especially when you get "What time do you call this son?". Also not forgetting becoming almost intimate with the PA columns in the back of the van, I'm sure you could see the familiar WEM speaker fabric imprinted on my forehead. These were the good old days. For those of you who are reading this and remember WEM, at the time the most iconic PA gear a band could have. If the band had WEM 'Festival' stacks, you'd made it, well, almost. Couple all of this with the receding euphoria of doing the gig and the general after show banter, these days will linger long in my memory, never to be repeated. Band travel had no rules and regulations, no health and safety to abide by. Most were compartmentalised, gear and personal. Some didn't have this luxury. Some Transit vans were used on the drivers 'Day-Job', a dual purpose no less. Building material during the daytime and a Rock n' Roll bus during the night. Not guilty, but I do recall one band's van being used to entertain the opposite genre. I can tell you the springs on those transit vans were built to last. This night we all recall one occupant coming back into the venue after being 'entertained', with a not the same hairdo they went in with and lovely streak of cement dust on the back of their jacket. All done with much mutual consent and agreement, the 'best possible taste' and the promise of a rum n' coke. Happy days. These vans could also be death traps. I know of one late night accident that resulted in the death of three local Midland musicians as tiredness overcame the driver. Only the night before they were seen at the club I used to frequent, Dudley's JB's. As the news spread, so did the grief and shock. I do recall there were a couple of other incidents, with other vans, of other bands. Both times the occupants came out alive, but to be joined in the front by most of the gear in the back of the van was not ideal. Being sandwiched between the vehicle in front and your own PA is not the ideal way out. They took the risks. These were the days before seat belts were fitted compulsory (1968) and wearing them even more so (1983). How I got away with being consigned to the back of the van I'll never know. A health and safety nightmare. The food was also greasy and sporadic, but we didn't care.

Coming back to Nick and the Dogs, little did I know that the Essex University gig we did that this county was to become my eventual, real home. Small world? The night after this gig we were back at the Barrel Organ as part of a new residency. I slept all day after this one. With another two local venues offering the band a weekly residency, things were looking up. Working three nights a week was a treat that I'd never experienced, however . . . The story as to why it never happened follows, but my last gig with Nick and the Dogs was in early 1978; yes, you've guessed it, at The Barrel Organ.

This band was just one that I never bothered to chronicle the gigs, yes, sad I know, such was my short stay. There were a few holes in its history that I never knew, or I'd conveniently forgotten. In order to correct, for this book, and to add in here I got in touch with John Wilson from the band. His brother Bob was heavily involved in the Birmingham scene having played with Steve Gibbons for many, many years. He probably is still involved. So, I got in touch with guitarist John, and he embellished the story of how this band came about. Prior to this my search of the Internet revealed nothing about the band but was a small part of the Brum Beat scene at the time. I can now put the record straight. I've also decided to add in the 'what happened after' just to complete the story with this band and its omission in the annals of history of the time and the scene. I won't do this for all the other bands I've played in, unless it's relevant. It goes like this.

Sky Trails & Pie Tales . . .

Guitarist John and singer Paul Slocombe were originally an acoustic duo. The band was formed around 1976 enlisting John's school friends, guitarist Nick Cleverley and drummer Howard Smith both joining as the duo morphed into a fully-fledged six-piece. Sax player Pat Corcoran came on board as was at art college with John and the original bass player, full time musician Derek Wood, who lived in the same row of flats just a few doors away from John. The band rehearsed upstairs at Pat's mum's house in Sparkhill, Birmingham playing the local scene over the following eighteen months. The usual haunts, The Barrel Organ, Barbarella's, Rebecca's, Cannon Hill Arena, and of course, the University Circuit. I do recall struggling up two, maybe three, flights of stairs at his mum's house with my bass rig. It was easier coming down. At this point (1977) Derek had left to join Birmingham's J.A.L.N. Band. This soul/funk outfit used to be formally known as 'Superbad' until producer Pete Waterman got his fingers into their pie. Derek ended up as part of a nineties line up of the Steve Gibbons Band, via time with Cissy Stone. John's brother Bob was also a long-time member of the Steve Gibbons Band. All terribly incestuous. Drummer Howard also features in the regular band that Steve Gibbons occasionally gigs too. What goes around . . .

After Derek's demise with Nick and the Dogs that's when I turned up after answering an advert in Birmingham's Evening Mail. Don't forget, no Internet in these days! It was all about keeping your eyes peeled and using land line telephones. I was just about getting my feet under the table after the handful of gigs when Howard and Nick upped sticks, Howard literally, both joining funk band 'Bumpers'. John, Paul and I stuttered on with local legend 'Dik' on drums, then crumbled completely. We never knew what Dik's real name was, he only answered to 'Dik.' As a postscript, in 1978, Dik went on and was instrumental in forming the post-punk, new romantic band 'Fashion'. These intervening years were crucial in

Sky Trails & Pie Tales . . .

the Birmingham scene for the likes of Duran Duran, also formed in 1978, and the infamous Rum Runner Club. The tapes that John, Paul, Dik and I made have long gone, lost to the great dustbin in the sky. These tapes were recorded, by saxophonist Pat Corcoran, at his house. Pat loved all of this sort of stuff. He built the PA for Nick and the Dogs, owned, and drove the band's Transit van. Such a commodity and a kind soul. His love for the music and all things related even spawned the name for the band. Pat's dog was named 'Mick', with Mick eventually becoming Nick and the Dogs. The band initially thought it would be better associated to guitarist Nick, as his band. With the event of punk, the name became a tad synonymous with that genre. Some punters may have been surprised with the sophisticated music, expecting something more basic, who knows? Eventually Pat became a teacher moving to Herefordshire, via the Isle of Wight.

After 'The Dogs' ended John auditioned for, getting the gig, with local Birmingham Band 'Hooker' who then became the 'Mean Street Dealers.' John and Paul also reverted to playing together again but parted ways when Paul moved to Cornwall in the nineties to start a new life. In later years John reunited with Nick Cleverley in 'Red House.' Nick has since retired but his son Chris now carries the flame on the folk circuit. John and his brother Bob still play, mostly on the 'cover band' circuit, sometimes with Dave Tickle, great name, John as bass player. Diverse. The close-knit Birmingham scene still exists as both John's brother Bob and Steve Gibbons are all next-door neighbours. Bob says he was never sacked from the Steve Gibbons Band, he just never gets asked these days, comes of being neighbours I suppose. For John, his flame now burns bright as his son, a London resident, plays music as part of Nkomba, a contemporary African folk band who play an energetic mixture of Malawian folk songs. Love it . . .

Sky Trails & Pie Tales . . .

Nick and the Dogs lasted about two years. You could say, was it was a steppingstone to further careers? For me it wasn't, not much really happened musically, I tried, but a quiet period beckoned.

It was Spring 1978.

8   The Years In-Between

Following the end of Nick and his Dogs the rest of 1978 was a bit vague. It was then and it is now. Musically I flitted about with no degree of success of finding anything suitable. I'd been spoilt really with the quality of 'Still', musically, and the fun and camaraderie of 'Nick and the Dogs'. It was hard to replace, and I didn't have much success in finding a band that I felt at home with. Over time my scouring the 'Wanted's' in the music press and the local Midlands papers, turned into an occasional look. The main source were the ads in the back pages of the Melody Maker, very full and bursting of opportunities. At the time the Melody Maker was just one of four national weekly music papers and the only one a most aspiring musician would read for gigs and work. Over time these ad's have spawned household names by attracting the right sort of player. The times I read the phrase 'No bread heads' in there, standard fayre at the time. The other dangled carrot was 'Gigs waiting' and the old chestnut 'Record contract waiting to be signed'. I replied to one band with this fictitious record contact in abeyance, all original material, a rock band. They were based in Corby, East Midlands. I was invited to audition. Early one Sunday morning I stuck my guitar in the van and headed east on the M6. It was a dismal day, getting more dismal as I approached the Steel town of Corby. It was bleak, misty. The auditions were held in a warehouse on an old industrial site. Trailing old factory dust everywhere I clocked in, literally, was given a time slot and joined the long queue of aspiring bass players. What an unruly bunch we were. Conversation was minimal, as it would be, we're all bass players! The prime reason was not giving your edge away or talk too much about your past. Those that were hungry to get the job listened to the previous applicants in the next room. It was hard not to as the sound reverberated throughout the whole building. I was quite a way down the queue, so listened intently, trying figure the format, verse, chorus, middle eight etc, nothing familiar. Halfway through the morning, the tune was changed. Great! Something else to get my head round. Then it was my turn. I expected to be asked to play what I'd been listening to for the last hour, sadly no. "Here's a new tune!". So, I'm presented with a demo run through by the band, no charts, no tabs and then asked to play. I had the key, that was about all. Totally unable to follow the twin guitar lead line riff, with no prior knowledge, or practice. I failed that section. By the time the band and I had quietly decided we were not a match with each other they threw in an old Free song. I was no Andy Fraser that day. The soul wasn't willing and all I wanted to do was to go home. I waved goodbye and wished them well. "Cheers mate, we'll let you know." Don't bother were the words rattling round my head. I never heard anything. I never heard of the name of the band again, the record contract remained unsigned. How many hopes and dreams have been scuppered over the years by the sound of a torn in half, of this so-called, promised, record contract?

I applied to many ads, both local and the wider world, well, outside of the Birmingham area. Some I was successful in passing the phone call chat and getting to actually play. Many floundered on the phone as their money ran out. Good old public telephone boxes eh! There were many auditions. One bloke thought he was Richie Blackmore, dressed like him, played like him, similar on-stage bravado, all in his front room through a five-watt practice amp. How I managed not to burst out laughing sitting on his parents front room three-piece suite as he tried in vain to summon feedback from his crouched position on the fireplace rug. You never saw a van, mine, drive so fast down the A45 from Coventry back to civilisation, only remembering to put my lights on after a couple miles. A couple of auditions were for

Sky Trails & Pie Tales . . .

pure 'covers' band. At the time not really my scene. I stuck it with one who promised to bring in more original material. We played this one song, repeatedly at rehearsal in some church hall. The Gods weren't happy. One audition was in a church. The brethren, if they'd bothered to turn up, would have been displeased as I rattled all the chalices on the altar, I apologise, forgive me. No, didn't get that job either. The closest I got was a band called Tudor Lodge. Great guitarist, good singer, very soulful, very much in the mould of Free/Bad Company. I liked them, thought worth giving them a go. This band persisted, but for a reason that has completely slipped my mind, the calls for rehearsal got less and less. During 1978 I got back in touch with the old drummer from the days of Labyrinthus, Chris Morson. We had a full rehearsal, but it never seemed to gel. Chris then went on to play with the fully formed band 'Bess'. This may have been the call he was waiting for, and old memories were still haunting us both, who knows? The rehearsal was stilted and difficult. With most of these auditions I'd got pretty fit and good at carting my heavy and bulky rig up and down flights of stairs with no help from those for whom I'm auditioning. Old top floor school rooms, someone's bedroom in the attic of an old Victoria house, the list is endless. Overall, it was pretty much fifty/fifty, I turned down as many offers as those I didn't get. At twenty-four I'd become choosy. Bored maybe? I started to look at the 'Wanteds' less, even to the point I helped as sound engineer, on live gigs, for a few local bands. Another string to my bow?

One of these bands were my old band 'Still'. After the Mk2 line up of this band had dissolved, of which I was a part, the Mk3 version became active following a member amalgamation with another band 'Clear Days'. One night at Dudley's JB's I bumped into Larry Homer. We had a long old chat, and it transpires they were looking for a sound engineer. Given I knew the band pretty intimately, the music, the ethos, I was the obvious choice. I must admit I reluctantly agreed to help them out being suitably encouraged at their next band rehearsal. The mixing desk was now mine rather than the guy who supplied it, along with the PA too. Feeling slightly embarrassed I took over the mix. I must have impressed as the general consensus of the band is that they wanted me to fulfil this role. I did. I also helped with a few other local Brum based bands. My old mate Terry Luckett's band 'Saloon' was one. I did a recording session for this band too. 'Saloon' was a tight three-piece band with Terry on guitar, Brian Roberts on bass and Paul 'Animal' Hale on drums. Where is that recording now? The rest disappear into the mists of time, knob twiddling and fader sliding.

1978 was a year I changed the day job, along with many other things. The circle of friends, read drinking partners, grew and shrank, I still kept close mates with those I'd become ingratiated with from college days; the core that congregated every Saturday night at JB's. These were nights that did fall foul of memory loss, but we all got home in one piece because we used to book the taxis' beforehand. Some nights there'd be anything from ten to twenty of us. The measure of a good night at JB's was how much you couldn't remember in the morning. Apparently, we saw some really great bands down there, some that went on to fame, fortune and a household name. We loved many of them, so we were told on the Sunday lunchtime session at 'The Shed'. JB's reputation grew exponentially as the place to play. The most famous story is that the club turned down Queen, in their early days. Freddie Mercury was on the phone pushing for another fifty quid, but the club offered a flat fee, plus fish and chips. The flat fee back in those days was a good deal, for a band from London. Neither party budged and that's why Queen never played there. They went on and became quite famous. For us lowly lot the most popular nights were the nights that hosted the likes of Supercharge, UPP and The Enid. All three very diverse

Sky Trails & Pie Tales . . .

set of musicians and music. Genre was irrelevant. There were more and for those part of JB's at this time will know what I mean. For us regulars at JB's we'd often be found rubbing shoulders with local musician Robert Plant, at the prime peak of Zeppelin. The place was full of characters and stories.

It was also round this time 1977/78 I was introduced to the delights of holidays abroad with your mates! I'd never been abroad before, never flown. What I say next may strike horror to some but could likely conjure up much memory 'warmth' for many. My first jaunt abroad was with two mates. I'd agreed, at short notice, to fill a vacant slot after a drop out and the holiday being rebooked with a company called Eighteen to Thirty. Yes 'Club 18-30'. These days it was a burgeoning company that catered for just this age group. So, you can guess what was on the agenda, not much sitting on the beach taking it all in. I recall my food intake over the two weeks of the first one was minimal. A strong constitution was needed, the holiday rep's even more so, coupled with a liver to match. This was the era that being a 'Club 18-30' rep was tantamount to winning the lottery, complete with high respect and envy, as long as you could cope with the intense regularity of a new bunch of people, every two weeks over the six-month season, to nurture and ingratiate into Club ethics and depravity. In the end I did four 'Club 18-30' breaks.

This book is not about what happened in other countries, I protect the reader, but we all had a fabulous time, you'll have to trust me. Nothing musical at all, I can assure you.

I changed my day job in 1978 coming complete with a big rise in salary. Apart from funding a burgeoning waste of money, as my parents would call it, the imbibement of alcohol, I was still able to save a considerable amount which turned on the ability to consider buying a

Sky Trails & Pie Tales . . .

property. I could work as much overtime as possible and did. I once did three straight weeks/weekends. Pay day was much beneficial, but I had no concept of day and time at the end. My first free weekend was glorious, I think. The savings grew until I was confident I'd got enough to put down a healthy deposit and cover all the other additional costs, or so I thought. Registering with a couple of local estate agents it threw up an acceptable, rather new, maisonette in Tipton. A top floor one bedroom flat, ideal. I went and viewed it and put in an offer. The sellers then thought they had undervalued it so, changed the asking price. I pondered. In order to meet the new price, I needed some quick cash. My parents were of no help whatsoever. Then it dawned on me I had something under my bed, something that wasn't being as used as much as it should. My Rickenbacker bass. Despite placing adverts in the local papers and one in the Melody Maker I had no phone calls and no takers. In desperation, I sold it to Modern Music in Dudley, at a knock down price. The extra money was just enough to be able to go back and accept the revised price of the flat, but I no longer had my pride and joy and the ability to play music. I rued the day. It was ironic that my first proper bass came from Modern Music and the Ricky went back the same way. It felt like door had shut, but I needed to get on the property ladder and move out of my parents' house. I occasionally wonder who now owns this bass guitar. The owners accepted my new offer and I just sat and waited for the solicitor's wheels to turn. I waited. I bought a cooker; I bought the necessary furniture. It all sat in my parents' garage. I paid the search fees and settled all the bills except the solicitors one. A couple of months past and I took a call at work from the flat's owners. They wanted more money. The price had gone up again! Good old gazumping. I agree that they said the market had changed over the last couple of months, but I'd agreed their two previous prices and sold my guitar in the process. The bottom line was that I couldn't afford it at

Sky Trails & Pie Tales . . .

the time and my mortgage had been agreed and set in stone. That night I sat at home and did my figures. Impossible to accept. Over the next couple of days, I was bombarded with many calls at work from their estate agent and a couple from the owners, I just needed some time to settle that I'd made the right decision. In the end I told them there's no sale and I've instructed my solicitor to close the contract and withdraw. It was the cheaper option despite being unable to claw back any money I'd already spent. I settled the bills. What happened next is the wife of the couple selling constantly called me at work, begging I reconsider, crying, then threatening me. I told the switch board not to accept any further calls and over a few days they stopped. It was the summer of 1979 and I'd needlessly sold my bass guitar.

So, what did I do? I had a choice, attempt to get a ticket to see Led Zeppelin at Knebworth in August, in which I failed miserably, or go on holiday. As we all know now this was the last time Zeppelin were to play a gig of this proportion. Up to this point I'd never seen the band live, despite being a local lad too. The closest I'd got a ticket to see them was at Birmingham Odeon a few years earlier. I'd got up early to join the queue that snaked around the Odeon at about 6am in the morning. In those days, pre-Internet, this was the only way of guaranteeing to get a ticket. The box office opened at 9am. It closed very quickly after. I had four people in front of me in the queue who also didn't get tickets. Back to the Summer of 1979 I went on holiday instead, to Corfu, Club 18-30, of course, with a mate of mine. I needed a break, an excuse to put the flat out of my mind, as well. It was a very wise move and a life changer on pretty much all fronts. Why? I fell in love, a holiday romance that was to change my life completely. Day one: Colin, (Luckett, brother of Terry) and I rock up to the hotel and I spy, probably the word is 'found' myself attracted to someone lying by the pool. Colin and

Sky Trails & Pie Tales . . .

I then go looking for a drink; start on the right foot I say. I think nothing of the girl by the pool till that evening's excursion. A voice "Anyone sitting here?" "No, feel free, join us." It was the girl from the pool, Jill. From that time on we were both pretty much inseparable. Beach Bar-B-Que the following day . . . shall I go on? There was a musical bond too. We both liked our music, albeit differing tastes, but some degree of "Oh I like them, seen them too." Over the next ten days we somehow got onto the subject of Rickie Lee Jones. Ms Jones was the 'one to see' at the time, with an impressive debut album just released. I'd missed out, again, in getting a ticket in Birmingham for her up and coming UK tour. Jill said she had a spare ticket for her London date. A little light bulb moment for me. "I'm happy to take it off your hands."

On returning back home this is why I then found myself sitting with Jill watching Rickie Lee Jones at the Hammersmith Odeon, as it was known then. I stayed at her flat in London for that weekend too. As September turned into October, I ventured down to stay with Jill a few more weekends. Not one critical point, not one discussion, well, one that I can recall, but I was to move to London and stay with Jill. After the flat gazumping episode and the impending downturn in manufacturing in the Midlands, especially for the company I worked for, I was also looking for another job. For some strange reason it made sense to cut the cord. Get a new job in London, of which I did and move lock stock and barrel and stay with Jill. Apart from my clothes and a van, all I had musically was a battered old acoustic guitar and my record collection. With hindsight, if I had bought the flat in the Midlands then the move to London would have never happened, but then I'd have never gone on holiday to Corfu either. Fate? I said goodbye to my friends and mates in Birmingham. It was November 1979.

Sky Trails & Pie Tales . . .

In between losing the flat and moving to London I sold all the rest of my gear. My Marshall amp and cabinet went to Terry Luckett. I'd originally bought this from another W&T Avery apprentice at Warley College of Technology, both of us bass players. This Marshall rig was a most reliable bit of kit. Never let me down. I later heard Terry's guitar through my amp, and it never sounded better, or warmer. I'd customised the amp with a stereo input socket, so I could use the stereo jack 'proper' on my Rickenbacker. Treble pickup through lead channel and the bass pickup through the bass channel. All very technical but it sounded great. The other bit of gear, my Acoustic bass bin, went to an unknown buyer.

As a slight digression, but related, this is a great example of how much my parents were against me making any form of music and the great lengths they went to stop me. After my mum had been admitted to a care home, I took the decision to sell her house in Birmingham, basically to help fund her care and for us not to have the bother of its upkeep from London. On clearing the property, we came across an old quote from a Midlands Music Shop. They had quoted my mum the cost for all my gear, guitar, amps and speakers. The date was years before I sold them to fund the deposit on the flat and my move to London. What she'd done was get a price with a view to selling them behind my back. When we found this quote in her house it was the first time I was aware of her intent. Can you imagine me coming home to find them gone with their constant, often stated view "You'll never make any money, waste of time, you won't be needing these!" Thankfully, they didn't. But just another example of how dogged in their determination to not encourage and support me. I occasionally wonder where I'd be now with their backing and if they'd have funded some music lessons? One of life's mysteries. My mystery.

Sky Trails & Pie Tales . . .

What happened over the intervening years and into the eighties and beyond? Well, Jill and I got engaged, bought a house, (finally) got married, had two children, James and Victoria, worked hard, loved our music. Over these years we saw many, many bands, all sorts. The famous, the not so, the up and coming and very occasionally, the awful. My record collection grew astronomically. With the event of the CD it took over and complemented the collection, especially after the initial hit and miss quality errors of transfer were sorted. I still prefer the physical product over the digital, but then that's the era I grew up in. In those days I usually had a long drive to work, sometimes over an hour, longer if delayed. Driving was a joy, mostly, and prime time to listen to music. So, what got me back into playing regularly and live work?

The day job got me back into playing properly. I was currently working in Essex at British Aerospace. I had elevated myself to head of my own department and were looking to expand the department. One application was from a genial chap, Richard Evans. He was selected for a personal grilling, by me. I've always maintained with interviews you can tell within the first few minutes if a candidate is suitable, no matter the job, or the responsibility. Richard's portfolio fitted the bill, just something that was inherent by flicking through, the way things were organised. Every interview I've ever done I've always asked the question of what the candidate likes to do outside of work. Richard said music, singing it and playing it. "Oh really." The rest of the interview was spent on music. He'd already got the job in my mind before this topic was discussed. We must have been in the room hours, talking music. Short story time. We offered Richard the job, he accepted, he joined the company. Very much a bond was forged. At times I found it difficult to be his boss, but we got the job done. It was 2001 when Richard coerced me into getting back into playing. Richard often played the Working Men's

Sky Trails & Pie Tales . . .

Club Circuit with his band. In a general daily office chat, he mentioned his normal bass player was unable to make a couple of gigs during the year. Jokingly, knowing that I used to play bass Richard suggested that I'd be a good fit. Not one to turn down a challenge I accepted. I bought an Aria Pro Series II, in black, what else, and obtained a Peavy Amp and away I went! The following six weeks were spent learning a 45-song set, remembering where all the notes were fretted, getting blisters and learning about thirds and fifths again. It was like getting back on a bike after falling off it, even surprising myself of what I could remember. I did have sore fingers for some weeks after though.

My return to live music, was on Saturday 21st April 2001 at Langham's, Tottenham. A four-piece band, bass, guitar/vocals, keyboard/vocals and a drummer. I'm afraid it wasn't the sort of music I used to play with 'Still'. I don't think that a Working Men's Club would appreciate a 20-minute rendition of the opus "The Garden". It was great to get back in front of an audience, despite their age, bless them, I had forgotten what a buzz playing live music is. I think the members of Still would have killed me twenty years ago if I had said I was going to play Jim Reeves (not Vic Reeves) numbers. I didn't let myself down and despite dropping a couple of notes I think I excelled. Even back then I was starting to miss the old Rickenbacker. The second gig was at the same venue, Saturday 14th July 2001, Jill and the kids were even brave enough to come. I never did find out what they thought, might be best to leave that one alone. Later in the year, 7th September 2001 (4 days before 9/11) both Richard and I were the background entertainment at work. This was a lunch time session to mark the closure of the site with some food, drink and music with our work colleagues, before the company moved lock stock and barrel. As for the day of 9/11 itself, I recall sitting in an office already packed up, waiting for the removal company to turn up and deliver us to our new office the following day. Someone rushed into the office saying a plane had hit one of the twin towers in New York. The rest of the day we spent glued to the television in the conference room. This event had so many repercussions, on many lives and businesses, including the company I was employed by. My family and I had also booked a break in New York in a few weeks' time. We still went, but the memories we brought back home weren't the ones we had planned. The most poignant was sitting in a first-floor burger bar that looked out onto the site, still smoking, now with the acrid smell tinged with disinfectant, it wasn't normal. The jolly muzak replaced with something sombre and reflective, coupled with every external window ledge steeped in a two-inch layer of dust are not the holiday pictures we either wanted to take, or have as the memory. As we all know, the world changed after 9/11.

These handful of gigs I did with Richard had stoked the fire again. Over the next few years, we did a couple more, mainly for charity and general good causes. The gig at a local school, 13th May 2006, was filmed. I'm not sure as for who's posterity, but I still have the DVD. Prior to this one, a rehearsal in an Estate Agent's cellar was memorable, but then I'm sure we've all rehearsed in the oddest of places, some even under odder circumstances.

I still hankered after replacing my fabled Ricky Bass. Good old 'Loot'. One was 'For Sale' £600. Very cheap for a genuine, original, Rickenbacker 4001. I called the person, sounded reasonable. Wanted cash, location Stepney in the heart of London's East End, very much old Kray country. What did I do? I find myself knocking on this person's flat door, with six hundred quid cash in my pocket, burning a hole! Door opens, head looks up and down the alley, "Come in, come in", door slams shut. They explain they haven't got much time and thrust this caseless Rickenbacker into my hands. "Can I try it out?", there's no amp or anything like that. So, I'm playing this bass, acoustically, in this person's flat with the thought in the back of my head of what will happen if I give them the cash? Sounds OK, no fret buzz, straight neck (an occasional fault with twin truss rods – must know your stuff). The most major difference to a standard off the shelf Ricky is that the finish of this one was nonstandard. I must say a professional job; the paint had been removed, along with the binding and re-lacquered. However, no serial number plate. By this time bells were ringing, but I knew what I was looking for to tie it in to an original 4001. Six hundred quid eh . . . stolen more than likely, an utter bargain if you ask me. Sometimes in our lives the clock in our heads stop, skip a second or two, and run through the scenario of 'what if I don't buy this, will I be disappointed when I get home?' and panic sets in. In what was probably a few minutes, but completely unable to picture it now, I agreed to buy, gave them the cash, grabbed the bass, flew out the door, down the stairs into the street, found my car (still there, complete with its quota of tyres) drove home very quickly whilst constantly checking my rear-view mirror. "Oh, that's nice. What you wanted?". Taking a deep breath and a well-earned cup of tea I plugged it in. Closing my eyes, all worked perfectly, sounded just like the old black one I had sold all those years ago. Same model, only the finish was different, but still had that quality only these basses can exude. When the dust had settled, I replaced the white scratch plate with a genuine Rickenbacker replacement, in black, of course, whilst checking all the wiring was intact and original. At the time of replacing the scratch plate, in the wooden well that catered for the profile of the electronic bits and pieces was the original paintwork. This bass was a sunburst model, now blonde. In one of these apertures was also a series of numbers. I e-mailed these numbers to Rickenbacker in the USA with an explanation of what I had. Not expecting any further contact, or even, at best, the year of manufacture, I had a reply the following day. Correct, they had no idea of the year of manufacture but confirmed it was an original 4001, made in America. I still have the guitar. It now also has a friend, a black 4003, bought brand new with one tiny 'dink'. Many pennies were discounted due to this minute mark, I made sure of that.

Back to 2002 I then started to take an interest in the music 'Wanted's' in the local papers again, this time bolstered and supplemented by an on-line presence. 'Loot' was a good source. What follows next became the beginning of what I loosely call 'Round Two'.

9 3am

It was mid-2002, good old 'Loot'. I came across one that caught my attention, can't recall why, but I phoned the supplied number. A rather well-spoken voice answered, Tim Renton. He played guitar in a band along with his drummer brother Andy. They said they had an American girl singer too who used to be signed to Columbia Records, impressive. I was invited round to Tim's house near Barnes, West London. Looking back now I must admit it was a strange evening. I felt they weren't really interested in me too much, but I'm sure they felt comfortable and had the confidence needed to take the plunge, talking more about what they had done. What didn't come out that night was that both Tim and Andy knew Mike Batt and used to be the people in those furry suits that were the 'Wombles'. In hindsight, if I'd known that then I might have had second thoughts, so maybe a wise move on their behalf. All the same I pursued and honoured the invite of an audition the following week, at Acton's Survival Studios. The singer never turned up and it was just the three of us, the brothers Renton and me. We ran through a few songs and worked on a couple. I asked what their plans were for the future, which turned out rather vague. They had no PA, plus the drummer didn't have a proper kit of his own. All very weird. So . . . I came home, went on holiday for two weeks, pondered it, wrote down the pros and cons and came to the conclusion that they weren't for me. I phoned Tim up and explained my decision and wished them all the best. The main reason for my decision was the distance that they were away from me and their basic lack of gear and vision. Not a good start for what was to come.

So, I started back on the adverts. I answered a couple, got an audition for a local 'Covers' band, not really what I was looking for but learnt a couple of tunes, turned up, played, and they said to come back the following week, which I did. At the second audition there was another bass player waiting. I played and stayed to listen to the other guy. He was obviously much better than me and I realised, at the time, I had to up my game, so I left straight away. I had another audition with another local band, 'Hedgehog', and again I felt I hadn't hit the mark. The world had changed since the late 70's. In the end my main reason was personal, and I felt I didn't fit in with their persona and general attitude and really couldn't see me playing with them, so I never asked if I'd got the job. It was then later that year that Tim Renton phoned me and asked me how I was getting on with finding a band. At the time I was pondering applying to play in a 'Shadows' Tribute band. Given the Shads had sparked something in me all those years ago, it seemed worth a go. I asked my old mate Larry, of 'Still' what I should do, the Shad's or the Renton's. He said the Shad's. What did I do? I went back to the Renton's.

When December of 2002 crept up, I decided to bite the bullet and joined this band with Tim and Andy Renton, along with singer Kathleen 'Kat' Pearson. The band had now got a name, '3am' and at the time, unbeknown to me, the name was already registered to Andy, having been used in the past. It was during these first few weeks of rehearsal, one of which Kat was late, that I found out about the Womble link. They; the Renton's, also had played with Robin Le Mesurier, son of John from, 'Dad's Army' fame, his mother being Hattie Jacques (Carry On films), in a pro band 'Reign'. All the time I played with 3am, I always felt that I never ever knew the full story behind these people. Both brothers had a closeted upbringing, went to private school, (where they met Mike Batt); privileged is a good word. Now Kat, as a singer had a certain style of her own, very unique, identifiable, but one which I felt didn't fit with what the brothers wanted to do in the band. Kat had

Sky Trails & Pie Tales . . .

also written some of her own songs, which we tackled and started to work on. There was one which always seemed to be problematic. To this day I have no idea why. I had started to record rehearsals, mainly for my own use to practice the songs at home and work on my style. After repeatedly listening to these there were one or two songs that I had shared with Tim and Andy, and it was Andy that pointed it out. Kat, in her own unique style, her own vocal inflections could cause the songs to sound out of key. Actually, they weren't, but to a casual listener it could be misconstrued as such. Given her past and having been signed to Columbia Records in the States it was an odd conundrum. From where I stand some twenty years on from this, I wish the band had stuck with Kat, embracing her voice and unique style bringing it more into the band, but we didn't. To this day I still ponder on what would have happened if we had. Kat has done some utterly fabulous things since. As 3am travelled into 2003 and we rehearsed more, it was becoming apparent that the band wasn't gelling, and we all started to be struggling with the odd song here and there. Maybe Kat is more of a freeform singer, I don't know, but overall, maybe she likes to sing things from how she feels at the time; the day; the room; her personal well-being, rather than sing the songs the same way each time. I can understand this and often do the same with my playing. It was Andy, who then sowed the seed in my mind that Kat is maybe not the right singer for the band. More of this later, but Andy was the master of the 'Hustle', getting his own way, mostly for his own benefit, and I fell hook line and sinker for it, bless him. Andy was the younger brother to Tim and fitted this mould perfectly. With this seed planted in my head, and me being me, with ambitions and drive exceeding my general daily routine, I went and placed an advert for a singer/songwriter in Loot, the paper in which I originally found 3am. After a few applications, mainly male singers, I received an E-Mail from someone that seemed to fit the bill.

Sky Trails & Pie Tales . . .

The mail was from Iain Black. He said that his partner, Helen Turner was a singer and sang in the style of a couple of the names I had mentioned in the ad, namely Janis Joplin and Elkie Brooks. However, Iain was quite adamant from the start that they came as a pair and Iain was the songwriter, who also happened to play guitar. He oiled the application stating that he liked the way the ad was written citing a couple of influences close to his style, mainly Fleetwood Mac and 1960's/70's blues/rock. What turned out with me looking for a singer/songwriter, I ended up with a singer and a guitarist, who also wrote songs. I spoke to both Tim and Andy we thought we'd give it a go, nothing to lose. However, Tim was very sceptical about having another guitarist in the band but went with the flow. Fast forward to Tuesday 22nd July 2003, an audition for Helen and Iain, at Survival Studios, Acton was arranged. They turned up at about 7pm. Helen preceded Iain. The band all quickly looked at each other, as visually she fitted the bill. Look and appearance are always paramount on first dates, as this was. She was very Stevie Nicks from top to toe. Iain bore no resemblance to Lindsay Buckingham. Iain's response to my advert was very insistent, to the point that 'we come as a pair'. Nicks and Buckingham's audition for Fleetwood Mac were role reversed, as we all know. The Mac were looking for a guitarist but ended up with him and a second singer. Fate? Christine McVie accepted her into the fold. Maybe Turner/Black would pan out the same, but in reverse? 3am's brief was singer/songwriter, not guitarist. First impressions seemed we were on the right track. How does she sound? We needn't have worried, for when she started singing, the difference it made to the band was immediate. Totally in a different league to anything else I'd witnessed at this point, a huge talent. I needed no persuasion. I had found what I was looking for and looking at Tim and Andy, they thought the same. Helen completely nailed the audition. The clincher was Joplin's 'One Good Man', so much so we ended up playing it at virtually every 3am gig. As for Iain, we went through about a dozen songs, some of which he knew well, some of which slightly less, but we all felt he was an accomplished guitarist. His solos followed in the vein of his guru/idol, Free's Paul Kossoff. It showed. As usual, I recorded most rehearsals and unbeknown to Helen and Iain, I did that night too. I still have the recording on CD.

They left and we had a decision to make. I needed no persuasion, like I said; I knew it was a done deal the minute Helen walked in. Some people talk about a sixth sense, well I had a sixth sense moment then. I can say that now, but Tim and Andy needed time to think about it. The addition of Helen would make the band totally complete, the perfect singer, and one that would front the band too on many aspects, but did we need another guitarist? Tim and Iain. Both had two distinct styles, both were songwriters, complementary? Time would tell. We were not sure at this moment. In the post audition notes, the pros and the cons, it was tight, could have gone either way. I think Andy and Tim discussed this at great lengths, especially the additional guitar stool to Tim. The singer decision was a done deal. Did Tim persuade Andy, or did Andy persuade Tim? Helen was the one we wanted, and the notes again prompted "Come as a pair, no negotiation", it was both, or neither. The die was cast, 3am became a five-piece band, with two guitarists. Tim took on the unenviable task of talking to Kat. The future beckoned.

As 2003 petered out, the band was to become a six piece. Where was this to stop? There was also even talk of introducing brass and backing singers over the years, being mostly driven by Tim and Andy's vision. The sixth member came in the form of keyboard player Chris Parren. Chris was known to Tim, via one of his badminton playing partners, having been introduced by his wife. Chris has played keys professionally for most of

Sky Trails & Pie Tales . . .

his life. He was part of Maggie Bell's 'Midnight Flyer', the band set up by Led Zeppelin's manager Peter Grant. He has also played with the Strawbs and featured on George Michael's 'Careless Whisper' and many other top-class sessions. A fabulous pedigree and an accomplished player. To be honest, at the time I struggled to know why he'd be interested in 3am, but there you go. Maybe a little persuasion and hustling by Andy and his brother Tim? Something that might have appealed was that if Chris joined the band we'd cover his share of rehearsal costs, bearing in mind his professional status. He still took his cut on gig fees, but for rehearsals we sort of hired him. Great work if you can get it. The other part of the deal was that if Chris had a better paid offer of a gig/session with another band he would take it. So, this explains why sometimes 3am were occasionally seen as a five piece. Set lists were interesting as there were usually two versions. A 'with Chris' one and a 'without Chris' one. A Chris-less one we'd have to drop those songs that depended solely on keys or sounded awful without. In the end the songs that we could draw on was pretty expansive. I liked what Chris brought, and relished the gigs when he was present, plus he was a character and one I could easily get on with. He understood the meaning of having to entertain. I learnt a great deal from Chris on this aspect.

After Helen and Iain had decided to join, the rest of 2003 was spent on rehearsals, building enough material for an hour and a half. Some of this material was classic blues songs given the 3am twist, which in the end we came quite good at doing, some were lesser-known songs, some were songs that Tim had written, and some that were Iain's. So, for every Tuesday night it was heads down at Survival. As 2004 dawned we needed some gigs. In the end it became a contest between Andy and me to see who would get the first gig. I started to approach various venues, mainly known music pubs. But it was Andy who got in first. He used to drink at The

Bull's Head in Barnes regularly, having lived only just down the road. Andy never drove. Again, I don't know why, perhaps he did, but that was another story that remained in the annals of Renton family history. So here he was in The Bull's Head. This place was very synonymous with live music, having a back room dedicated to the stuff. Every Monday there was a 'Stormy Monday Blues Night' run by Pete Feenstra and his business partner George McFall. Sadly, George passed away in October 2010. It was George that Andy persuaded, probably hustled, and got a booking for 3am to play. The date was set, 16th February 2004 and we had something to aim for. Most memorable for all the right reasons. I know I'd done a few with Richard, my work colleague, but this I could class as a full-fledged line up and a serious gig, no pressure this time. It went well; it went very well indeed.

It was at this gig I was introduced to Dave Thomas. Dave had travelled from Norwich specifically for this debut gig of 3am's. Dave had played with Tim, Andy and Robin LeMesurier in their band Reign many years ago. Prior to this his talents featured heavily in 1970/1971 Prog outfit Blonde on Blonde. With 2022's resurgence of interest in both Dave and this band I was approached by Dave to help rekindle Blonde on Blonde for the twenty-first century. Sadly, my then schedule was unable to give Dave the commitment he needed. We both looked at and took Plan 'B'. Dave was someone I would cross paths with again, in years to come, as part of the Malaya Blue Band. He was heavily involved with many bands and jam nights in and around the Norwich area. Very much a bluesman through and through, well known and well liked. He even sat in with my band, Trev Turley and Friends, one night. I also depped in his band for one gig, a boisterous afternoon session at the annual beer festival in Norwich. I nearly didn't make that one. Norwich is notorious for not being able to park in the city centre. I'd unloaded at the venue then drove miles to

Sky Trails & Pie Tales . . .

find a car park with a free space. As it was beer festival week, it was unusually busy, for the non-drinkers. I ran back to the venue just in time to start the first set, a nightmare. Being in a band, parking is and can be crucial. The ideal solution is to load in and out right next the venue, with direct access to the stage, ideally, then being able to park as close as possible, for free. It's not always the case. London's 100 Club is notoriously difficult. The alley at the back of the club is limited and patrolled up to 6:30pm, plus the Congestion Charge and all manner of other catches. For me, if I can backline share with another band's bass player, it's easy, hop on the Tube with my guitar and a small flight case. Recently, I know it's expensive, but a taxi in and out, is the least stressful, taking in my full rig too and then able to go for a couple of beers afterwards. One band I played in we played on a boat. No access to park nearby, carrying the gear miles, as it seemed that way, over a tiny gangplank. We never lost one single piece of equipment in the water, an achievement in itself. The same band played Kenny Jones' (Who, Faces drummer) Hurtwood Park Venue once. On getting home after this gig one member had a few items missing in their van; guitar and PA equipment, thankfully flight cased. The venue was closed when these items were found to be missing. An early morning call and drive back to the venue found these items still in the middle of Kenny Jones' car park, untouched, where they were left the previous night, in exactly the same spot. Lucky is a good word. As Kenny's site and Polo Club is at the end of a long approach road and reasonably secure overnight, they were in luck. Some bands are not always this lucky. Over the years I've always gone back to cast one lasting eye around, just to ensure mine and all the other band members gear is not there. There is one rehearsal studio in Newmarket that was always keeping an eye on items for us, left behind, usually by the same person, not necessarily band gear either.

Sky Trails & Pie Tales . . .

Due to my 24/7 persistence of pursuing gigs and starting to develop my 'Little Black Book' of contacts, of promoters, of venue owners and of booking agents, the gigs started to flood in, 2005 was a busy year, working most weekends. Over time I'd got pretty good at it with a decent bit of respect from within the business and the fraternity. As with most bands starting out it always seems to fall to one person, one band member, to take on this role. For 3am it became me. At the start, it was enjoyable, a challenge, the thrill of the chase, with getting the gig a brief high, only to come down and look for the next one. On this subject, the very first London 100 Club gig I got it was an utterly emotional moment. I literally did a little dance. The folks in 3am were just as overjoyed as me, bar one. Iain's first words to me were "You should have checked with us first before accepting it." I even heard the rush of air from my rapidly deflating balloon. This first 100 Club gig was a grab it quick opportunity, a moment in time, never repeated, want it, accept it. I grabbed it with open hands. The calendar showed the date as all of us being free, as explained in a moment. What 3am didn't know at the time is that within three months of this 100 Club booking the band had lost three members, doing just another nine more gigs. Yet another fragile example of this music business. Hatched chickens are not always there to be counted.

Over 2006/7 we peaked, but it was hard going. At the time I was building on the growing contacts and booking gigs, almost a year to eighteen months in advance and it was getting slightly easier, but always a 'hard sell'. The hardest part was getting the band to commit to them. I'd devised a calendar that each band member would populate with known days of unavailability at the beginning of each year and then update on a rolling basis. Great idea, or so I thought. That way, when I was offered a gig, I could instantaneously respond to a promoter, booker, or agent as of commitment, or suggest an alternative date. This was to avoid the

"Thanks I'll come back to you; let you know" syndrome. Being able to respond in an instant raised the bands professionalism. However, some venues were impatient, couldn't wait to hear back and I lost some gigs. Having to negotiate with the other five band members was hit and miss, tiresome, time consuming and became wearing. I can smile now, but every January Helen and Iain's blocked days/weekends grew in count as each year passed. For the rest of us it was the odd day, or annual holiday. We felt more committed if that's the right word. In order to free up negotiating with the band on these blocked days, the kudos of the gig was crucial; the higher the value, the better chance I had. Over 2006 – 2007 we could have done so much more, we did a lot anyway, but the process I had put in place, thinking it would make my job of booking easier, started to wag my tail. Some days it would drive me emotionally. I plodded on. Over time, Andy, Tim and myself often had the conversation in how to honour these missed opportunities due to the unavailability of the singer. We thought about going out with a dep singer, but dispelled that idea as she's a hard act to dep and would do more harm than good. We could run the risk of losing some of the fanbase, not knowing who's going to turn up to sing. Plus we could also have lost Helen. We thought about starting a parallel band, under a different name, with a new singer and one guitarist, playing material not normally associated with 3am. That idea didn't last long as it would mean starting from scratch again as regards building the profile and one, I did not relish doing that again, especially with all the work needed to keep the 3am gig roster rolling. In desperation, I can't recall who suggested it, but we looked at the possibility of replacing Helen and Iain. The vote was for one of viability and worth pursuing. Back in 2004 we had been booked to play the 'Blues Bar' in Grays, a football ground social club. I'd booked this through an old acquaintance of mine, Mark Sibley. I'd seen him play here before, singer and harp player, good front man, strong voice. Cutting a

Sky Trails & Pie Tales . . .

long story short, as I have no idea what year this was, but I found myself talking to Mark on the phone. He was open to 'giving it bash'. We fed him a handful of songs to familiarise himself with, he of us too and arranged a secret and covert audition at Survival Studios, on a non-3am rehearsal night and waited for Mark to drive from one end of Essex to Acton. These rehearsal studios could conjure up all manner of interesting people. One regular was drummer Paul Cook who's most notable previous band was the Sex Pistols. His kindly behaviour was much tempered from the days of anarchy in the UK. However, the night Mark turned up we were constantly looking over our shoulders, watching and waiting for the door handle to twitch, expecting Helen to walk through the door. It went well and, after Mark had left to drive home, we all thought it was viable. It would be a completely different approach, male singer, good harp player, the very essence of raw RnB, one guitarist, and we all felt we could rearrange most of the material and still build on the 3am we knew. In the end Mark saved Helen's and Iain job. He didn't join. I'm still a friend of Mark, occasionally seeing his current band, The Feelgood Band. A revelation of this nature is an example of the inter-band skulduggery that occasionally goes on in maybe most bands, some surfacing in stories like this; some remaining lost to time and memory. It's the music, nothing personal, well, mostly. In general, it was a close call for 3am. We embraced the problem. I eventually got to the root of their issue on the day I was grilled for a couple of hours by the other members of the Bare Bones Boogie Band in 2013. They only, ideally, wanted to do one gig a month, that's twelve a year, not overly committal, I know. Why this wasn't mentioned all those years ago I'll never know. While the rest of 3am struggled with wanting to gig as much as possible, two members wanted to do less. In fairness, I'm surprised nothing was said and they tried to temper the gigs by other means. An unknown stalemate was reached. Maybe nothing was said due to the possibly of creating upset and worry that the band may have replaced the two people raising the issue in the first place. In this situation, we nearly did! Looking back now it must have been a 'Gig-Tug-of-War' on both sides, with possibly an unacceptable status quo for all parties. That's bands for you.

3am did 152 gigs over four and a half years. All sorts; big, small, pubs, festivals. From the sold out to the one man and their dog. One or two with stories to tell, most forgettable. We were the last band to play at one venue, closing the door behind us. I had one owner constantly coming up and telling me to turn down. I played the second set with my amp off. They still complained. I laughed when we collected our paltry fee. I think they just didn't like bass players; I could be wrong. The last ten 3am gigs were all high-profile festivals and theatres, even playing the annual Guilfest, a main stage slot no less. Things were going well, until . . .

At one 2006 festival, we supported 'Roadhouse' who after our slot came looking for 3am's singer Helen, they were most impressed. Roadhouse were well known for having dual female singers fronting the band. Visual appearance was part and parcel too. Helen was taken aside; head hunted no less and offered a lucrative position in Roadhouse. Going back to the original condition of the response to my advert for a singer/songwriter, the one of 'we come as a pair', then as Iain wasn't targeted in the offer too, Helen turned them down. Good on her, I thought, at the time. Dear reader keep this in mind as you read on. This was to pop up again and again. The Nicks/Buckingham Bond was strong in them. Shortly after agreeing to join 3am, Helen and Iain married, on holiday, on a spur of the moment decision, their bond being cemented further and crucial in the demise of this line up of the band, the formation of the band that followed and the breakup of that band, the Bare Bones Boogie Band. It still persisted when I

Sky Trails & Pie Tales . . .

asked Helen to sing on my legacy album, 'Cherish Ever' in 2020. She declined, probably because the invitation sadly didn't stretch to Iain. I already had a big bucketful of guitarists to plunder.

During these 3am years I bought guitars, I sold guitars, some I kept, some I didn't. One was, for me, very much a holy grail. I'd seen Sheryl Crow and Paul McCartney's occasional bass player Brian Ray use this one, a Guild. It dwarfed Sheryl's diminutive stature. Over the years I'd kept an eye out on the usual bidding sites. A couple made themselves available, but I either missed them, or were overly priced. It was very much a sellers' market. As they were snapped up the availability escalated, in the wrong direction, they teetered on the edge of extinction and became like 'gold dust'. Then I saw one, on eBay, current home in the States. I watched it like a hawk. It was, even back then, heavily distressed and gigged to match. The user had worn the wood away where his thumb had rested and glued, yes glued, a soft pad on the back of the body, purely to make it more comfortable to use. It had seen the sun too, probably by hanging on its wall hanger. The varnish had crazed and the binding yellowed. It was red, a deep read, just like Sheryl's. The bidding crept up as the duration of the auction headed into single figures. Not a 'Buy-Me' option. In the early hours of the morning, I'm up at 4am (UK time), watching the clock count down, alarm clock synced to eBay time. Sixty seconds to go I hit the 'Bid' button with my previously primed maximum bid. I had become a bit of an expert in the value of these guitars over the years, so knew what this would likely go for, but this one was in a poor state of affairs, but still functional. I received two messages. One told me that my bid had been registered, accepted, the other was telling me I'd won the auction. It was March 2004 4:42am in the morning and was experiencing that cold, cold sweat that travelled from my forehead, over the top of my head, down the back of my neck waking up all major follicles on the way. This guitar now had a new owner. I went back to bed but couldn't sleep, would you? So, I got up again, made a cup of tea and turned my machine back on again. I settled the bill and read the couple of e-mails from the seller. How on earth am I going to get this in my hands? The auction was a close-run thing, despite the lateness of my intent, the history showed that I was nearly out bid by two other bidders, one with four seconds left. Thankfully I'd entered a maximum and the bidding site worked in my favour. Two and half days later, via international courier, I caressed this much battered and worn-out bass, it was still red, it was thirty years old. The bass was originally sold as new from a little shop in Maine and had flown the ten hours to England. All the hardware was in a workable state and played lovely; I made sure of that at the next band rehearsal. The next three months the guitar went on holiday and spent some time at Essex's top luthier, completely devoid of all hardware, being brought back to the day like it was when it first left the factory. All the hardware was given a full spruce up with just a couple items being replaced with identical items. Hardware and guitar finally met up again. The 'thumb groove' had gone as had the awful glue marks on the back of the body, it was a complete 'Repair Shop' make over and worth every penny. Some people criticised me for doing what I did, saying I should have kept its visual history of playing. The faults of the neck and the body were too apparent once the luthier had removed the varnish and paint, it wouldn't have lasted long in my hands. The frets had never been replaced either, it needed some TLC; it got it. Lovely guitar. Apart from this one there have been a constant stream of bass guitars, some have stayed, some didn't like living with me and I don't blame them. The most bizarre buy was via another on-line sale site. I think the person who was selling wasn't aware of its value, but I won't dwell on that. It was a risk I was prepared to take; a purchase that almost had to happen such was the mistaken value. A lovey Fender Jazz. The covert meeting place, if you could call it that, was the concourse of Stratford main and tube line station, at rush hour. "How will I recognise you?", "Oh, you will!". It was pretty obvious, as the case was placed on the concourse floor, opened and then shut. I had a quick glance to check the originality of this bass, and it was a genuine USA model. I never ran my fingers and eye up and down the fretboard. A huge risk but one I was prepared to take, and, in the end, it turned out fine, a bargain no less. The train station filled up with even more jostling commuters as I passed the envelope stuffed with twenty's to the seller, grabbed the guitar case and hastily made my way back to the Underground. I never saw or heard from the seller again. Covert mission completed. I must stop buying guitars like this. Another was a cash buy for something black, another Rickenbacker, in 2017. Something that had never been played, more of an investment up to this point I think, until I got my sticky fingers round it. It had travelled from the US to Doncaster and then on to Kent in a short few weeks. It needed to be played and eventually was happy and content with its new owner. I've only ever bought one completely brand new, in fifty years of playing. The same has happened with hardware, amplifiers and speaker cabinets. I've had them all. Marshall's, Orange, Laney, Roland, Gallien Krueger you name it. Same as with effects and pedals. I'd hate to add up all the money I've spent on gear over the years, trades included. I'm still doing it as technology marches on.

3am released, well, all made at home, two very 'Cottage Industry' CD's. Both were recorded 'Live'. The first was at the Bull's Head, Barnes and the second at the now defunct Red Lion in High Wycombe. Andy knew someone who had a small set up complete with a digital editing suite and was reasonably cheap. Listening to the recordings now it shows, especially as home recording technology has moved on since that of fifteen years ago, the quality being so much better today. However, taking each album on their merits they are a 'Live' snapshot of where the band was at the time, but then we were desperate to get something released and to sell. The finished audio quality was adequate. The Bull's Head artwork was all black, the Red Lion one all white. All very digital, Black & White, Yes & No. Any orders were handcrafted, each personally by Andy. Without consultation he'd done all the artwork and sourced the components. I personally preferred the white one, in both looks and listening quality, but was still not up to a studio recorded album. On both CD's I struggled with the recorded audio quality of my bass and never really liked my sound and felt it was not really representational. I have no idea, even today, why it wasn't recorded very well. On some tracks I'm inaudible, but on others the bass appears to be digitally treated to something that really doesn't appeal, to me. Andy, or his digital editor, just got on with it and we were presented with the finished item, no chance to tweak, temper, or correct. Even today I struggle to listen. At the time this was a great little band, but poorly represented in this instance and on this format, in my view. Half the band thought we ought to get a proper studio recorded album, the other half thought this was adequate. Chris Parren sat on the fence, a true professional musician, don't rock the boat. The lines in the sand had been drawn following our 'White' album and the recording fissure and debate grew over time, sometimes without the consultation of the other party, on both sides and it got worse. With the passage of time the two factions only bickered and moaned in their own group, rather than having a sensible discussion as to how to resolve with everyone. Unfortunately, I had a foot in both camps of view and ended up with the complete picture that no one else in the band had. My choice was, which horse do I back? I went with the flow in each trying to appease all, but no one won, least of all me. In the end I couldn't keep the

Sky Trails & Pie Tales . . .

peace any longer. The lines of communication had broken down, including mine.

Within the band, on the odd occasion, this subject of a professionally recorded studio quality CD was debated and went on for the best part of a year. A solution could never be agreed. Both Tim and Andy, because they had been brought up on the way things used to be done back in the 60's/70's thought that the same would apply, was one view. They looked for a producer, not wrong, but very expensive. The other camp, Helen, Iain and I, were not prepared to explore the Producer path. It was obvious the start of the rift and became the two distinct camps which appeared in the band roughly during 2007. As previously mentioned, we never knew which camp Chris belonged too, probably his own, I never asked. Eventually, mid 2008, without any consultation, Andy announced he'd found someone who'll record, mix and produce an album, all for a fixed fee. Brilliant, great news, we were, after nearly four years going to get a proper album made. This would cost the band £1000 and eventually cost the band dearly, in another aspect. Andy always played his cards close to his chest, until it was too late to change minds and back out. He said I'd like the bloke who he's found as he's an ex Brummie. This was Bill Gautier. Bill had been around the block, recording and producing many bands. He had his own studio in his back garden and had recently been recording Paul Jones and the Blues Band. So, we all thought kosher and turned up one Saturday in July 2008 at Bills house. The studio had been booked for Saturday and Sunday and the plan was to record 5/6 backing tracks on the first day, then all vocals and overdubs on the Sunday. It was apparent to me that when I turned up on Saturday, as I was always the first to turn up, that Tim and Andy had already been there, probably the night before and had already set up and sound checked. The drums were damped and miked in a specific way, something that would have taken awhile to set up. Tim's

Sky Trails & Pie Tales . . .

guitars were also on wall hangers. At the time, I didn't realise, but maybe they both had had a head start? Had Bill recorded part of the songs already? Anyway, we all set up and cracked on. It's worth pointing out that Chris Parren, (keyboards), was not there on the first day. The pattern of the day was to record, maybe a couple of takes, take a tea break, then go back into the studio and record another couple, and so on. As the day wore on, maybe because it was a nice sunny day, the breaks got longer and longer, and these breaks came out of our studio time budget. At the end of day one we had some semblance of a decent backing track for each song. Day two was supposed to be overdub and vocal day. Eventually, only the guitars and the keyboards were recorded. Chris eventually turned up on the Sunday. It had been Tim's idea that Chris was to add some sampled brass to one of his own songs. Tim had told Chris what the BPM (Beats Per Minute) was of the song and Chris had dutifully learnt and pre-recorded the breaks on his keyboard. However, when these were played over the top of the backing track, recorded the previous day, they didn't sync. The BPM of the backing track was faster than the one Tim had told Chris to work to. During the preceding day there was no mention of us in having to work to a click track. The only solution was that Chris had to redo and record these fills in the studio. Now, I do take my hat off to Chris. The fills were fast and given Chris's aging fingers he struggled, but all credit to him, he did it, the consummate professional. Chris in his later years, started to have trouble with the joints in his hand. I suppose playing keyboards most of your life didn't help. Guitar over dubs and solos were completed, via a myriad of takes, taking up even more time, between the tea breaks. Helen didn't get the chance to record her vocals that day, returning the following week to Bill's studio, under Andy's supervision. What transpired, as to the how, the why and the who, I don't know, but Helen's final vocal takes seemed less raunchy. The final recording was Helen, but not the one I'd got to hear over the past years. She did what was needed and left this session having run out of time and money.

This recording session was before and leading up to our gig at The RhythmFest over the Bank Holiday period on the 30th of August 2008. Unbeknown to us, this was to be the very last 3am gig. Most of the band were unaware but the studio recorded material was being mixed at Bill's, without band intervention. A good thing, or a bad thing? I wasn't there at least. Anyway, we did the gig, packed up and watched some of the other bands and generally took in the festival. Andy told us "Not to panic" when asked how the album was coming on. Assuming and hoping he was involved in the mixing process. At least some band inclusion. The next rehearsal was on Tuesday 2nd September 2008. As usual we all went through the material required, in preparation for the next gig; nothing was said about the CD we'd recently recorded. As we were packing up to go home and just about to leave, Andy produced a 'Listening' copy of the final, as mixed, CD. Helen, Iain and I were given a copy. I got the impression that Tim and Chris had already heard it, maybe they had as I can't recall if any comment was made by either of them. I was still slightly stunned that Andy knew he had this CD with him, knew when he was going to hand it out and go through a three-hour rehearsal session without saying a word. Andy's parting words were to listen carefully as there's a lot of stuff going on . . . Boy was he right!

Driving home I was probably a distraction to the other drivers on the road. I put the 'Listening' copy into my CD player and pressed play. Maybe it was wrong of me to formulate an opinion even before I heard it, but what I heard didn't match expectation. Nothing initially wrong, the quality was so much better than that of the bands previous two 'Live' albums, but it sounded like another band I was listening to, it wasn't 3am, almost to the point it was like another band playing our songs, very

Sky Trails & Pie Tales . . .

unrepresentational. Helen didn't sound like Helen. There was a lot going on, some of it I'd not heard before, Andy was right on that count. The mix was very keys driven, but not a bad thing and made me wonder, in places, if we actually had a guitarist, or two. Plus, where did all this extra percussion come from? I had a good idea. I was starting to be curious as to how my little bass break in one the songs was going to come out. When I played it in the studio it set the feel and groove for the section that followed, I was very pleased with way it came out during the recording session. On the CD it had become distorted and seemingly oversampled, almost to the point I questioned if it was actually me. Shock is a good word, and I had that halfway round London's North Circular, not really the ideal place. Here I am again, like the two 'Live' recordings, I'm hearing nothing that represented what I thought I sounded like. I gave it another listen. This was wholesale editing, without an ask, with in my opinion, a potentially drastic outcome. I didn't like it at all. In the end I had to stop the car and call Andy to ask what had happened to the bass in that one song. He wasn't very forthcoming with the explanation. He said it sounded better (his view); I thought it was appalling. I pressed him. In the end he said both he and Bill had sampled it and added the samples as a double octave etc. Clever, but would have been nice to know what was coming. Andy said to give it time, and that there's a lot going on (too right there) and that I'd grow to like it over a period of time. Really . . .

The next morning, I listened once more to the CD; a third time. This was to be the last time I listened to it, for many years. It took me these three listens to decide it was not representative of the band and most of all, not representative of the focal point of the band, Helen. I even let Richard Evans at work listen, just to make sure I hadn't missed the plot, or the point. He confirmed my worst thoughts, "devoid of emotion and just a piece of round plastic". He'd seen the band a few times and said it's not really a 3am album and wouldn't buy it. If he didn't fancy buying a copy then, who would? This 'Listening' copy then languished in a box of CD's, in my attic, for over a decade, unheard, unloved. Only when I got to sorting out a song to represent 3am on my legacy album in 2020 did I crawl through the dust and cobwebs to extract this CD with a view of seeing if there's anything useable. Being recorded in Bill's studio it was of high enough quality. As it fell under the auspices of never being released, I'm sure I could find a track on here that, even after twelve years, I could use. The first track was a Tim Renton song 'Red Hot and Blue', the one with the infamous Chris Parren 'brass' line/piece. These twelve years seemed to have been good to 3am, or maybe the circumstances at the time of first listening had matured. 'Red Hot and Blue' sounded strangely fresh and indicative. Very much Chris to the front. This will do for my album, and I felt I needed not to listen to the rest, so I didn't. I ripped a copy of this song in the highest audio resolution I could muster, committed it to my hard drive and put the 'Listening' copy back into its wallet returning it back to its home in the attic, where, I assume, it will remain until my house is cleared.

After navigating the North Circular that night in 2008, my thoughts turned to the others in the band; I wonder what they thought? I phoned Iain the following morning to gauge his thoughts. He said it's not too bad but wouldn't let his mates listen. This I thought was a clue especially if he'd keep this closeted from his friends. Helen was disappointed too, but purely based on the lack of consideration for others, especially during the mixing and production process. Andy and Bill must have put in an inordinate amount of time and effort at this stage as it was so apparent in this 'Listening' copy. Can what we hear be rectified, tweaked? With hindsight, it would have needed a major overall at this stage, so a 'Like it, or Lump it' scenario seemed to beckon and be the only outcome. The three of us, Helen, Iain and I, agreed to challenge the mix, the running order and the oddities at the end at the next full band rehearsal in a couple of weeks' time, more inter-band behind the scenes skulduggery. In these two weeks I laid low, not wishing to prompt an online argument, which occasionally gets misconstrued, misunderstood. The face to face, the whites of the eyes are usually good indicators. Bear in mind this was before 'Zoom' technology. The three of us knew what was needed to be said, to be challenged and hopefully sorted and turned up at Survival Studios on Tuesday 16th September 2008. It was a remarkably quiet preceding two weeks. The evening followed the usual pattern and not one word was mentioned about the album. As the evening wore on the impending conversation, I knew what was coming, seemed to get louder in my head until half an hour before packing up time I took off my guitar and sat down. I took a deep breath, looked at Helen and Iain and asked what the thoughts were of the CD. Tim said it was great. I don't recall either Andy, or Chris, saying anything. I asked about the possibility of changing the mix, the running order, the sound of my bass. I must have mentioned the view that it doesn't really sound like us, a bit bland, bit more of a keyboard driven band than a guitar one etc . . . Tim said we can change this, but couldn't understand why, he loved it. Andy then stands up rather abruptly, throws his sticks down, "I've had enough of this rubbish" storming out of the door in the process. A quiet and shocked cloud descended in the room. I packed up, said goodbye and drove home, to ponder what next. At work the following morning I got a text from Andy Renton at 8:01am. It read:

"Don't take anymore bookings for the foreseeable – you will need to hold auditions for a new drummer – I will see out the ones already in the diary."

Sky Trails & Pie Tales . . .

That was it then, Andy had decided to quit the band. Once I'd passed this snippet to Helen and Iain, it didn't take very long for the three of us to decide to leave too, but we waited, a full working day. It was plainly obvious to realise we'd all had enough and knew that the band had reached its limit, probably both musically and personally, it just took Andy's catalytic E-Mail to focus minds, along with the diverging camps in the band and lack of communication. The album was the last straw that broke the back of this camel's line-up. A shame, after five years. Over teatime and into the early evening it didn't take many E-Mails and quick calls to formulate mine, Helen's and Iain's exit from 3am. I suggested we ought to form our own band with a new drummer. I didn't get much instant take up on that, so assumed some pondering was needed and left them alone. Given Andy's text earlier in the day I agreed, purely out of consideration to Tim, that I call him and pass on our intention. I became the spokesperson for Helen and Iain. Later in the evening, after Coronation Street (a UK TV soap based in Manchester) I called Tim. It was a very one sided, short, conversation. I wished him and the band well, without an explanation of our reasons (I didn't get the chance), but I'm sure these were plainly obvious. I've conversed with Tim since, but after the day Andy 'dropped sticks', I have not seen hide nor' hair of Andy. In one day 3am had lost four of its five permanent members. The remnants and lion's share of 3am, I suppose, now resided with me, Helen and Iain. If we formed a new band, as I'd suggested, we would be unable to carry on masquerading under 3am as the name was registered to Andy. We'd have to find a new name for our band and a new drummer, if we decided to carry on.

In the days after, it was seen on the internet that 3am were still alive and kicking, still with Andy as drummer. Either Tim may have talked him round, appealing to his better nature, or Andy may have withdrawn his early morning text to me, or maybe there was a wider remit; I'll not go there. My dogs remain asleep. I'll never know. Again, this comes with the territory of the music business. I'm sure we all have similar stories to regale. Over time I became the scapegoat, someone must have to be I suppose. Sometimes it was very hard for me to read. I'd been kept in the loop, being forwarded from other third parties and friends of mine, the 3am Newsletters and statements that followed. It got a little too much for me. I called Tim from Sainsburys car park on the Friday afternoon that preceded Andy's text and had to explain what was happening. Tim was most understanding, to the point we had a gentleman's agreement on the issues and situation as they stood. Thankfully most of this disappeared shortly after, a man of his word. I just had to make sure that the source and reason of the initial fracture was Andy's text.

I sat in my car that day, for quite a while. What about the response from Helen and Iain? My suggestion languished. Shall we form a band together? It was not long after I had a digital 'Yes please, we'd love to' to my idea. The new band had no name, no drummer and no PA, but a few remnants of gigs I'd booked and could recommit, reschedule, from 3am. Up to this point I'd cancelled all the 3am gigs I could with no repercussions, or have any effect on my reputation. Most were accommodating and sympathetic. Those that were more legally binding I held in abeyance before deciding what to do with them.

3am were a great little band and looking back, an ideal bunch of musicians for me to get back into playing proper live music again. Very much like 'Round Two'. Looking over the gig list 3am was very much a good quality Pub Band as those type of venues mostly featured. The musicians, especially Chris Parren, were a talented bunch in each of their own category. I was initially musically challenged which helped my playing no end. I learnt a lot, but I learnt more about the non-playing side of the business, the gig booking, PR, road management, logistics. I think the rest of the band were happy to let me do this, book the gigs, book the odd accommodation when required, send out the flyers, all the stuff a manager would do, even to the point of circulating itineraries and even compile the set list. Over time my 'Little Black Book' of contacts developed exponentially. Some gigs all the rest of the band had to do was turn up, play and go home, with me collecting the fee and dividing up. Most of the time I loved doing all of this. In most bands, especially those starting out, there's always someone who takes on this role, whether reluctantly, or not. It was during this time I also joined the Music Managers Forum to develop this role further. More of that in another chapter. However, and I didn't know at the time, the weekly rehearsals at Survival Studios had started to inflict a slow creeping damage to my hearing. The rooms at Survival were quite small at the best of times, some very small. Most weeks you had six musicians all with their amps and rigs pointing inwards to a central mid focal point. Loud music has always been a buzz, sometimes literally, after the gig, but as we know now, regular exposure can dull the frequencies, especially at the higher end. 3am were a band that liked the volume, and this often increased as each weekly rehearsal went on. Each session was three hours long. This exposure pattern carried on into my next band, eventually covering ten years. It was only in Malaya's band that I realised the damaged I'd self-inflicted. 3am turned it up and we loved it.

The 'Andy Text' was almost a relief to the solution, not ideal, but could be deemed as a chapter closing episode. The only disappointment I had was that the last ten 3am gigs were all really good and of high profile, as the time and effort I'd put in, as regards the PR and the gigs, was starting to pay off, naturally spawning the bigger and the better bookings and potentially extract the band from the occasionally soul destroying 'Pub Circuit'. Our, and my, very first gig at The 100 Club was a treat and a prime example in itself. The thrill of treading those boards with of all those that preceded in mind was indescribable. It was a great gig and thought that after this night coupled with all the hard graft I and the band had put in things would finally be coming good. 3am were never to reap this. They are still a working outfit, with Tim and Chris as the only original members. But what did I do next? Did Helen, Iain and I successfully pick up the pieces?

Ginger's and my very first gig (ever) – 18th July 1972
Morson/Me/Jesson/Morris

Still Mk1 - Rushton/Homer/Lake/Me/Matthews

Still Mk2 - Homer/Parry/Lake/Me

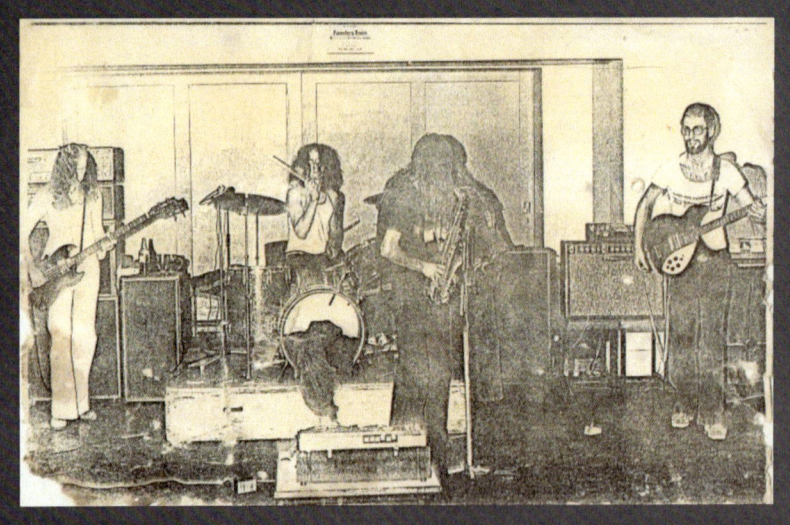

Ferret – Birmingham University
Me/Hill/Ellis/Goodwin

Nick and the Dogs – Poster for residency at
The Barrel Organ, Birmingham

Bare Bones Boogie Band - Studio albums
2010 – 2012 - 2013

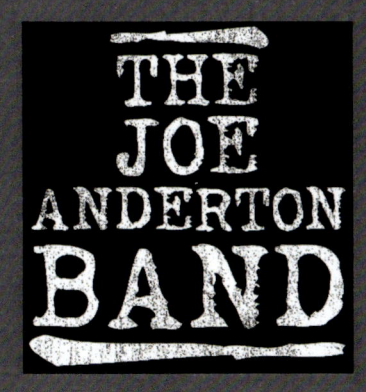

Joe Anderton Band – Live Album

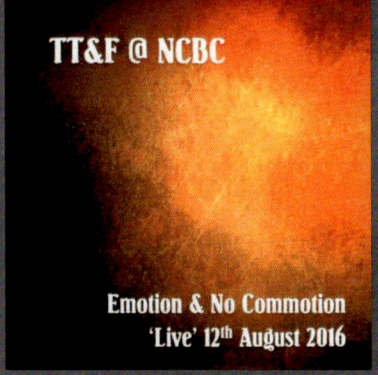

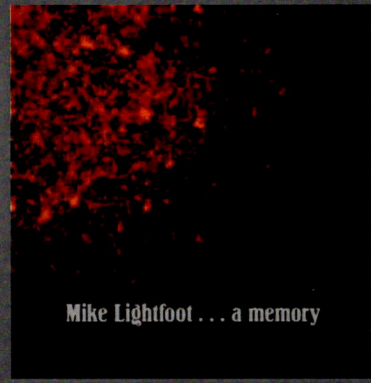

TT&F @ NCBC

Emotion & No Commotion
'Live' 12th August 2016

Mike Lightfoot . . . a memory

Two 'Limited Edition' releases, both recorded at the New Crawdaddy Blues Club. 'Emotion & No Commotion' and the Mike Lightfoot charity fund raiser.

Malaya Blue Band – Blues on the Farm, Chichester
Cooper/Walker/Marshall/Me/Malaya Blue/Dring
21-6-2015

Malaya Blue/Me

Joe Anderton Band – The Borderline, London
Anderton/Me/Hayes 23-9-2017
© Al Stuart

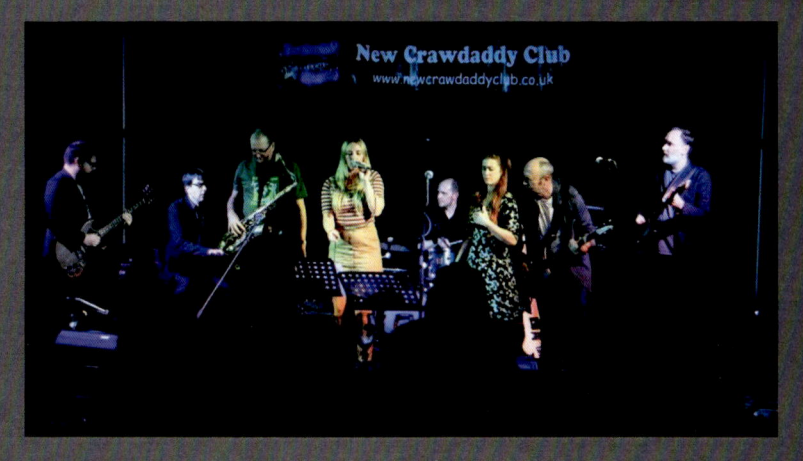

Trev Turley & Friends 12-10-2018
Howes/Cooper/Marshall/Dove/Dring/Yve/Me/Walker
© Graham Chapman

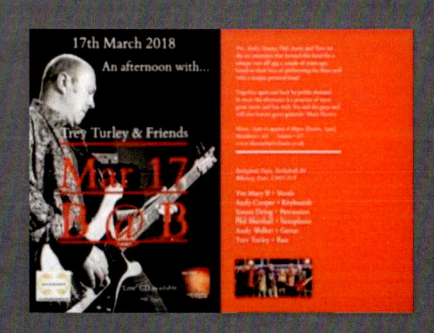

Trev Turley & Friends Flyer

Me/Steve Holley – BB Kings Club, New York City, USA
1-9-2009

MoJo Preachers – Apex Theatre, Bury St Edmonds
Walker/Hammerton/Me/Furness/Van Selman
1-9-2019 (Pix © Laurence Harvey)

MoJo Preachers 2019 album – 'Man Made Monster'

Original Melody Maker 'Wanted' advert and
'Autumn' band sticker © 1977

The original painting by artist PJ Crook entitled 'The Enlightenment'.
As used for the cover of the legacy album 'Cherish Ever'.
(© PJ Crook)

The original plaster cast and painted piece of artwork as created by Jenny (Rob's then wife) and used by Rob Lake as inspiration for the lyrics for the song 'House on the Hill'.

All the previous pictures, in some form or another, featured in the 24 page booklet that accompanied 'Cherish Ever'. These two below were omitted but are exclusive to 'Sky Trails & Pie Tales'. Not wishing to omit a picture of the band '3am', here is the only decent picture I have and of my London debut.
The Bulls Head, Barnes, London 16-2-2004

Renton (Tim)/Renton (Andy)/Turner/Me/Parren/(Black)

. . . and it all started here in 1969 with '3am' as 'Reign'.
Renton (Tim)/Doss/Renton (Andy)/Le Mesurier/Thomas
(© Tim Renton)

The Random Earth Project: 2022

Carleton Van Selman

Kym Blackman

Larry Homer

Finally . . .
Some years in between these, forty-three to be exact.
What happened? A lot of water has flowed under these
two bridges and many of the stories are in this book.
The guitar might look the same, but it's not. I still have one, the
other I don't. Different models anyway. Spot the difference.
(Clue: One is a 4001 and the other a 4003)

The Great British Rock and Blues Festival, Skegness 18-1-2020
(© Tony Cole)

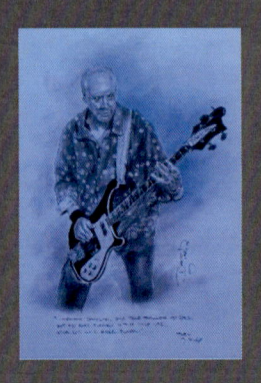

(Left) West Bromwich Town Hall 21-1-1977
(Right) A painting for posterity © Duncan Lamb

10   Bare Bones Boogie Band (BBBB)

For the next six years, from late 2008 this band was to become all-consuming. However, for me, the last year of this band was yet to be another story, but more of that later. It took up a lot of my time and daily thoughts. Apart from the musical aspect, carrying on from the previous bands non-musical activities I had dived into this with both feet, accompanied with my 'Little Black Book' of contacts. But first we needed a name, a drummer and a PA, minor points I suppose. The name came from Iain with a descriptive and instant idea of what the band was about. Yes, the Bare Bones bit fitted like a glove, especially after our previous band. The Band bit was a given, but the Boogie bit, I was never convinced. Sure, we played the odd tune over the years that could be classed as 'boogie'; however, we also did blues and rock too. One or two reviews of live gigs and albums also picked up on this and were oddly confused. We got used to it over time, as did most, shortening the name to the BBBB; less ink on the tee shirts, the flyers and the posters; always a silver lining. One lunchtime at work I came up with the design for the logo, duly accepted and I went about registering this, taking a leaf out of 3am's book. We now had a name and a reasonably instantaneously recognisable logo, but still no drummer. I seem to recall an advert was placed for one, could have been good old Loot again. A couple applied, one I thought was worth looking at and one that came recommended to Iain. Once again Survival Studios became the place to convene an audition. On one night they trooped through the door, sticks and breakables in hand. As my potential rhythm section buddy, I thought I'd have the last word, wrong. The person I favoured was energetic, expressive, not easy to initially play with, but a likeable character. I would say he and I could have been quite a dramatic rhythm section, challenging

Sky Trails & Pie Tales . . .

nevertheless, very much a man after my musical heart. The other drummer that surfaced was solid and with hindsight, the better choice for this band. I was outvoted. Welcome Andy Jones. Over the years I've been known to flit in and out, outside of and within, the drummer. It took me a long time with Andy to get inside his drummer's head. The very first gig the BBBB did was without Andy. It was an old 3am booking with the drum stool duly filled with a dep. It was also Iain's first outing as a solo guitarist, rather than being able to have a second guitarist as a foil. I can't speak for him, but sensed it wasn't a walk in the park for him having to provide both rhythm and lead parts, with the old material we used to play dictating such. We got through the debut with much nodding in the direction of the dep drummer and focused on the next gig with Andy, which just so happened to be the Grey Horse in Kingston, not Jamaica, in West London. The Grey Horse was a well-known music pub, especially for its 'Jam Nights'. The first gig had highlighted the need for much arrangement, or shall I say rearrangement of the material, especially in the guitarist's department. Over time and from where I now sit these early days of the BBBB were crucial in the way the musicians plied their trade and developed the future style of the band.

I cracked on with approaching promoters and venues for gigs. There was one gig that was a bit of a carry over from the days of 3am. I'd been in negotiation with various London Boroughs and the organiser of a marathon being held. It was not 'THE' London marathon, but an offshoot with the focus more on the charitable side. I'd managed to get the band, 3am at the time, a slot at one of the small stages dotted around the course. The request was to play, entertain no less, to the surrounding crowd and each and every runner who had the misfortune to pass by our little gazebo. It was a gazebo and a hastily erected one at that. During these negotiations with the organisers and my signing and agreeing to the contract 3am had splintered. I honoured the contract with a substitution, the BBBB. In the end it was quite fortuitous as the pitch of this so-called stage was near the Greenwich Observatory, at the top of a hill, overlooking the Thames to the Naval College. A prime spot. All the runners would have to run by us, turn around at the top and then run past us again on the return. A double BBBB exposure! The date of this was a day that new drummer Andy was unavailable; bring in the dep, again. On the actual day of the event, the race, we turned up at dawn, at the allotted time, during a heavy rainstorm. This rain remained unabated. It got worse, especially on seeing the circumstances we had to play under, yes, the feeble garden gazebo. The rain came in from all sides. Part of the contract was that a PA was going to be provided. This we never saw. We never saw one person from the organisers of the event either. Looking out of their window in the early hours of the morning maybe they thought we'd never turn up, but we did, such was our commitment. Plus, I'd signed this binding contract. Over all my time of playing music, if there was a contract I had to sign then I'd abide by it, to the letter, I've never reneged, or not honoured anything legally binding. The rain continued to bucket down in Greenwich at which point we started to think we could be risking our lives if we plugged into the mains, but where was this plug? So, we didn't. I managed to get hold of the organiser and, rather apologetically, said under and due to health and safety issues (mine and ours) we'll be unable to play today. "Oh, that's OK" was the reply. We drove home back to a late breakfast, just missing the road closures for this event. If we'd have got caught in the closures then we'd have had to stay all day.

As with most new (read unfamiliar with the public) bands looking for gigs it was helpful if we had some music to share and circulate. The band hastily recorded two songs at Soundmagic Studios in dark deepest Essex, running off a few copies, as a single CD for sale at the odd gig too. One song was an original, the other a BBBB inspired version of Joplin's 'One Good Man'. This cover was the song that got Helen the gig with 3am and she did it rather well in her own style. It must have worked as we were booked for thirty odd gigs in 2009, some were quite major festivals and one our debut at the 100 Club. It all culminated in a short set at the Dome in London. Not the main O2 Arena as it's now known, but a rather bijou club as part of the Dome's complex, but good enough for me. In amongst all the gigs over the years we became the last band to have been booked to play Charlotte Street Blues in London. We were due to turn up the night it closed, receiving this news in a short E-Mail a few hours before we were due to leave. Another fine London venue falling by the wayside. 2010 followed in the same pattern with more festivals, one of which we brushed past both Bob Harris (Old Grey Whistle Test presenter) and Paul Jones on our way to the 'Green Room'. One gig we did in 2012 we brushed past Jack Bruce in the corridor. We had to follow his band on the day. The promoter of this particular gig, yet another no fee one we did as it was in aid of charity, had coerced Jack Bruce to play four numbers with his then scratch band, with which he duly complied. The day of this event was focused around Jack Bruce. He didn't disappoint. A packed crowd lapped up all the old Cream songs. The crowd wasn't as full when we took to the stage shortly after, no idea why! Returning to the opportunity in the corridor of close contact with Jack, I froze and became too respectful saying nothing. However, Iain, our guitarist, summoned up the courage and proffered his hand to Jack. Mr Bruce pointed and proffered his elbow to which Iain sheepishly shook. It transpired that for many years Jack refused to shake hands after the injuries he sustained following an overzealous and 'not knowing their own strength' handshake. This day was the same one that Andy Fraser (Free's bass player) was in attendance too. He was currently in the UK doing

Sky Trails & Pie Tales . . .

some PR. A good friend of mine at the time, who had his own radio show in Nottingham had secured Andy Fraser to appear on his then live programme. The presenter, knowing the esteem that I held with Andy, mentioned this to me. I must admit I was very quick in my response, sending my friend some of the latest material from the BBBB. What transpired was an on-line live radio show discussion with Andy Fraser touching on the subject of yours truly and the BBBB. Nice drop of PR and most appreciative. This radio programme aired a few days before this charity gig, attended by both Jack and Andy. So, I felt even more humbled when Andy came bowling over to me and shook my hand, all preceded with a bright "Hello Trev". For me this made up for not shaking Jack Bruce's elbow! Andy was such a nice person, giving everyone in the room time as he circulated. All rather poignant, as within a short time after this charity event both Jack and Andy passed away. The framed, signed and dedicated piece of paper I had from Andy hangs in pride of place. For Jack, on this day, he charged a fee to have a private audience and to sign an album. I'm sure 'selfies' were extra, who knows? I didn't cough up. Whilst on the topic of signed 'bass player' memorabilia I've done quite well over the years. I have a signed and dedicated backstage tag, complete with lanyard from Tal Wilkenfeld. I'm forever indebted to Tim Aves and his son Owen for this. Guitarist Owen is Tal's favoured 'go-to' player for her band. Tim was invited to a show of Tal's in New York one night. On Tim's return to the UK, I'm presented with this signed pass. I returned the favour of paying Tim for some studio time. Tony Levin is another. I have many copies of his defacement, on many items, books; albums; programmes. Nice person, even to speak to despite my son, who was very young at the time being with me, and Tony talking more to him. These people, Tal, Tony, John, Andy, Chris and many, many more have had a huge, albeit subconscious, effect on my playing and style. Very strange and odd in how they manifest themselves with no conscious effort. Wonderful players and musicians.

One story that does need to be regaled, cast to tablets of stone, is the night the BBBB played a pub in Huddersfield. As part of the package, other than the fee, we were provided with accommodation. After the gig we had to drive miles to another pub and were so late that even the afterhours 'Lock-In' crowd had long gone. The landlord eventually came down and let us in. He duly served us our free first round and soon after announced he's off to bed with the immortal line "Help yourself". Now, it's miles past midnight, we're in a pub, the door is locked, the curtains are pulled, and we have free run of the bar, and we're a band, what can go wrong! An attempt to drink the bar dry failed, but we had a jolly good go. Breakfast was memorable, just about.

During my time with the BBBB, apart from the fleeting brush with the rich and more famous there was one I have to mention and this one I even had the chance to play alongside of him! It was the first of September 2009 and I find myself, with my wife, on a city break at BB King's Blues Club in New York City. After a hard day of being a tourist we needed some food and alcohol. BB King's Club was nearby. Low and behold we find us in the lower bar with the house band playing the blues, amongst other things. Eventually nature called and my wife says she'll go up to the bar and get another round in, good girl. Whilst she's up there and I'm in a state of relief, the band take a break. The drummer of the house band is at the bar, next to my wife and hears her English accent. "Where are you from?" he asks. "London". In the ensuing conversation he tells my wife he's the house drummer tonight. "Oh, my husband plays bass", "Is he here tonight?", "Yes, he's in the toilets", "Is he any good?" (I'll leave you to decide what my wife said to him next.) The drummer says, "We'll get him up in the next set then." This is how I find myself playing at one of BB

Sky Trails & Pie Tales . . .

King's iconic clubs, in New York City, a few pints into the evening, with a borrowed bass guitar, under strict instructions not to make it greasy. At this point I'm not sure if I was told, or knew who the drummer was, but I'm hugely indebted to Steve Holley for the invite, his bravery and risk in letting some kid from West Bromwich play in the band. Steve was in the last incarnation of McCartney's band Wings and has been a long-standing member of Ian Hunter's (Mott the Hoople) band, The Rant Band. Very much a tenuous link back to when I first started playing with my so called 'Bible' being Ian Hunter's book 'Dairy of a Rock 'n' Roll Star'. Small world some might say. Déjà vu others might say. I had difficulty sleeping that night, I was still buzzing. I wanted to tell a few friends of what had just happened. I posted a few messages via social media, nothing! Of course, everyone's asleep in the UK, how dare they, I'm just five hours behind, story of my life. As for what my wife said to Steve Holley at the bar that night I'll never know, but whatever it was, it worked, thank you. As an aside, there are things that my wife has said to many very well-known people in this music business that might be best left unmentioned. However, there is one story worthy of mentioning. This one entails Robert Plant, one time singer of a well-known beat combo and happened during a BBBB gig. I'd got the band booked to play the Queens Head, Wolverley in the West Midlands, twice. This pub is well known as Robert Plant's local. He was there on both occasions. The first one he sat outside, almost unrecognisable. My wife was on 'BBBB Flyer Duty' and in trying to attempt a read by Robert encouraging words were shared, only for Robert to mention his ailing years and associated conditions. Round one to you Mr Plant. The second time we played there was the night after a London Gig of his and he was much better attired. The previous week I'd had some conversation with Robert's sister, about something completely unrelated and slipped into the chat about my band being at the Queens Head. Bless him, he turned up during our set and approached us. Mid song he was right in front of me, he winked and then disappeared into the toilets as the door leading to them was to my left. We never saw him again that night. The humorous part of this encounter was that both Helen and I witnessed it whilst the guitarist was totally oblivious. He had his eyes shut whilst attempting to ring as much emotion as he could from his guitar, mid solo. Round two to you too, Robert. In subsequent years this encounter has been used in the odd drop of PR as Robert Plant in coming to see the BBBB. Not guilty and really not the case. On the back of this sole Led Zeppelin encounter is another, again at a BBBB gig. This time it was at London's own 100 Club. We were supporting. Before our set the word went out that a certain Jimmy Page had been spotted. He, the guitarist of the same well-known beat combo as Mr Plant. That night Jimmy was with Ross Halfin, also known to take a mighty fine picture of the rich and famous, mostly musicians. Cutting to the chase, Jimmy and Ross weren't present for our set, for which our guitarist was probably mightily relieved, as the penultimate song in our set that night was 'Since I've Been Lovin' You', that well known ditty off Led Zeppelin Three. We come off stage and blend into the crowd only to find Jimmy Page in front of my wife and I. Much digging Helen in the ribs and pushing her forwards in the general direction of Mr Page ensued. "Go and say hello". She eventually did and my wife took three pictures. As for the conversation between both guitarist and singer we can only make up our own speech bubbles. Like Robert, Jimmy never did come and see us, it was just good old twisted and fabricated PR. But this is the music business, a business built up on hype, manipulated truths, borrowed room presence. Don't always believe in what you read.

Radio shows, either in-studio, on-line, live or recorded, were another great PR vehicle. Over time we'd got adept at it. One live on-air chat was conducted on a mobile phone in a car park with minutes to spare before a show,

Sky Trails & Pie Tales . . .

I kid you not. We did many shows for Dave Raven and Martin Clarke. Martin's were always held live, in the small studio of Radio Wey. There'd be six of us crammed into this tiny studio, including his producer Heather, now Martin's wife. Heather always announced the weather after the local news bulletin, being introduced as "Here's Heather with the Weather". I think I took it too far referring to her as Miss H. Weather. Martin was a great supporter of us over the years and his shows were always great fun. Albeit we couldn't get a drum kit in there, but we regularly performed live versions of our songs on his show. These were most joyous times. Especially when the bass player found, in a box, in an annex room, an adult sized rabbit suit. Much jollity ensued. As for Dave Raven's sessions these were always held on the upper floor of his houseboat moored on the Thames. We did many, as I did with 3am and Malaya. He liked the ladies did old Dave. Dave has since passed, and we all miss him greatly. Dave's set up was more in keeping with recording live music sessions, the main reason being you could get a full drum kit in across the mooring, up the stairs and into his dedicated studio. Most sessions were videoed and can still be found on the usual streaming websites and platforms. Dave was a hugely passionate and professional radio presenter. He knew his stuff and was very much respected within the fraternity. Dave was also qualified to provide a health and safety service to all houseboat owners in the locality, a role in which he did with great professionalism and enthusiasm. It was a well-known fact that Dave Gilmour (Pink Floyd guitarist, for the uninitiated!) had a houseboat moored nearby and Dave Raven was always coy in keeping facts under lock and key when prompted for stories by other people.

Paper PR was another good source for this band, we did well over the years with many fine reviews in many magazines. 'Blues in Britain' (editor: Paul Stiles) and 'Blues Matters' (editor: Alan Pearce) were often kind and generous in their reviews and articles, as were 'Classic Rock'. Some overseas magazines, both published and digital, garnered high praise, such was the appeal of the band. Paul Stiles, in one edition, he had the BBBB mentioned on seven pages of features and reviews, including Helen as featured 'Cover Girl'. Alan Pearce, now deceased, was a great advocate of mine and both 3am and the BBBB. Over the last few years of 3am and all of 'BBBB Life' he did what he could to support. We graced the Blues Matters stage at the annual January Skegness Festival a few times, thanks to Alan. I could always call him up for a chat anytime. Sad to say after the demise of my duration with the Malaya Blue Band, our relationship came to an abrupt end; not from my doing I hasten to add and not for the want of my efforts. All my calls, messages, e-mails went one way, never returned. It was almost like a switch had been thrown. Maybe his ears might have been tainted? Who knows? This is the music business, isn't it? Prior to this one of the last things Alan did for the BBBB was to include a track from the band on the Blues Matters second sampler CD. The deal set up was that I paid a portion of manufacturing costs to Alan, to the magazine, for return of a quantity of physical product. If all sold at the agreed price, I'd get a return on my outlay. Easy, or so I thought. This I never told the band, or made public, till here now, in this book. There were a few delays and production issues with this album, so much so that during this the band had folded and I received my album allocation after the band had split. To this date I never got my money back, never covered by the band (but they were unaware) and there's still a big box in my attic containing many copies of this album. I'm sure we got some passive PR from sales of this album by the other artistes featured but was all to no avail. Same could be said about the PR company 'Outlaw' as run by musician Clare Free, at the time. The BBBB's first two albums we did, or rather I did, most of the PR, the pushing etc. On the third one, 'Tattered & Torn' we agreed to release

Sky Trails & Pie Tales . . .

with help from 'Outlaw'. A pre-generated PR package was circulated around the magazines and the radio stations, courtesy of Clare, co-ordinated with the time of release. Prior to this, independently to the band (again they are unaware, as I never told them, rather than have 'that discussion') I'd had an agreement with Clare that I'd pay her a monthly retainer leading up to the release date. Both Clare and I conceived a plan, a strategy, in the six months leading up to the release in order to keep the bands name in the ears and the eyes of the 'taste makers' of that time. We both thought it was worthy. The band had, until now if they read this, no clue. Very much a covert operation. I think it worked and three figures well spent. In this time the band had unprompted (by me) press in Classic Rock magazine and its Blues spin off Classic Blues, plus was featured in the top fifty best albums of these magazines' charts for 2013. Probably due to the six-month retainer? Or maybe the album was that good? Or could be yet another case of it's not what you know, but who and came with a price? Over the years I've got to know one very kind, and a lovely person too, who independently reviews into these magazines on a regular basis and still does. Even now he's still at it, writing features and articles, all coming with a preceding respect that his words demand. Dear old Henry Yates has reviewed every album I've released ever since. I first became aware of his work for the story book that accompanies Joe Bonamassa's album 'Dust Bowl'. I got (paid) Henry to write the liner notes for the BBBB's second album 'Blue' too. Our long time friendship has endured over time.

Given the great, good and positive start, we invested in the necessary and much needed PA. My contribution came in the form of a decent monitor (foldback) system. This, coupled with the two-track studio taster the band had all the pieces of the jigsaw in place. I even started a mailing list and a monthly newsletter! Thoughts then turned to a full album. By this time Iain had written a few of his own songs, most of which had been arranged and were now in the set. The set had become a mixture of the bands version of a few covers and an increasing body of self-penned material. We returned to Soundmagic Studios in 2009 and over two long weekends had the basis of the first album. This was released at the beginning of 2010. Over the bands reign, if you can call it that another two studio albums were released: 2012 and 2013. All three had minimal artwork and was always the subject of intense conversation, with the last one, I believe, being the final straw, which fuelled of what was to come. Each bore the logo of the band and became known as, 'Red', 'Blue' and 'Tattered & Torn', reflecting the colour of the logo. All were very well received in the press and the public in general. The second album 'Blue' even had one song nominated in the 2012 British Blues Awards in the best song category along with eleven others. We didn't win, or feature in the top three, but was meritable, nevertheless. The song was called Fallin' for Foolin'. It started life and came to rehearsals as a short up-tempo song. It never seemed to work or fit in with the band. I suggested to slow it down. We slowed it down and down until a four-minute song became a seven minute one. For me it was always a joy to play, so open, so soulful, not overly complicated, but had heart. I'm sure many musicians have graced the 'less is more' school. This song was one of those. Silence can be a note in itself, if used well and in the correct time frame. Anyway, it must have raised awareness in the high hall and long corridors of the then British Blues Awards committee, as it appeared in their choice. The second album took two years to write and record and the third and last one, just one year. The second was carefully crafted, but the last one was done under great pressure, not only to write, arrange and record, but to hit the ideal release date and to maximise annual availability, plus, to reap the benefit of the small amount of success of album number two. You couldn't have had two differently crafted albums. The third and last one

Sky Trails & Pie Tales . . .

broke the band. Of all three, the last one is the one that appeals to me the most as regards mix of material. A point in which I'm a firm believer is that when under pressure the best work often gets created, a focus of creation, but how the pressure is absorbed, or deflected, or dealt with, within the band, is crucial in how the train comes out of this tunnel. Many of the most notable songs in the world are written under duress, pain and emotional turmoil. The blues is a complete genre of this. How many women/men and pets have left their owner to cause them to write "I woke up this morning . . ." The last album seemed to appeal to most and even made the top fifty chart in Classic Rock magazines best albums of 2013, with a fine review to match. However, during the recording and production, with good old hindsight, there were many pointers, behaviour and words said, that the rest of the band were not happy with the bass player, whose idea it was to form this band in the first place. I'll spare you the details but it all came to a head one evening.

It all started with the circumstances leading up to our 100 Club gig on Tuesday 24th September 2013. On the day of the gig we had sold more tickets from our allotted quota of one hundred, guaranteeing us second slot on the three-band line up. The middle slot was most revered and was the BBBB's. The other two artistes on the bill, who shall remain nameless, both came with the same manager who was also rather well-known, who came with some clout and was very good in promoting the up and the coming and getting his own way. He expected his bands to headline, which was a given, the other being a support to his main act. The terms of the promoter, as regards the two support slots, were allocated on who sold the most tickets to their fanbase, with the one selling the least going on first. The BBBB had outsold the other support act by a large margin. During lunchtime of the gig, I was contacted by the promoter saying that the BBBB, despite outselling the other support act, were on first. This I declined to accept. I pointed out that I'd put in a lot of effort in selling the minimum contracted allocation of forty tickets, but in the process had outstripped this quantity. This was the deal, and we took a percentage of the tickets sold. The more we sold the larger the fee. My time and effort was to be in vain. The promoter said he'd talk to the manager of the other two bands and let me know. Fair enough. Within a few minutes the phone rang again. The manager was in no position to negotiate, to the point he'd told the promoter that if his two acts were not on second and last then he'd be pulling them off the bill. In effect, the Bare Bones BB were told "go on first, otherwise no gig" with much loss by the promoter in kudos and money. I said I'll talk to the others in the band. I did, still having the words of the manager, via the promoter, ringing in my head "It might be in his (my) best interest in accepting this offer." Given the timescale, my 'not very pleased' I didn't have much time to temper, I was rather annoyed, putting it mildly. My 'sensible hat' remained unworn. But this is the music business, isn't it? My frustration spilled over onto my band mates, but I got no support there. The three to one vote dictated I had to accept the situation. Sad to write, but if there was ever one point in this band that the last gossamer thread of being a band was broken, then this was it. It snapped like a taut elastic band. As for the internal air of the band you could cut with a knife. In the end I got back to the promoter and we agreed to do the gig as first on, hoping that all the people who'd bought tickets from me would turn up when the doors of the club opened. I kept clear of the manager of the other two bands on the night, best policy I thought, for both camps. I had no intention to cause conflict, or at worst damage my reputation. I remained quiet. The BBBB had a good turnout for our set, the second act less so. As for the headline act I'll never know. I was halfway home on the train by then.

Sky Trails & Pie Tales . . .

This night, this gig, was a prerequisite as to what was to come. I should have read the frosty signs, but I didn't, as all was to be revealed the following week. Rather a vivid memory, it was Wednesday 2nd October 2013. I turned up for rehearsal as normal. I needed to clear the air regarding the previous gig. I was primed to be open and honest to the others in the band, proffer an apology, if necessary, and explain the situation I had to handle. The 100 Club issues I had to deal with on my own, unsupported and hope they understood my emotions, my reaction and what drove it. Some degree of support would have been appreciated. To be honest, any prior emotion was never directed at the others in the band they were my friends, weren't they? All was to be revealed, over the next two hours, or so. When they came into the room, I don't care if people dispute this, but my sixth sense was doing overtime. Anyway, I opened up, I said my bit, gave them an apology, bared my soul, call it what you will. What I wasn't prepared for was their flood gates to open and what became apparent to me was their colluded criticism that lasted for over two hours. Things were a bit strong. This one-sided verbal bashing covered all bases, much personal critique, nothing positive. Some awful things were said, I'll spare you the details. If I'd have known, I would have worn verbal body armour. Over the two-and-a-half-hour session that this lasted, it became apparent that all three of them must have had a prior meeting to discuss and agree their critique and plan of discussion. Historically, I'd always booked the gigs, booked the accommodation, did most of the PR, all the networking etc, for nearly 13 years, having done the same role with '3am', but there was always the occasional difficult and egotistical person I had to deal with. One had surfaced at the last 100 Club gig. The band had started out with me doing most of the non-musical things. Iain could write a tune, so we all pretty much left him alone with this, arranging and refining at weekly rehearsals. Over time and with this look back at past events Iain did get a bit more involved

Sky Trails & Pie Tales . . .

over the last couple years of the bands life running and designing the bands website, publishing the monthly newsletter and administration of the mail shot list. These tasks were ones I had historically done, but in hindsight, were these taken away from me in readiness for this night in October? Who knows? A brand-new monitor system had also been bought, replacing the one I had initially funded. Not that I minded as it was one less thing for me to bring, but another pointer, a sign, in preparation for this night? Apart from all of this administration that most, if not all, serious bands have to deal with there's also the personal side. This night it transpires they had a few other issues here too. Over time my hearing was on the wane. I didn't know at this point, I found out this evening in particular, but my volume had been creeping up in order for me to hear myself. A musicians blight. I couldn't offer this as an explanation at the time, or at worst realise I had to do something. That wasn't for another couple of years. So, I continued to absorb the flack, the vitriol. It got personal, my style of playing came for a turn under their microscope. Ever since the days of 'Ferret' I've developed a bit of a 'free-form' style of playing always looking to play something different, better is the correct word; experimenting with the song, each time I played it. Yes, I played the correct notes at the right time as each song dictated, but the frills and trills could vary. Many years ago, at a session on Dave Raven's boat, cum studio, Iain had remarked during the interview that he thought my playing added 'Colour and Interest', so up until this point I was merrily bowling on down that road, adding the free-form colour and interest. I now find out this evening in October that it wasn't appreciated anymore. Rules and playing etiquette were laid down. Then came something that was a 'make up your mind' moment. What was said became the working title of this book, but over time removed in order to protect the source, I shall keep it personal. At this point of the evening, I thought this was a classic 'Musical Differences' reason. In this these five words it was the moment I'd really had enough, but I thought I'll sit here and see what else is said. So, I did. Work and life balance was a key feature as well. I read this as less gigs, as the words "one a month" were mentioned. However, a pre-agreed solidarity of the rest of the band tempered their conflict. At this point I'd spent my share of my fee of rehearsal time listening to this, it was nearly nine. How did it end?

By this time my guitar was back in the case. Do I just get up and walk out of the door, saying nothing, wiping all that time, effort and money I'd put in off the slate? In effect walk away. No, I thanked them and gave them three options. Sack or replace me; I leave; or give them another chance. In my mind I'd already gone by then, an hour before. A rather painful silence followed, not in their script. Helen said "Have we upset you? You're cross aren't you." I ignored that and walked out the rehearsal room biding them a "I'll let you know sometime tomorrow." That was it. The drive home was memorable, because I can't remember it! But in my mind that was the day I'd really had enough. It wasn't fun anymore, tedious and just another 'job'. Anyway, the whole story, the whole evening, I regaled to Jill when I got home. I went to bed, slept on it, and most of the next day at work . . . The only thing in my mind was that, yes, no more. This following day a late evening E-Mail from Helen, possibly fishing for my response, prompted me into honouring my previous night's statement. It was nearly midnight and after seeking much advice from my wife, family, close friends I thought best I honour a reply. I said I'll carry on, based on their previous evening's words, but in reality, my mind had told me to look elsewhere as well as doing the honourable thing by honouring all the contracted gigs I'd got and booked for the band. Yes, I'd left the Bare Bones Boogie Band. It was Thursday 3rd October 2013.

Sky Trails & Pie Tales . . .

The following few days was spent working out which gigs I had to and would honour, especially those that I'd entered into a contract with, and those that I could drop without too much of an effect on my reputation. Some bookers and promoters were very sympathetic, understanding, the others I let be. Personally, like life in general, I don't like letting folks down. So, I looked at the remaining gigs confirmed for the rest of 2013 and decided to leave well alone. I just had to grin and bear it, playing with people that suddenly weren't my friends anymore. It just became like a business agreement. The first gig after 'The Chat' was Stevenage's Red Lion. We always went down well here; we did that night. The promoter, the late Trevor Keeling, had supported me over the last ten years booking both the BBBB and 3am many, many times, had no idea of the inner turmoil. Things weren't right in the band that night, my glances, expected nods, to the other members during key musical moments and changes fell on stony ground. During this time of year, it's always the norm to look forwards more than usual to booking, scouring for gigs for the following years. I'd already had a couple of decent bookings confirmed. Broadstairs Blues Bash and the Limelight Theatre in Aylesbury being a couple. I just needed some more time to think. To plan ahead, what to do next. I stopped looking for work, but not completely. During my time with the Music Managers Forum, it had often been implied, advised more like, that many promoters, venue owners prefer to be approached by third parties when bands are seeking work, rather than a band member direct. It exudes more weight, more kudos, more professionalism, so I was told. I'm talking about booking agencies and managers. Until now I'd fulfilled this role, on both counts, not only with the BBBB but 3am too as both bands never had a proper manager, or a booking agency working on its behalf. As this band ground to its inevitable halt, I looked to investigate if this was true, and real, as I had time on my hands. Without going into great detail, these theories and advice were proved founded. I registered a business, I still have it, to deal with and take on such activities. During these fallow months I was offered a couple of bookings, but never accepted as they fell into 2015 and outside of this band's life. Initially I only targeted those venues and promoters that I'd drawn a blank with over the years or didn't wish to go down the route of dealing with a band member. It was quite apparent that this route proved profitable and backed up the advice I've had over the years and from the MMF. One venue who I'd personally approached for a booking, as a band member, and refused point blank, couldn't have been more enthusiastic when approached by a third party, but same band. My point proven. My advice to any budding (serious) band is to get yourself a manager, at best a reputable booking agency, to do this for you. Hard work to get accepted, but even if a percentage is taken, it comes with a certain value and lessons the burden on the band somewhat, even in these days of the 'Cottage Music Industry'. The ideal solution is if a business-like minded friend of the band takes on this role of manager, then the costs could be absorbed within the mantle of the band, as this was the case with my band that followed the BBBB. For this one, in good faith, I just fed all my contacts to the manager of this band, and they did the rest. On most, I did initially open the door and they took the necessary steps that followed. In the end all my 'Little Black Book' of contacts were shared, I could say I was bled dry, bit unfair, but this is the music business, isn't it.

For me, 2013 was when the band lost its appeal and in the end 2014 was just a year to coast to a grinding halt whilst keeping one eye open for the next opportunity. I did and used this time to sow a few musical seeds. A private gig was one, as part of Geoff Tristram's band 'The Free Spirits'. It only exacerbated matters. The rest of the band must have sensed my commitment was on the wane. 'The Free Spirits' were a scratch band assembled by Geoff in order to play at his 60th birthday party in the Midlands. All Free and Bad Company songs; eight of which I had dutifully learnt following instructions and telephone guidance from Geoff. The actual night was a resounding success and of great joy despite all of us never having played together. Even Robert Plant's sound engineer, Roy Williams, was there and suitably impressed, despite the shambolic tightness of the gathered. No, Robert didn't turn up despite the invitee list being most of the past attendees of JB's Club. However, dear old Johnny Bryant did, who's initials were used for the club. He even got up and sung a couple songs; more like adding a few backing vocals, whilst grimly hanging on to his pint glass. Johnny used to sing with local legends Little Acre, a ten-piece conglomerate of the 70's. Little Acre had two fabulous female singers Glenis Smythe and Laura Spencer. Don't let on but there was a young lad at the time who had a soft spot for this band, a yearning no less; or maybe it was the girl singers? I'll never know. Geoff's party was in April sometime and a couple of weeks after some corrective surgery I'd had so I was off work and Bare Bones duties with plenty of time on my hands. An ideal time for the BBBB to scour for a replacement, or so I hoped? It was around this time I also decided to take early retirement from the day job. This made complete sense to me, a fresh start, as a professional musician no less, as what else could I be?

The last seventeen gigs the band did were really quite painful for me as they were the ones after 'The Chat'. I honoured them. One of these in particular, I feel quite embarrassed about it now, but given the circumstances, it was what it was. Iain's company held an annual works event. This one was at the 100 Club. The BBBB were invited to play a short set. Being brutally honest I didn't want to be there, no fee, but in good faith honoured it. The train journey in was the usual London rush hour madness, complete with delays on the underground that particular night. I was late and ran down Oxford Street whilst all the time trying call the band. No signal. Texts undelivered. Show time was the time I arrived at the desk of the club. I saw Helen and Iain on stage, no time for apologies, or explanations; plug in and get on with it. I proffered an explanation after the short set, but I could cut the air with knife. I gave them my free drinks tokens and retraced my steps back up Oxford Street and on the Central Line, no delays this trip. This unavoidable incident, albeit not my fault, may explain why on the very last BBBB gig at the Limelight Theatre Andy turned up with minutes to spare. Maybe he never forgave me? I'm sure they were able to use my free drink tokens at the works event at the 100 Club and had a raft of apologetic texts from me once the mobile network found their phones. Rock n' Roll? At the Limelight, the very last gig, I was on autopilot, professional to the bitter end. The last note was still ringing out as I headed out of Aylesbury. If I'd let it, it could have been overly emotional, but I didn't, I wore the Teflon Coat and goodbyes were minimal and brief. It was a shame, and some have said a waste. I'd turned down some rather good gigs for 2014 and there was an offering of potential gigs in Europe with a respected agency, as my negotiations were all going in the right direction, who knows where this would have led. I declined these after the last Limelight gig. Things were bright but snuffed out. To this day I don't really know why this band fizzled out. I have many theories, but for me it ended on that cold October night in 2013, but then each band holds it worth, it's value, to each and every member. We all take something, use it, and make sure we don't make the same mistakes next time. For the BBBB there were some great highlights and also some utter moments of despair, for us all. We played some great gigs and the odd awful one, but don't all bands. I'd even succeeded in getting the band booked for two appearances at the legendary Glastonbury Festival, but I must admit the one man and his dog gigs make the better ones more appreciative. One club in Rochester was as bizarre as they came, full house for the first set, empty the second. Same thing happened at the Swanage Blues Festival. Different reasons. Where was the promoter for these? One was not in the country the other could have been at home. Some ought to take the role a bit more seriously rather than expect the band to be in the line of fire. The punter can be a fickle thing at times. As for Glastonbury, we were booked for two slots in 2013, the year the Rolling Stones appeared: a very late one and a Saturday afternoon one. My book of contacts and the right people to talk to had come good. The application I put in was placed right and must have been of the right ethos and quality. We even got a fee. In the end it was not to be. This was the year a dozen or so peripheral stages were culled, sadly these included the stages we had been booked on. Even now, I find it quite emotional, thinking of the potential appearance and the overall weekend in particular, but I take heart in that the hard work I'd put in securing this booking was the plaudit, not only of my personal grail, but the band in general. Every year many, many bands apply to play this festival. Some via the formal routes, some via the informal ones, some even apply in the annual 'play at Glastonbury Festival Competition', a huge amount never hear anything, ever again. I count myself lucky, or worthy, no pun intended. (The working farm site is called Worthy Farm, keep up.). Playing this festival would have been the easy bit, I'd already done the hard part.

With the dust well and truly settled I delivered what was legally theirs and took what was legally mine, settling and closing all open financial accounts and bolting both business and personnel doors. In 2014 I was nominated as one of six bass players in the final 'best of category' in the British Blues Awards for that year, you can't write this stuff. I didn't win, but the nomination may have turned a light on in someone's head in Norwich towards the end of the year.

Sky Trails & Pie Tales . . .

11   Malaya Blue & Band

With the demise of the BBBB my thoughts turned to 'what next'? Given the past ten years of constantly having the waking thought in my head of pursuing bookings, gigs etc; and looking for that next opportunity it was a welcome break to not to have to bother. I relished the break but soon got itchy fingers again. Strangely enough the word had percolated and wasn't long before I was contacted on the old grapevine by one Tanya Piche. Tanya was ensconced in the wilds of East Essex, and I knew a little about her. She has a unique voice, one that I would call distinctive, probably not everyone's 'cup of tea', but doing the honourable thing I suggested she send me a sample of her material and CV, in her search for a bass player for her band. An obviously hastily compiled, computer burnt, handwritten jewel case and CD turned up in the post. Around the same time, I received an E-Mail from the then manager of one Malaya Blue. To date I had not heard a thing about her, despite her album 'Bourbon Street' being lauded in the Blues Magazines. It was heavily PR'd in Blues Matters Mag but somehow, I'd glossed over it. At the time I was a long-standing annual subscriber to this Bi-Monthly A5 sized magazine, but more of what happened to that later. The contact, from memory, was sparse, could have been a phone call as well, not sure, but I didn't pursue as she was based in Norwich, a mere 100 odd miles away and I thought logistically unworkable. I politely declined and listened to the Tanya Tome. I was undecided and a little hesitant at first and was roughly a 70-mile round trip for rehearsals as part of the Tanya Piche Blues Band. Fending off a very persistent Ms Piche, as fate would have it, I received in the post about this time a complimentary copy of Bourbon Street, from Malaya, plus a nice PR picture! Fair enough, another persistent woman after my

Sky Trails & Pie Tales . . .

meanderings on bass. Maybe my 'Little Black Book' of gig contacts from the previous ten years appealed too, who knows?

I took 'Bourbon Street' from its professionally made digipak and slipped it into my player, Track one, hmm, this sounds OK, a voice and style I hadn't really experienced, mellow, smooth, almost with a touch of jazz overtones. Nothing expected in the Prog arena here, but I was possibly open to a change, or the time of day was right, who knows. A few more tracks in and I'm slightly warming up here, so I drop her manager a message and we start chatting, on-line, whilst I'm listening to the other tracks. Then I got to 'Lady Sings the Blues', co-wrote with Andy Littlewood, just piano, guitar and voice. If there was ever a track, a composition that made the scales swing in a positive direction it was this. I stopped chatting on-line, my concentration became focused. Most impressed of what I heard; this was eventually conveyed into the ether. As mentioned, if there ever was a point in time that the carrot dangled in front of me became the hook, then this was it. What I was unaware of was that all my comments to her manager were being relayed to Malaya, in real time and fuelled a parallel discussion. Her manager ricocheting my words backwards and forwards to his client.

What happened next was that I agreed to meet up with the both of them, one evening after work, for an informal chat. A halfway meeting in a public house was arranged in Exning, Newmarket, The Wheatsheaf. It was 3rd December 2014, another Wednesday. I recall finishing work a bit early to miss the commute traffic home. You couldn't miss Malaya, very much dressed to impress! I assumed the other person was her manager, it was. This hindsight malarky can make a situation, a meeting, into something else, yet I was drawn in by what was offered on the table. A very ambitious package was placed, they'd obviously thought about this, probably to the point of scripted. She, or probably her manager, was putting the next generation of a band together to open the next doors of her career. Sounded fine to me. They wanted a new bass player, but again, with hindsight, the main draw, I think, was my ten-year portfolio of collected names, forged contacts and venues for bookings, but I was happy to help, naïve possibly? It transpired that her manager was a tad lacking and green in the ability to get 'work' at this point, but had contacts and 'influence' elsewhere, of which I was lacking, so a fair deal I thought. It so transpires that they offered me the job, bass player and assisting as unsolicited 'gig getter'. As far as I was concerned and my understanding was that it was a full-time role as part of the band proper, not contracted, not as a 'Session Musician'. I mention session musician as this becomes a key bit of information in the story as it unfolds. The other thing that appealed to them no end was that in nineteen days' time I would become a full time 'professional' musician, devoid of ties and day-job, at their beck and call, 24/7. Anyway, I didn't accept straight away but agreed to let them know by the weekend. It took me two days to get back and accept; fate sealed? Thus started my long-distance love affair with Norwich and the road that linked both the cities, Norwich and London, it still goes on as I write, but with less of the road work.

I passed my decision onto Tanya. Subsequently I shall forever be the bass player that 'made the wrong choice and was lured by Malaya'.

So it began, over Christmas, to get gig ready, learn the material, commit the arrangements to memory in readiness for a first rehearsal and impending gigs in the New Year. Shortly after accepting I was asked my opinion as regards a drummer, another position that needed filling. I was sent clips of a couple potential candidates. One of which was obviously unsuited, the other completely, but would he join? His CV was impressive. Best drummer in 2010's British Blues Awards, gigged world-wide, even headlining at Glastonbury. He joined, good old Simon Dring. Unbeknown to me the rest of the band had been assembled from her managers contacts in the Norwich area and one person from a previous collective, all of which you need to bear in mind as part of this story and assemblage which unfolds in later chapters.

Winding the clock back somewhat. Malaya arrived on the Norwich (Blues?) scene following being asked to sing and to contribute to producer/musician Andy Littlewood's album which became 'Bourbon Street', thus successfully launching her career. The album was very well received and in the meantime a band and a manager needed to be sourced. She made herself known on the blues 'jam' circuit in Norwich with a view to enlisting the better and more suitable musicians to form a backing band. This she did with taking the whole of what was known as the MoJo Preachers (remember the name, you'll need to for later). Prior to this, MoJo keyboard player, the talented Carleton Van Selman, had been approached by her and had already worked with her during the Summer, at Carleton's suggestion, as a duo cum trio, which made perfect sense at the time. Following two gigs with the MoJo Preachers, as her backing band, it culminated in a 'cherry pick' of musicians by her then newly appointed manager. Some accepted, some declined, some were told they were surplus to requirement. It was then that I was pursued. Making a fresh start in 2015 it was on one day early in January that myself, Malaya, Simon, guitarist Andy Walker, keyboard player Andy Cooper (another well known character on the Norwich circuit) and Will Johns assembled at Blue Shed studios in Soham for the very first rehearsal of The Malaya Blue Band. It went well, very well.

Sky Trails & Pie Tales . . .

I mention Will Johns, guitarist, singer, songwriter, son of producer Andy Johns and Paula Boyd. Paula's sisters are Pattie and Jenny who between them married Eric Clapton, George Harrison and Mick Fleetwood respectively, thus each became an uncle to Will. It was inevitable that Will, having been encouraged by EC at an early age that he would pursue a similar career. This was the first time I'd met Will, let alone played alongside of him, but we struck up an instant, somewhat cheeky friendship. We shared a car and chalet during the weekend of the Skegness Rock & Blues Festival of 2015 at which the Malaya Blue Band knocked them dead at the late Friday night, gone midnight. slot at Jak's Bar, now demolished and the Sunday afternoon 'acoustic' session. I smiled a lot that weekend. Will was brought on board for the occasional gig not only to lend some musical weight but to be a more familiar name to those unaware of Malaya's starting pistol.

The first gig was in Lowestoft, a back-room pub on 18th January, a nice little warm-up, then onto Skegness for the annual Butlins weekend blues bash at the end of January. This three-day festival is the first major blues gathering of the season, attended by many of the same faces each year, very much a comforting opening to the season. I'd actually played this weekend twice before with the BBBB and knew what to expect, knew my way round and rekindled many acquaintances. Much 'Hi/Hey Trev' was endured followed by a thumbs up and smiles and the occasional beer thrust into my hand. One such lunchtime session involved me managing to empty an entire pint of Guinness over Richard Townend. This event has now gone down in the annals of history as 'GuinnessGate' with Richard keeping a safe distance from me whenever we meet. Oh, how we can still laugh about things. My much personal popularity over this weekend was looked on with some disdain, especially from the core team; a seed was possibly planted at such an early stage, read on.

Sky Trails & Pie Tales . . .

Over the next eight months the band gigged and embarked on a schedule of events designed to raise the bar and increase the public awareness of our employer. I personally did 26 gigs and a handful of 'live' radio performances. I was only depped once, but that's the way my cookie crumbled. A lot of these gigs were via my past contacts and relationship with promoters and venues I'd worked up and established over the previous ten years before joining this band. In most cases I was happy to kick start the enquiry passing over the donkey work to her manager and being a much more acceptable way compared to the way that I'd been used to working. Some promoters trusted my judgement knowing that my recommendation wouldn't go awry, or disappoint, even if they were unaware of who I was offering. This band was really no exception, given the calibre of musicians. By the fourth gig I'd been introduced to a rather remarkable saxophonist, Phil Marshall. I'd never played alongside of him and the first time we met was actually on the stage at Blakeney Harbour Rooms; we supported Laurence Jones. Phil rolled up and played like he had always played in the band. As the evening rolled on, I sensed that Phil and I had something more in common, our sense of humour and ability to 'entertain', some may say confident stagecraft. Over subsequent gigs, when Phil was able to join the band, we developed and honed this, to the point that at one gig we possibly took it a step too far; taking the attention away from Malaya was deemed a tad sacrosanct as we were to find out. We were thought it was entertaining, having 'fun'. Phil's family include a rather well-known relation, his uncle, now sadly deceased. Both Phil and Uncle Jim were indelibly linked with the same surname, Marshall. To the uninitiated Jim Marshall is better known in the musical world as the 'Father of Loud'. His brand of amplification and speakers are well known and revered all around the world and continue to be such icons in themselves.

Sky Trails & Pie Tales . . .

Back to Phil and myself. As the gig list evolved so did the band and over one weekend in June it became obvious that the classic line up for this band was to be Marshall, Cooper, Walker, Dring, Malaya and myself. The two gigs in question, over a three-day span, at the New Crawdaddy Blues Club in Essex and Chichester's very own Blues on the Farm Festival were, I would say, the musical pinnacle. The band had hit a groove, an in-built driven chemistry that most bands seek to attain. The odd nod, the odd frill led to other things, let's say intuitive playing. This line up were to play just twice more at two slots, over one day in July, at the Birmingham Jazz & Blues Festival. This booking was gifted to me from the promoter who I'd known from his days of running the infamous Henry's Blues House, upstairs at The Crown Pub in Birmingham, in days of old. I loosely knew of Jim Simpson before this, as did many, growing up in the Midlands late 60's into the 70's. Jim managed the band Earth, which morphed into Black Sabbath, until his position became untenable in 1972, the rest is, as they say, in the history books.

Malaya Blue and her band were introduced at Blues on the Farm with great expectation on a warm Sunday afternoon after having lit up social commentary from the gig on Friday at the Crawdaddy. I still have the audio feed, as mixed on the night, from the sound desk of the Crawdaddy Club. I must get round to sprucing it up and getting it archived properly one day. Back at the Chichester Festival, it just got better as the set rolled on. Phil and I are stage right, as you look at it, and having a ball, playing off one another and just having fun and hopefully rubbing off on those in the crowd. It doesn't really matter which song, but Phil took a solo, pushed to the front of the stage he responded with glee and awe, earning a well-received round of applause. During his solo I noticed a stool to the rear of the stage, no idea why it was there, but it was. In the name of entertainment, after Phil's solo, I grabbed this stool and placed it behind Phil, who thankfully was on the same wavelength as me sat down and I proceeded to dab his forehead with one of the provided towels. Much mirth and jollity ensured; we thought nothing of it. Entertainment no less. Malaya and the band took their bows and bagged another great gig. However . . . The next rehearsal, to spruce up some less played numbers ready for Birmingham, saw the band light up again till the mid rehearsal tea break. I've mentioned sixth sense before, well, I got it again as I sipped my tea on the sofa. You just know sometimes when things are going to be said, things that have been agreed and discussed prior to the event. Malaya receded into the sofa cushions as the leader of 'Team Blue' regaled the feedback from the prior two gigs and what was needed to make things even better. All heads in the room nodded in agreement. However, both Phil and I were singled out, made an example of in front of the others in the room that it was deemed unacceptable to have too much 'fun' on stage, to the point that the attention and post gig commentary was taken away from Malaya. A fair point, but I thought it could have done been done with a bit more respect, a bit more decorum by taking the 'offenders' to one side. It was from this point that I realised I wasn't a paid up 'band-member' but another session musician. My role and position were disposable, untenable maybe? The effect of this 'don't do attention drawing' resounded long throughout the band. Social commentary lit up once the band members, less Malaya, got home in the evening. Looking back now its amusing that one seminal event, in effect one sentence, how it had a marked effect on the moral and commitment of the band, all the time leaving Malaya with no 'dirt' on her conscience; isn't that what managers are for? At the end of the day the Birmingham gigs were a tad odd to say the least. The band, as a professional outfit excelled, but there was something lacking, something I and the rest of us couldn't put our fingers on. Shame . . .

Sky Trails & Pie Tales . . .

These two Birmingham gigs were to be the last time the classic line up of this band would play together behind Malaya, but I gathered them up again as part of my own band Trev Turley & Friends (OK I couldn't think of a better name to go out under). This task is regaled under its own chapter, later on.

As a slight diversion it was around this time that dear old BB King passed on. The blues world respected his worth and value to this genre so much so that local Chelmsford promoter, Nick Garner organised a tribute day to BB. This was basically a day of extended jamming; with as many musicians Nick could muster that were available to play for free in BB's honour. I put myself up for house band bass player, along with drummer Glen 'Bo' Buck. We played twelve bars all day, for about eight hours, interspersed with the odd complete band who performed in their allotted slot. Apart from the sheer joy that this day brought us all; those who organised it; those who played and those who witnessed it; it will be remembered for the celebrity stories from the people that BB had actually touched. One such story was from John Verity, ex Argent. He was signed to the same label as BB and regales a great story of the day he met BB, it's out there on YouTube, somewhere. I subsequently asked John if he'd like to play a few bars on my legacy album, 'Cherish Ever', he was more than happy to and did so with such glee. I sent him the track, devoid of guitar, and was in receipt of a rather outstanding solo, even to the point his outro perfectly matched the sax break, without even hearing it. Musical Déjà vu! For me, playing with some fine and great musicians that day will always be held in high esteem and humbleness. John Verity was one, as was saxophonist John Altman. John Altman's pedigree is second to none, as a musician, arranger and just a lovely down to earth person and one I cannot exude as much as I could. I don't intend to regurgitate, and name drop all the people he's played and worked with over the years, but you can find that

Sky Trails & Pie Tales . . .

out in his own autobiography 'Hidden Man'. I will say he was great friend of George Harrison, all of the Monty Python crew, Bjork and was there playing alongside and encouraging Amy Winehouse at the start of her career. There were many others; go find and read his book. Later on, in 2015 both John Altman and I would work together again, this time it was in Malaya's band. John was brought in to cover sax for the evening. Not an overly memorable venue in the backend of Benfleet, Essex, but shut your eyes and it could have been the Royal Albert, the Hall, not the Pub . . .

The Malaya Blue band ploughed on with gigs up and down the country with nine in July and four of these over three days. All these had a mixture of regular band musician and brought in dep, as and when the required person was unavailable. The ethos became that the gig is paramount rather than the person and the chemistry. To the fan, the punter who followed the band it must have been on their mind as to who will feature at each gig. For me a great challenge, an experience to be honest, very much a learning curve, especially when a drummer I've never played with before appears before me. For you bass players I'm sure you'll agree with me that the so called 'Rhythm Section' has to have some degree of empathy. This bond, this chemistry, for me, is paramount. Over time I like to get inside the drummers' head, to the point it becomes intuitive to me as and when certain fills are played. At these points I can go with the flow, embellish, and make it look like to the observer it's rehearsed, or comes with a constant level of regular gigging. With a dep, for me, the phrase 'seat of my pants' comes to mind, occasionally. With Malaya's band both Simon and I had played enough together to have an understanding of what's required and of what to play and, in some instances, what not to play. This was evident on the day when we recorded the double 'A' side single 'Hope'. No disrespect to all the other drummers but I struggled to convey what Simon and I played at certain points, in an instant, during a gig. In the end I just left the drummers to hack it their way, to their own comprehension and I followed in the wake whilst still in the format of the song. Interesting times, sometimes not overly joyful, but opened new avenues. With the last dozen or so gigs I played the interpretation of each song could be different from gig to gig, depending upon the band make-up on the day. Perhaps it was the era I came from, but a band was always 'The Band', the same group of players. If one missed out, then so did the band. I've always said The Beatles wouldn't have been The Beatles with one member depped, I still subscribe to that ethos. I felt it a shame that the last handful of gigs I was to play with Malaya could have been better and the spark, the chemistry, was slightly lacking due to the constant musician merry-go-round. They were still enjoyable, but never like that period of May/June including those two London dates at The 100 Club and the Jazz Café, heady times, loved it!

There was one amusing gig we did, at the Dereham Blues Festival and highlighted the issue of depp-ness. Malaya's backing band, as we'd now become, for this gig was reduced to a three piece; myself, Andy Walker on guitar and a dep drummer. Some of the songs, Andy and I, took to areas of musicality that never existed in this band. Poor old Malaya struggled with what was going on around her as we were in effect 'jamming' the concept. Thankfully Andy and I managed to signal to each other when the next verse started otherwise, we'd still be there today!

I mentioned about the day we all assembled to record her double 'A' side single Hope/Let's Reinvent Love, all new material. Hope was something her husband had written whilst Reinvent was a Phil Marshall piece with lyrics courtesy of Malaya. This day was the day drummer Simon Dring had first heard the song Hope. This will be interesting I thought as I drove up to The Grange

Sky Trails & Pie Tales . . .

Studios, Thetford, Norfolk. Paul Long, he of BBC outside broadcast dalliance and long-time producer of BBC Radio 2's weekly blues programme with DJ Paul Jones, produced. Charts duly arrived; we did a couple of run throughs to ensure Simon was au fait. Then went for it. The backing was myself, Simon, Andy Walker on guitar, Malaya on guide vocals with her husband Graham ensconced on piano in the middle of the room. Having not been briefed that her husband would be an active part bought a new aspect and hugely influenced what I played. I'd already had the two pieces worked out prior to the day, but now with this new and additional piano line it initially threw me. Fret not, thinking on my feet, I simplified the lines I played and voila 'job done'. Even to this day when I listen to the final versions it still amazes me as its not 'Trev-Like' at all. I was most pleased and proud with the final mix after Phil had added his sax later in the day, despite an awful play back mix in his headphones, playing, as he said to me 'blind'! His intuition comes over very well knowing the recording hardship endured. Additional organ was added remotely by Andy 'Mr Hammond' Cooper. As usual Paul Long extricated the best performances out of everybody with such ease and charm that only he can do, plus a myriad of overdubs in all the right places and a one-person virtual choir. Shame that these two recorded versions never appeared on her follow up album to Bourbon Street, as they were re-recorded later in the year with yet another version of the band: another different bunch of session musicians. However, the version of 'Let's Reinvent Love' that we recorded this day does appear on my legacy album 'Cherish Ever', privately released in 2021, some six years later. Copies of the Hope/Reinvent Love single do occasionally surface but are becoming rare.

During the last couple of months, the band were writing, working up and arranging new material that had been written by the members, with lyrics supplied from

Sky Trails & Pie Tales . . .

Malaya. This was all with a view for the follow up album. One piece was one of those songs that I wrote an intuitive bass line, almost from first listen. I was very much inspired and pleased the way it drove the song to a different level, almost giving it a different feel. I looked forward very much to recording this, but it was not to be. At the end of the day, as events panned out, roughly about half of the material on the album was written, or should I say co-written with this band. Credits to the co-writers are hopefully still received in the form of a regular royalty cheque. The performances never happened.

The last gig I played with Malaya was on the last day of August 2015 at the Black Swan Hotel, Brighouse. From memory this was some kind of 'Women in Blues' event. It was an odd evening as I was made to sign a receipt for my fee at the end of the night by her manager. I say odd because for all previous 25 gigs this had never happened. How odd I thought as I drove home from sunny West Yorkshire. My fears were not in vain. Wind forward to Tuesday 8th September, I'm at the Hackney Empire for a King Crimson concert and I get a text from guitarist Andy Walker, saying he's been summoned by 'Team Blue' the following day for a chat. He's been told there's one other, he suspects me. Ominous. Anyway, I forgot completely about this, the music I'm listening to is too good. Early in the following day Andy informs me he's been 'Let Go', surplus to requirements, an 'ex-guitarist' (for those of you who remember Monty Python). I knew what was coming as the other members of the band not affected by this decision were told the previous day, but you can't keep a good secret to yourself can you, especially when it involves one of your 'Band Buddies'. Learning from the events surrounding the BBBB chat of a couple of years prior, I thought it best to let the conversation be driven from the other end and to be polite, unemotional. Eventually I get a message that I'm needed for a Zoom call at one p.m. I

Sky Trails & Pie Tales . . .

know what's coming but even this one didn't fail to impress. In my day job, to provide real money for my family and a roof over my head, as I've never ever earnt enough money to sustain this from music, ever; I too have been the giver, as also the receiver, of what could be bad news depending upon your circumstances, so never easy at the best of times. I've even been on a two-day course to educate the class in 'How to sack someone with minimal pain and emotional embarrassment'. This Zoom call was a corker and didn't fit any of the course notes I'd kept. Her manager talked; Malaya sat behind. Forty odd seconds, probably less if I just consider the dialogue.

This is really a dim one as I try to recall the sequence, but went along the lines of, once the audio had been connected:

Team Blue (TB) "Hello Trev, how are you?"
Me "You go first."
TB [Long Pause] "Malaya and I have been discussing and we are going to have to let you go."
Me "Fair enough, suits me, good luck."
TB [Pause and then the Zoom feed goes blank]
Me [I terminate the link my end]

I laughed. No explanation, all surmised reasons. Sweet and to the point. The following chat that lit up social media afterwards was much more enlightening, illuminating and probably filled in most of the gaps. These peoples' thoughts and support were most endearing; some I was very surprised to read who they came from, not to be mentioned in this book, for their sakes and probably mine. One or two were well positioned and highly regarded in this so-called music business. At the end of the day, with this band, I had played some excellent music, some of it different to what I've played before; appeared at some fabulous and memorable gigs, a couple I would have never had the chance to play. I'd also been given the opportunity to meet, some to play alongside, many fabulous musicians, some of whom I remain very good friends with to this day. However, my most useful contribution was probably the share of my portfolio, if you can call it that, of my ten years of contacts with promoters and venues. If at the end of the day it helped to get the name of Malaya Blue on a road map, then my job was done. I suppose . . . As for asking me to sign for my last gig fee all I can sense is that I wasn't trusted to be honest enough to own up to have received it, with them knowing what plans were just round the corner. I'm of the opinion that these things, these so called 'seeds of untruth', came from others along the way of my so-called playing career to date, or maybe it was a 'digging for dirt' exercise with others to validate personal decisions. Thankfully I'd never be one to lie that I never received the fee, not in my nature. The fee you ask? For this last gig? Fifteen pounds. It didn't cover my petrol home.

As a slight postscript, following this, one by one the other band members who'd been party to the impending decision honoured all their commitments, their contracts and became apologetically 'unavailable' as time proceeded. A shame in my view, as the backing band line-up of Phil Marshall, Andy Cooper, Andy Walker, Simon Dring, and myself really had forged a bond to develop; the latent promise was never exploited. We were a great band, period. However, I did assemble these guys together again for a handful of gigs and one recorded live album in a year or so. Plus, these stories got into another songwriter's head to pen a tune and some striking lyrics. This was my good friend, songwriter and musician Richard Townend who wrote 'Sweet Loretta'. This song was featured on his album 'Gold Fever' along with the lyrics printed in a lavish coffee table book of scored music, pictures, and a story to accompany each song. This was the story for 'Sweet Loretta':

Sky Trails & Pie Tales . . .

"He picked up the bass, wiped the strings and placed it in the case, and then into the car it goes in a ritualistic ceremony played out before every performance. He had a long drive, but this road felt more self-assured, it had a purpose, there was a navigator and this time it was somehow different. With years of effort blown away by miss-judged hot air emanating from people's view of their own worth, he was now not in the mood to organise but had the desire to be organised. He needed a rest from this nonsense and this band, with its potential, was just the ticket. Of course, there needs to be a level of confidence to move forward, but there also needs to be a reality check once in a while, since Show Bizz is, as it says on the page, business. The previous band had sadly misjudged their appeal and whilst reaching for the stars had trampled on the flowers which had given them beauty. Hobnail booted steps where ballet elegance was required. The CD, to keep him company, was slipped into the slot and the voice resounded from the car speakers, it had for months. The songs, now so familiar after hours and hours of due diligence learning, helped the tedious journey become almost enjoyable, he was excited. He picked up the bass, wiped the strings and placed it in the case, then into the car, the gig done. It was similar to the last one and probably the next one would be the same, but at a different venue, with a different crowd, but all considered it would be the same. He cautiously walked to the management and made small talk, then broached the subject of future intent. "Where are we going? What is the plan? When will we get paid?" Of course, these were taboo subjects. There was talk of recording, there was talk of a plan, and there was talk of many things, except money. So, the elephant continued to sit in the room, as it does in these circumstances, eating away at the relationships and biting into the fabric of goodwill. A long recording session done, there was a distinct autumn feel in the summer air, the coldness of a crisp and precise conversation replacing the genial even jokey atmosphere that had once prevailed. There was

plan afoot and it did entail a boot, although no one on the shop floor knew that just yet. The silence spoke volumes. Meanwhile in an office not a million miles away: "Can you do; Oh, you can; Yes, that's great; Thank you; Yes, the fee will be;" and so the secret plan was executed, names booked, finance secured and the casualties were about to feel the cold blade of ambition severe their ties. He picked up the bass, wiped the strings and placed it in the case, then into the car, then the phone rang, it rang urgently. 'Hi how are you?' he enquired. There was a subdued and sullen voice, the response was not what he is expecting, it said, 'I am afraid we are going to have to let you go, your face don't fit the radio.'
It happens to us all . . ."

© Richard Townend (Reprinted with his permission)

Nothing specific but strangely relatable, strangely synonymous, to us all maybe, regardless of instrument and standing within the business and chosen community. I was replaced by Roger Inniss; which was comforting. A fine player, someone with mutual respect and someone with whom I've remained friends. Not only that his six-string bass fretboard is easily mastered by his hands and his technique, but his impressive pedal board is even bigger and infinitely harder to work, well, I thought so.

What did I take away from playing with this band? Lots to be honest. Whilst the music, and sometimes the actual genre was not overly 'me', I learnt to adapt, learnt I could play other types of music. Probably the most major lesson was the notes 'not' to play. The space between the notes is just as important as the notes themselves, sometimes silence is powerful. Malaya had a unique voice, easily recognisable and I personally feel it was a missed opportunity for her and the original band to develop into something quite formidable. All the musical pointers were there. As for her and the team she chose to surround herself with during my time and in her band from this point onwards then not really a subject matter for this book. My respect and personal influence remain intact, I did my bit to push things along, but like life in general, we're not in charge, we just deal with the fallout and move on. Personal opinion is a strong card to hold, we all have one and is often misunderstood and can be occasionally used against the person who holds these cards. Those who decide to place the card on the table are unable to retract once placed. It was also during this period that I was starting to understand that my hearing was depleting, especially covering certain frequencies, especially the sung (and/or spoken) voice, but like most things at this time I turned a deaf ear, which was very true and poignant in equal amounts.

The 'wanteds' beckoned once more . . .

12 Joe Anderton Band

The rest of 2015 was filled with the odd dep, yes, even I succumbed. One was for Dave Thomas at the annual Norwich Beer Festival. Dave is ingrained in this story way back when from the early days of Pre-3am. Soft spoken, a true 'Blues-Man'. I occasionally had a brief chat with him when Malaya and the band were playing in Norwich, when he was seen sculling round. As 2016 became a new page on the kitchen calendar wall my thoughts turned to another quest, another grail, another point to make perchance; the idea I had became something of a reality. Since the end of my association with Malaya it had been suggested to me a couple of times that I ought to put my own band together. This subconsciously nibbled away. Given the musical chemistry that my band mates in Malaya's old band had, it made sense for me to use them as core members, nothing to lose? The first couple of months of 2016 were spent in putting this jigsaw together, all I needed was a vocalist to fill the shoes of Malaya. I eventually found one; fast forward to chapter thirteen.

In May Nick Garner ran another sequel to the previous year's BB King Day event. As 2015 had gone so well, it was thought that this could be repeated so both Glen Bo, and I signed up for house rhythm section again. The line-up wasn't as eclectic as the previous years, but still proved interesting from mine and Glen's point of view. There were some old faces, a handful of new and some names I'd never heard of. Who's this Connor Selby? We all gathered at The Basement Club In Chelmsford and proceeded to crank the handle once again. Musicians came and musicians went, Glen and I churning out endless twelve bar blues, until two teenagers turned up. I paid attention when they started, a nineteen-year-old Joe Anderton and an even younger Connor Selby. Such obvious talent at such a tender age. The older, nay elder, 'Blues Men' and aging members of the audience had often said who's going to take on the blues for the future, well, it was here, right in front of our eyes. Solos were swapped between these two, turns at the mic too during their short set, but I'd heard enough. It was time for me to help to be a mentor, not a Svengali. Both impressed me no end. I'm no talent spotter but like to think I can recognise 'potential'. I'll put my neck on the line here; on the day Joe, for me, was the talented one, just something, something I couldn't put my finger on, the old sixth sense again! Connor had a great touch and a great style, obviously from hours of playing along with the masters at home, but Joe had this 'X-Factor'. OK, blame me now for watching, occasionally, this TV talent spotting competition but the programme title is the best way to explain. It's also worth pointing out that this event, this day, was the first time that both Connor and Joe had played together as was to prove quite seminal in the future of both of these two young musicians. At a suitable break in proceedings, I approached Joe's dad Steve and gave him my business card and said if your lad fancies on forming a band, being part of a band etc, get in touch, have a chat etc.

He did and cutting a long story short Joe and I formed a band; The Joe Anderton Band, however, a drummer was needed and found; Dave Tettmar along with rhythm guitarist Andy Hayes, both former members of Rosco Levee and the Southern Slide. Rosco has since gone on to join forces with Rosalie Cunningham of Prog band Purson affiliation. Dave was an exemplary inventive drummer, one that listened to what was going on around him and reacted accordingly. For me, a dream and a pleasure to play alongside. Andy didn't do solo's, he was just there, as a pure rhythm guitarist; take him away and you'd notice, key and very important. Within six weeks of Joe and I playing together at the BB King event we'd formed what became The Joe Anderton Band, or

Sky Trails & Pie Tales . . .

more succinct, The JAB. First gig was at Chelmsford's Fling Festival, nice and local. The line-up was Joe, Dave and myself. Into the fray and the unknown with very little rehearsal, but with great intrepidation. It went well; it went better as the set progressed; what was a sparsely filled tent for the first song, mostly friends and family, became solid, standing room only spilling on outside. We thought 'we're onto something here'. The three of us realised how easy and natural it was to play together, our age difference and experience knew no bounds, or barriers. It was so natural and instinctive, and it showed. Gigs at the Great British R&B Festival and in the locality of Essex followed, then The 100 Club in late January 2017. The 100 Club was, for me, for us all really, an incredible night, one of those nights that will remain in the musical memory for a long time.

Joe had been booked as part of Solid Entertainments 'Tuesday Blues' Night, a three-band line up. It was the night Aynsley Lister always headlines, always his spot, regular as clockwork. The deal with the promoters is that each band who supports get a quota of tickets. You sell at face value and keep a percentage as the bands fee; the more you sell the more money you make, simple. Yes, in essence 'Pay to Play' but if the rules don't appeal then don't dive in and accept. Also, to make it more of an incentive, the two support bands vie for the first and second slot on the bill, with the headline going on last as the third slot. With this arrangement, the second, middle slot is and always has been the best slot. The late comers have arrived and those that have to leave to catch last trains etc are still there. I've even known some well-known bands, some headliners, insist they have the second slot and seen the club empty before the other support take the stage for the final and third slot. Terribly unsupportive of the general gig going public, but not much can be done, unless the promoter puts an end to headline artistes swapping from last on to second to last on. What an opportunity it was for a young nineteen-year-old to be playing at one of London's iconic venues, having also virtually doubled the sales of tickets of the other support act, verging nearly on three figures sold. There was something brewing and bubbling under as regards the boy Joe. I must admit, Joe was nervous, wouldn't you be at his age? But he'd had his hair cut, bought a new jacket and grabbed this gig with both hands. What unfolded was not short of miraculous. A slightly unsteady start, but after the second, or third response from the near sold-out crowd it gave Joe the impetus and he surfed the wave that followed. A set of a mixture of his own material and rearranged 'interpretations' filled the fifty minutes allocation. The previous gig to The 100 Club we'd played a version of Neil Young's 'Down by the River', an extended version no less, much light and shade and huge swaths of emotion; changing groove from what was expected, to swing, to pseudo-jazz and all stops in between, such was Dave Tettmar's confidence to hold it all together and lead from the front. I joyfully followed in his wake. 'Down by the River' was a big part of the set at The 100 Club, probably for fifteen minutes as we let the song breath and unfold, creating music before ours and the those jammed up at the front of the stage eyes. Brought the Club down, well, figuratively speaking. What a great start for Joe and his band. It bolstered the view I had and what I saw in Joe at the BB King 'Jam' Day.

Dave had done his quota of drumming, for now, and promised to cover his seat with a dep, for at least the next gig, maybe more. What we didn't know was that Dave never drummed with the JAB again. A shame as far as I was concerned. He was 'key', maybe he knew it? All the good work and 'buzz' that had quickly been worked up was somewhat deflated by the next gig. Joe was booked to play two sets at Broadstairs Blues Bash in February. Dave had arranged a dep to cover his vacancy. I believe it was his flat mate, an incredibly talented musician but one I knew more as a keyboard

Sky Trails & Pie Tales . . .

player. A drummer too? Dave said his mate would drive in and bring Andy too. Made sense. So, we're all there ready and waiting, set up waiting for the drummer and the guitarist to arrive. The start of the set tick's past, no sight, we're starting to get twitchy now. Joe agrees to do the first set solo, just him and guitar. No issues there, he's more than capable. So, he carries on as the rest of us are on sentry duty watching and waiting for the other two to turn up. I try calling. No reception in this remote part of Kent. We do wonder if a call would come the other way giving an ETA, a reason. As Joe nears the end of his first set a car turns up with smiling faces and lots of waving. 'They're here!' is heard along with frantic unloading and setting up and rejigging the second set. Thankfully we'd had a short and brief rehearsal a few days before, so I knew that the keyboard player was more than a capable drummer. No thrown in at the deep end for me as the experience I'd had with the drummer merry-go-round in Malaya's band helped no end. In the end it was a bit of treat, not the same as Dave, but we achieved the aim. Given the delayed start the difficult bit was absorbing this and covering the fees etc. Fair enough, but for the drummer this was his job, his only source of income, so honour of his agreed fee was paramount and took a fair chunk. I was sympathetic and let my 'cut' go and lessen the blow to Joe and the band in general as regards financial outgoings. Comes with the territory. I may have said this before . . .

There was humour too. Any visitor to the male toilets that night would be able to look up at the time of 'relief' and see the poster for the Broadstairs Festival. Top of the list was Joe's gig. It read 'Joe Ander**S**on Band'. Maybe I was in the wrong place after all? Oh, how we laughed, and it lessoned the disappointment a bit. I'm reliably informed that a young Mr Ander**T**on prised open the frame containing this poster and secretly removed it. It now resides on a bedroom wall, somewhere in dark, deepest Essex.

Sky Trails & Pie Tales . . .

After this Joe and I agreed we needed a more permanent solution in the drumming department. Joe, much to my surprise, is a very good drummer, as I saw at rehearsal, but as the main singer, guitarist, front-person difficult to drum too. Joe writes a very good song too and has an uncanny knack of coming up with memorable 'Hook Lines'. Very much an all-round musician. Enter Joe Fowkes – new drummer, young person. This Joe I believe was an old friend of the other Joe and I also believe they'd also played in other combinations outside of the JAB. More rehearsals followed to work the new Joe in, with more gigs up to last one in September. Andy wasn't always available and often the JAB was a three piece, the two Joes and myself: old man and two youngsters. Odd? Over these last handful of gigs, I sensed Joe (Anderton) wasn't all too happy with the drum stool occupant and the outside band hassles. I'd applied and managed to get the JAB a coveted 'Jessica Foxley Stage' slot at the annual August GB R&B Festival in Colne. These are for unsigned, up and coming artistes/bands that many have gone on to great and good things. A lot of PR and scrutiny are given to the eight selected, so I thought this is a great opportunity for the band and for Joe more importantly. It was, but Joe was pondering his options, very much a mature head on a young person's shoulders. That same day as the JAB strode off the main stage my mind turned to fulfilling my commitment to another band appearing on the other main stage.

I had been contracted to dep on bass for Dove and Boweevil, who's own bass player was getting married at the time. A much enjoyable gig. Singer Lauren Dove and guitarist Mark Howes are much revered in my book and many other people's books too. I'd got to know them from the Norwich circuit, in which they inhabit as on their doorstep, plus with introductions along the way from my time in Malaya's band. I'd also reviewed an album of theirs for the Blues Press so was reasonably

Sky Trails & Pie Tales . . .

aware of their material. For some reason I was first choice when their bass player was off being matrimonial and honeymooning. This Colne dep was sandwiched between two other gigs with Dove and Boweevil for all the same reasons: very much enjoyable and so pleasing. Lovely, lovely people and just nice to turn up and play without all the extraneous brouhaha.

The last appearance of the JAB was as support to Henrik Freischlader at the Borderline in London. Connor Selby was the other support, a sign? Personally, the Borderline was a venue that was on my bucket list of places to play, and I could eventually tick this off. As with all the JAB gig's it was joy to play and support Joe; give him this opportunity, hopefully kick start something for him. Maybe my way of giving something back to those that follow. I've often used the analogy that my 'out' door is much closer than others 'in' door. But the JAB was to come to an end. Joe spent a lot of time backstage at the Borderline with Connor, like I say a sign of things to come. Joe called me soon after and said that the last couple of gigs I'd got him he was going to do as a solo artiste. Fully understood the reasons he gave me. I continued and continue to this day to support him one hundred percent.

Joe did the Ilfracombe Blues weekend and the Skegness R&B Festival in January 2018 as a solo artiste. The annual Skegness slot was on the 'Introducing Stage', a one and only chance to impress, with a winner each day given a main stage slot at next years festival. I'm not in favour of music being a competition, never have, never will, but this is the way the cookie crumbles. These are the rules, terms and conditions of acceptance for a coveted slot here. The Introducing Stage was the last gig Joe did under the JAB banner. The on-stage video backdrop displayed the words THE JOE ANDERTON BAND, as the operator hadn't been told, or just failed to change it. Joe sauntered on stage and in order to break the ice he

Sky Trails & Pie Tales . . .

pointed out the video back-drop screen and made a humorous comment as regards the no-show of the rest of his band, funny and throw away, but some in the audience took it seriously. Sadly some, who knew of my involvement with the JAB took it on themselves to proliferate and spawn their own, and incorrect perceived reason of my absence around the grapevine. It took a while to dispel and circulate the correct reason; unnecessary. I'm very good at being able to blot my own copy book but take a dim view when it's untrue and by someone else. In this instance I didn't let Joe down, never did and would never do such unprofessional wickedness. I often wonder how circumstances would have turned out if the full band had done the 'Introducing Stage', even more so with original drummer Dave and that line-up. Who knows? Déjà vu?

I did twelve gigs with the Joe Anderton Band and like to think it helped him no end to raise his profile via some high-profile gigs, again courtesy of my 'Little Black Book' of contacts in order to get his dander up as a latent teenager; wind his internal spring for what was and is to come, whether I'm still here, or not. His dad Steve often tells me and thanks me no end for what I did, but it was nothing and I've done it for all the bands I've been associated with etc. The thing with Joe, and Steve, is it's appreciated, recognised and I have no feeling whatsoever of the dreaded phrase of 'being used'. Up to this point and I must admit I felt this has been the case with a couple of bands though. The music business, at whatever level, there is much evidence of 'borrowing' & 'using'; like I've said it before it comes with the territory. We all use each other at some point, it's what makes the world go round, but there are a handful who are 'serial users' casting those who have been drained of use to one side, potentially becoming overly deluded and eventually believing their own hype, their own PR. Then there's the phrase 'believing in your own lie'. I shall leave that nugget well alone . . .

Sky Trails & Pie Tales . . .

During the time that the JAB was active I did the first of two Trev Turley & Friends (TT&F) gigs in Essex and Norfolk respectively, then releasing the Essex gig as a live CD, captured straight from the New Crawdaddy Blues Club mixing desk on the night. This release was 'as mixed', and I was most surprised at the quality. More of this in the next chapter. Given the quality of the mix and balance we thought we'd do the same when the JAB played the same club later in the year, after my own band. The intention was to use the recording for PR and generate some income for the band. The night of the gig we supported Saiichi Sugiyama and his band. Saiichi was going to provide his own sound engineer rather than use the clubs and our set would be captured this way. Not wishing to upset the apple cart I was hesitant at first because the TT&F recording was mixed by the club's sound engineer and was, to me, a known quantity. I just was respectful of the headline/support unwritten rules and kept quiet, creating no waves of discourse. I knew my place. Now with somebody else recording and mixing it was, for me, an unknown quantity, but I was assured it would be fine and they would take the recording away and remix accordingly. You can sense the way this is going. Saiichi said he would mix and produce remotely which he did, but even I could tell the subtle aural nuances were not really the same as with the TT&F live recording. At the end of the day, it was what it was, as an off the cuff live recording, warts and all. Seven tracks, five of Joes own songs and another great version of 'Down by the River', not as good as The 100 Club gig, but good all the same. I did decide to pay to have the JAB Live album remastered at a third-party studio just to give it that bit of 'edge' and I think it was money well spent. This turned out to be the only CD/Album of evidence, in a recorded format, of this band. This JAB/NCBC recording of 'Down by the River' was the one that made me think it could be bettered and why I chose this song to re-record on my legacy album 'Cherish Ever' as the seminal song to represent this era and the JAB in

Sky Trails & Pie Tales . . .

particular. Plus, the 'Cherish' version featured both Joe and Connor on guitars and vocals.

As a postscript, after the dust had settled and Connor had dispensed with the first line-up of his own band and then going out under his own name, Joe became an integral part of his new band collaborating with Connor on song writing duties. The classic Joe Anderton 'ear-worm' hook can be heard on some of the co-written material. Joe still goes out under his own name occasionally but more often than not he's with Connor. Already he and Connor have played at Wembley Stadium as one of the support bands to The Who, plus recently at one of the summer series of concerts at Hyde Park, as support to Pearl Jam this time. A worthy booking garnered by the connections of "It's not what you know but Who you know". A very bad pun, but with an element of truth in it as I keep this story under wraps. It's not part of my one here.

This short period playing with Joe and the JAB means a lot to me, it was and will always be cherished. It ran its course but was hugely important to both Joe and myself and I wouldn't have changed it for the world, and yes, I did form my own band. A little bit of that follows next.

13   Trev Turley & Friends (TT&F)

I have mentioned that I put this collective, this band together at the start of 2016 during my time and parallel with the Joe Anderton Band. It also spilled over into my time with the MoJo Preachers in 2018. In that time, we did just four gigs, but what great, enjoyable and incredibly memorable gigs. I'll explain.

This band came about after the demise, well, me being kindly 'Let Go' from Malaya's band, so in a weird way it did me a favour as TT&F would never have happened otherwise. Shortly after and with much support from the grapevine some suggested I ought to put my own band together. Probably to be 'In Charge', control the hiring and firing etc, but for me this ethos rankles. I understand the process, but can be driven by success, by set goals, by inflexibility and uncompromising blinkeredness. All I wanted to do was to play music, to people, in the live arena, not too fussed where to be honest. I took this idea of 'My Own Band' and went with the flow. I really had no desire to go through the process of advertising for musicians, auditioning, building up the interest, buying a PA, rehearsing, seeking and securing gigs, making sure everybody's available, on & on. I'd had enough of that with the ten years I did it for 3am and the Bare Bones Boogie Band, especially as main booker and gig seeker. Very much a thankless task and often unsupported, and occasionally criticised, "That was an awful gig, why did you book us in there?". That was why the Malaya Blue Band was less stressful on this front, much more pleasurable. I was happy to share my 'Little Black Book' of contacts and let someone else drive the chasing, the persuasion, do the pleasantries and be the false faced 'Mr Nice Guy'. Dealing with some promoters and some so called 'venue owners' can be downright tedious, but overall, most are really understanding and welcoming. However, having to carefully nurture the odd one, or two, for fear of upset (we can all be narcissistic, self-righteous, and self-important can't we, probably us musicians even more so?) it can be occasionally galling and wearing. Purely from my experience, more over recent years, as the music business became more 'Cottage Industry' and thankfully much better at it, some of these 'promoters' still had strong beliefs & ethics; convincing their 'family following' that they now wear the Emperors New Cloak. Some, OK maybe many, have day jobs, as like a musician in current climes, they too must make ends meet and deep pockets come to mind. A thankless task. Both musicians and promoters depend upon one another, are indelibly entwined, but depends upon where each are on the ladder. I'm not going to go into all the combinations, that's for another debate and could be another book, maybe a guidebook on how to succeed with success in getting gigs, regardless of stature. Once the only important grail was to become signed to a record company, this has been diluted by the internet and social media in general. The general public has only so much, maybe too much, choice of music at the click of an icon, at the scroll of a screen, all riddled with a lowering of attention span. (Damn you inventor of the 'Digital CD Skipping Button'; never happened in the day of only vinyl). There's only so many waking hours in the day and with new bands and new music being poured into the digital ether on an ever-increasing daily trajectory going to a live gig seems less important these days, especially after the eighteen-month to two-year hiatus that was ruined by a worldwide pandemic over 2020-2021. Yes, Covid, C19, a misplaced Wuhan Test Tube, call it what you may. During this Lockdown we all forged a world, adapted no less, to deal without our weekly live music fix, it wasn't so bad. Zoom Gigs became the de rigueur; a blight on society as far as I was concerned, delayed and often un-synced. Appalling replacement entertainment. I've never been a fan of this medium. Soulless, in my humble opinion. The only time I've 'Zoomed' was the day I collected my P45 following a forty second chat from a digital front room in Norwich. As venues closed due to unsustainability and lack of support, this has made the smaller venues even more important to the burgeoning musician, less overheads for starters.

Today's Cottage Industry Musical Greenhouse has opened its skylights and let the green fingered amongst us nurture a new strain of promoter; a good thing but can be one who occasionally is much more resilient to requests for a gig, making sure that the 'flock' come back for more, week in, week out. Who knows? Given recent years, from my experience, I'd say that roughly from 2018 onwards the promoters' parameters, the rules and the 'book of excuse' has dominated in the world of gig getting and the givers. The power that the promoter currently wields can work for their roster, for themselves and against it too. Even to the point that the oil on water can, and I've seen it, make an artist and destroy an artist in an instant. Same applies in the promotion world. Dealing with these kinds of folks these days, at this level, my advice is to use the unwritten 'musicians rule book'; be careful, tread lightly, do your homework, ask around, but most of all be pleasant before getting into bed and above all don't blot your copy book. Sometimes we only get one chance. That said, to the promoter, the choice of artiste these days that must be on offer to book is daunting, I don't envy them. Recent years I've seen the bar raised, musicality, performance wise, appearance and entertainment value, all qualities a burgeoning artist needs to consider. Quality succeeds. I don't envy them and the phrase that comes to mind is 'Please yourself, as there's no way you're going to please everyone else'. Good luck to all who sail . . .

To avoid all of these promoter politics (mostly) and to deal with only the 'known', I had this bright idea, yes, I do occasionally get them, to think about calling upon the remnants of what was the backing band for Malaya Blue. We had a chemistry and they are some fine quality musicians. The first call I made was to Paul Dean, promoter of Essex's New Crawddady Blues Club. "Paul, what if I were to put the old Malaya Blue Band together, with a new singer, would you book them?" No pause, a resounding and instant "Yes" was the reply. Paul was so disappointed when he found out the situation of the fracture of the old band, so jumped at the chance. Seed sown. I contacted saxophonist Phil Marshall, Andy 'Mr Hammond' Cooper, guitarist Andy Walker and 'Tin Basher' Simon Dring. Much enthusiasm came flooding back to me with the suggestion I ask Yve Mary B Barwood to sing. In essence, I had the agreement of five people, if you include me, a potential booking and just one jigsaw piece to find. At this point, this juncture, my intention was to do just the one gig, more like a 'point to prove' to me that this band should have, and I firmly believe could have, gone onto to greater and better things if left to gestate, to cogitate and develop under its previous charge, who then would have reaped the benefits too. Again, another one of life's mysteries and now unknowns.

I was aware of Yve from the Norwich scene since 2015, she worked the scene up in Norfolk incessantly, sang with many but mostly Lauren Dove and guitarist Mark Howes and came recommended, from memory possibly by Andy Cooper. I think at this time she had, or had been part of Morganway, so a pedigree established. I called, she agreed. I had a band. What to call it? No idea whatsoever. It was Phil who said call it by your name then folks can relate to me, know what to expect or, in his words, "can blame me if its rubbish". It wasn't going to be anyway. It took me awhile to be comfortable with 'Trev Turley & Friends', or TT&F as it got affectionately called. I called Paul Dean and we agreed a date, Friday 12th August 2016.

Sky Trails & Pie Tales . . .

Songs and set lists were conjured up between us. Quite easy as there was a mutual amount of love for Eric Clapton, the blues, some standards, some known, some not so, a couple of old Malaya Blue originals crept in there too. We thought it was acceptable to stick the originals in there as they had been co-written with a couple of the players in TT&F. Home practice ensured with one full blown rehearsal at Blue Shed studios, the old haunt, so job done, the band was ready. As normal I'd done the usual amount of PR and postcard flyering I generally do, so between Paul and myself we covered as many bases as possible. Just needed the brethren to turn up on the night . . . and they did, in their droves.

The New Crawdaddy Blues Club came with a professional PA, lights, FoH (Front of House) mixer and sound engineer. I've known these guys for many years having been a regular punter at the club myself. I also knew that there's usually the case that a feed is taken off the post mix desk and is used to capture the night, digitally, for posterity. I asked, can you record the evening, but don't let on to the band? They did. It also captured the in between ramblings of some ex-Brummie bass player as I attempted to M/C the evening and hoped to inject some humour. My intention was to entertain. I think we did. As the evening wore on my confidence grew in the chat department and the music was, in someone else's post gig comment 'sublime'. Aim achieved. Have to say Yve's voice was spell binding. The intention was not to replace Malaya, Yve didn't, but brought something of her own, something gentle, something mesmerising. I got critique when people saw the set list, another rendition of 'I'd Rather Go Blind'? But Yve did complete and utter justice to this song, to the point I missed my cue as I was listening to Yve. Overall, the musical content was to be familiar, to give comfort and high on the entertaining factor. Some would say we were a 'covers' band. I disagree, more of an 'interpretational' band. A standing ovation at the end dispelled any doubts and during the night for the usual staid, quiet and respectful audience they used to get at the club, there was plenty of nodding of heads. The whole band impressed, for once my seed of an idea had blossomed. Yve's taxi driver for the night was guitarist Mark Howes. We dragged him on for the encore for a much lengthy rendition of 'High Time We Went' complete with rapid bars of swapped solos between both guitars, keys and sax. Unbeknown to me the rest of the band had agreed that during this song each member would disappear as I introduced their 'Limelight Moment', to a point I was the only one left. I hastily mentioned over the PA that I was the one that was paying them and suddenly I had a full band again. Laugh? I had the last one.

As we packed up and loaded out, I was grateful to hear that the whole evening had been captured in all its glory as one single high resolution digital file that appeared in my E-Mail In-Box a week or so later. Much time and appreciation was spent in separating the tracks from my in-between ramble, then adding a bit of polish at Soundmagic studios to master the complete selection. I couldn't put the whole night onto one CD but selected the highlights and went to manufacture. One hundred copies of the CD 'Emotion & No Commotion – TT&F @ NCBC – Live 12th August 2016' were duly delivered. I hand numbered each of the limited edition which sold in an instant. Chapter closed, or so I thought.

Word got out, the CD was reviewed in the Blues Press and I and the band were wanted for an encore in Norwich! The last gig of the season just before Santa arrived. Much of the same as the Crawdaddy ensued, this time with the addition of Dave Thomas (he gets everywhere) and the wearing of Santa Hats. An overnight stay had been organised and was, in hindsight, wise. Happy Christmas. We let Dave play as it was his and his cohort Steve Morphew's regularly organised

Sky Trails & Pie Tales . . .

blues night. As I write, this event no longer runs, another victim to the virus and changing attitudes.

TT&F took 2017 off as the band needed a well-earned rest and reconvened in 2018 at the Barleyland Blues Club and a final goodbye at the Crawdaddy, both in Essex. The Barleyland gig is a nice Saturday afternoon gig, very well attended and all can get home by teatime for the evenings 'feet up'. This one pretty much followed the same pattern and the set from the first Crawdaddy gig. The final nail in the TT&F coffin was one momentous evening at the Crawdaddy. The date, if needed, was Friday 12th October 2018, mid-way through a busy month for the MoJo Preachers, more later of that. TT&F had expanded to an eight piece for this last hurrah. I don't do things by halves, with a wage bill to match! To the current line-up I'd added vocalist Lauren Dove and guitarist Mark Howes. Some sense of arrangement was done, especially in the dual vocal department, but mostly we went with the flow given the quality and expertise on show. This was the feature of this group of musicians, an inbuilt intuitive nature of how to play together, I was going to miss it after this night, but I didn't as there's more to come, but not with TT&F.

Back in the days of the mid to late 1970's I followed and was in awe of a band from the Midlands, 'Little Acre', a multi-instrumental ten-piece band. Loved them to pieces with duel female singers. They also had Johnny Bryant on vocals and harp. It was Johnny's initials that were used to name the legendary JB's club in Dudley, more of this story and my association with club is elsewhere in this book. So, it was another boxed ticked to get both Lauren and Yve for TT&F. Long had I wanted to be in 'Little Acre', but don't let on to singers Laura Spencer and Glenis Smythe as my eight-piece line-up was as close as I was going to get. Lauren and Yve did not disappoint. The evening followed the well-trodden, four gig path, complete with a radio mic wander into the audience courtesy of Phil and myself, more cheeky banter from me and the obligatory colluded agreement of the band at one point to stop playing completely, bar me, again of which I had no idea, despite me warning them not to repeat the 'walk off' of the first gig. I didn't mind to be honest and I'd have been disappointed if they hadn't plotted something unbeknown, such was the relaxed ethos and respect. Again, with this gig, like the first one, I had it captured digitally from the mixing desk, but on-stage rigs and more of them was just a tad of a step too far to get the balance right. If it had been a mic in the room then possibly better, but this was not the intention this evening. The intention was to entertain, say goodbye to TT&F and have a bit of personal fun; all of us, and we jolly well did.

Chapter closed: Once again, good idea, seed sown, blossomed and sent to recycling ready for a new bunch. Point proved maybe? Four gigs, two years, one live CD – Limited Edition (read collectible now), a lot of laughs, good fun, respect and still in touch with each other. Can't say fairer than that. As more of a postscript, not a great earner, but costs were pretty much covered, but try putting a value on the joy this band and the music we made – PRICELESS. Add into that the memories of those that came to see us, support us, then something money can't buy. As with most gigs of later, more recent days, with the event of the mobile phone and its camera technology, if you go searching on YouTube you will undoubtedly come across footage from some of these TT&F gigs. I still think the name of the band could be better, but it'll do.

14 Fleeting Combinations And Odd Bob's

After the demise of the Joe Anderton Band with TT&F still hanging on in there, I was approached by Olivia Stevens back in early January 2018. Olivia went under the alter ego of Ruby, as in Ruby and the Revelators. A Bognor, read south coast of England here, based band. I was loosely aware of her soulful voice and her proactive push on anything that she's involved with, bless. At the time she was scouting round for bass players with her band, and I responded to a call that she had made a long time ago as regards her request to me "It would be nice to have you on board". Tabs were duly sent and a call to audition. Nice day by the seaside I thought. New band and a new drummer, who was also being auditioned the same day. Results were in; let's give it a go. Oliva has a strong soulful voice with the ability to breath soul into the most mundane song. A couple of gigs were lined up. A private party (good payer) in Chichester and the 'Welly'. Hove's Duke of Wellington has some sort of reputation as a purveyor of decent live music, so I was told, and was drawn back to the pub circuit. Armed with a set of crib sheets, as there was quite a wide range of unfamiliar material, I bashed through two very energetic gigs.

It wasn't to last as my competition came in the form of a local bass player. I lost. 'Location, Location, Location'. At the audition I also sensed a tightly wound-up personal rubber band between other members. It's this old sixth sense again. Maybe I could make more money by being a clairvoyant? With hindsight, no great loss, but it was a joy to witness 'Ruby' do the 'Biz'. In the end the drummer became the bass player and the merry-go-round turned again. I was no longer a 'Revelator' of Ruby's. We've remained in touch though. The last I saw

Sky Trails & Pie Tales . . .

of her was at my dear friend Barry Hopwood's Garden Shed, or more commonly known as 'Barry's Blues Barn'. A place to purvey acoustic (mostly blues) live music without annoying the neighbours too much. Must briefly mention this 'Blues Barn' of Barry's. Completely crafted in the middle of his garden and loosely based on an old Mississippi 'Shot-Gun Shack'. His intention was to create a place for his collection of music memorabilia but took on another life when he started to put on acoustic artistes, mostly solo. Attendance is by invitation only and very private and limited to how many can be crammed in. At the time of his very first gig there I wrote a piece for Blues in Britain magazine, about his 'Blues Barn', his plans and this first gig. Turns out I was the first ever author of published PR for Barry. He still has the article, framed, and in pride of place on the wall inside. Since then, his notoriety has risen and now has a long list of some rather notable musicians requesting they play there. A classic 'from small acorns grow' idea and having the foresight and support to create such a unique platform just two steps from your lounge. 'Barry's Blues Barn' is now known far into Europe and by the time I finish writing this likely to be much further, possibly worldwide.

This next anecdote is sparse and vague but required in order to give a good example of the Hunter S. Thompson quote regarding the music business being a 'cruel and shallow trench, cum corridor'. Some names I've removed to protect the innocent and the guilty, but a great example of how some, no matter at what level, can manipulate the facts to their own benefit. However, in this story, I still have no idea as to what benefit this became, and to whom. This happened, all very factual, but I can look back now and find great amusement.

During my very short tenure with Ruby, if it can be classed as that, I again opened my 'Little Black Book' of gig contacts, initially to help, but with a view to personally play a few venues in which some previous bands I'd been in would have been deemed as unsuitable. I managed to secure a smattering, with one in particular, later in the year. I thought nothing of it, happy to help another artiste even if I wasn't going to appear as part of the band. And then I forgot about it until October that year, 2018, as part of the MoJo Preachers. The MoJo's were approached, or more specifically me, at short notice to fill a gig in October at the Blakeney Harbour Rooms. Blakeney is reasonably close to the main hunting ground of the MoJo Preachers, Norwich. I assume we were asked with a view to enticing a few folks to the Blakeney gig. This is where it went wrong and maybe I shouldn't have asked, but I enquired to the promoter as to who's dropped out. "Who are the MoJo's covering for?" Really just to gauge our suitability, like for like. The answer that came back was Ruby and the Revelators. "Oh, that's a shame". "Yeah, they've bust up" was the unsolicited promoter's reason. We agreed a fee, confirmed, and said we'd be there, thanking them profusely, as you do.

Roll on a day, or two. It played on my mind, perhaps again with this thing called hindsight I should have said nothing else, none of my business. I was about to learn a very harsh lesson, none of my doing but instigated in all good faith, being helpful no less. If you cast your mind back to early January, I'd managed to secure a gig at a particular club, for Ruby's Rev's in October, which just so happened to be close, a few days after the now unable to make it Rev's gig in Blakeney. Given the excuse, to me, by the Blakeney promoter as Ruby's Rev's are no more, I thought, purely out of good faith, that as I was the one that initially got Ruby the gig at the club a few days after the Blakeney gig I better mention it to this other promoter. Wrong.

I dropped this other Club Promoter a line to mention that the MoJo's have been asked to cover a vacant slot

Sky Trails & Pie Tales . . .

(Blakeney) due to the previous incumbents being no more. I also reminded them that as the booking at their club was initially part due to my enquiry, I thought I best mention this fact in case Ruby's Rev's so-called demise would affect their club booking. Out of pure goodwill I suggested that the club investigate, as in my words, I'd hate to be blamed for a 'no show' especially as it was my name on the initial booking, albeit now I wasn't linked, in any shape, or form, to the band in question. "Just passing the message on." That was all. I even suggested that if the club was stuck for an immediate replacement, do come back, as I and the MoJo's might be able to help, but not as a replacement, never the intention. Bit of a Good Samaritan move on my behalf. That was it, or so I thought.

What came back from this club's promoter was utterly staggering. A complete misunderstanding and implied accusation, amongst other things. I still have their E-Mail. For legal reasons, despite being nowhere near the truth and the twisting of my original goodwill and intention it's best left under the stone of legality, despite being a great story in the mode of 'Kiss and Tell' and falls well into the court of a 'Pie Tale'. In the end I gave up explaining in my response when it seemed to unearth more unfounded accusations. Apparently, I was as dab hand at multiple voting, I never saw that one coming.

Back in the days of 3am, as I seemed to be getting all the gigs, arranging the travel, booking occasional 'stay overs' and generally doing the role of Tour Manager I joined the Music Managers Forum as a paid-up member. This was to look for some support, and hopefully some advice and guidance, within the fraternity, as regards the role of musician cum manager. I got some key pointers and the MMF helped no end in the development of me, my experience and of course the 'Little Black Book'. I kept my annual membership going from my time in 3am into the Bare Bones Boogie Band. In 2008 I was invited by The BRIT Trust to sit on the one thousand strong nomination committee for the 2008 BRIT Awards. I accepted. I assume I was asked given the role I'd developed with the MMF and to broaden the BRIT's nomination process across the whole spectrum of the music business. Being a member of the MMF was no doubt key. Without going into detail, the selection process was extremely slick, fool proof and daunting all in one. It opened my eyes and ears to music and artistes I'd never heard of. 2008 was the year of Adele. The precursor event to the event you all see on the television was held at the Roundhouse in London. This is where the nominees are announced for each category in the BRIT's proper, i.e., the sifting and results from the 1000 strong nomination committee, one of which was yours truly. I went to the Roundhouse pre-nom nomination announcement party. Slick and an eye opener indeed. A very young Adele was one of many showcased that evening. Given my Prog Rock education she was not overly appealing, to me, but it was obvious there was a latent talent emerging. She's done rather well for herself since. Nice to have been one of the few that night that heard her sing, the start of what has become her legacy in the space of a few years. It also taught me a few things of what to look out for in other artistes. Those who have that extra factor, sadly it makes all the difference in this day and age; especially in this overcrowded, over polluted pool of mundane talent, deluded, or real, or God-Given. I was very humbled to be included on the BRIT's nomination committee for the next couple of following years. I felt tried, trusted, valued, and respected. Accusations were never on this agenda.

So, with no supporting and supplied evidence of their e-mail content by this club/venue owner/promoter, with a normal day job, it was time to walk away, take note, buy a long stick (to keep them at bay) and wander up the hill of moral high ground. As to what happened since 2018 it beggars' belief. I'm not an overly religious person but find it strange that sometimes the guiding light doesn't always fall on the righteous, but this is the music business we're talking about here. It goes without saying we no longer converse or cross each other's paths anymore. Life is too short.

Mind you, there are some, most are, genuine, nice, open and honest people in the business. I could list them out, but then I'd guarantee to upset the ones I've missed out, or they could then assume the worst. Over the years, at all levels of the business and no matter the genre there's some really helpful and genuine folks. As I've got older and the circle of people I circulate with changes (read trust), I would say the more well-known they are the more lovely and kind they can be. I mention this later in the book, but this has become more noticeable in 2022, post Covid/Lockdown. Maybe the enforced break has given musicians, well, all of us, the time to reflect, reassess, be nicer, loose the ego and the air's and graces. But, and a big but, a very small number have come out the other side with none of these characteristics. I will leave this well alone. The classic phrase that comes to my mind is 'keep your friends close and those that aren't, closer'. Good old Hunter S. Thompson. Amen . . . Somewhere there's a moral to this story and this chapter. Let me know if you find it.

Sky Trails & Pie Tales . . .

15   MoJo Preachers

During the days of the Joe Anderton Band I was writing album reviews for the Blues Press, one of which was 'Confessions' by the MoJo Preachers, a Norwich based band and released in 2016. The MoJo's were started by both Andy Walker and Sophie Hammerton, grafting on Carleton Van Selman a little later. At the time I was unaware of the link of this band to Malaya, but that story is told in chapter eleven. 'Confessions' was made during the time guitarist Andy Walker had been seconded to join forces within Malaya's band and where I'd met him.

During Andy's absence his place had been filled with the guitarist (Nick) featured on their debut album. On his move to the Midlands a replacement was required, and pretty sharpish. With the sharper points smoothed off, the MoJo's approached Andy once more, despite his wayward venture and offer of riches with the Malaya Blue Band. A series of 'sounding out Andy' weekly blues jams, a couple of rehearsals and a gig with his then current band the DC Wilson Band, by keys man Carleton Van Selman, resulted in the re-invitation. Chance jumping by Andy was quick to follow. Over time, 'sights' within the band were raised and it was deemed to seek a more suitable bass player to hopefully achieve these new goals, which eventually transpired to cover and replace the complete rhythm section too. As Andy and I had been 'let go', from Malaya's band within hours of each other, my name appeared as a prime suspect and an ideal candidate. The 'let go' bond was still strong between us as we were the only two members of a very exclusive club and fellowship; M's LGC, (work it out!).

It was early in 2018 that Andy Walker, now back in the MoJo fold contacted me with a view of an invite and an audition with the MoJo Preachers. They had some gigs coming up. This time the boot was on the foot, I was replacing someone. Not nice, as being in this reverse position with both the Bare Bones and Malaya Blues Band I knew the emotional implications affecting the departee, however, it was nice to be asked. I had an inkling of the music and the standard of musicians I was due to join in having reviewed their debut album 'Confessions'. The review mentioned keyboard player Carleton as a prime draw. Some of his playing and arrangements were very appealing to my Prog Rock ears. Tempting no less. But the whole package wasn't your conventional 'Blues Band'. Singer Sophie Hammerton also ticked the 'unconventional' boxes too. I agreed to audition. Songs from their debut album were familiarised and I drove up to Norwich one evening in April 2018 and parked up by the old rooms next to Saint Andrew's Church, Trowse. The complex was more commonly known as the 'Create Rehearsal Rooms', next one down from the graveyard. A resting place for another bass player perchance? I turned up, I played, we had a chat, I drove home, I was liked, I was offered, I joined. The date was Friday 27th April 2018.

The first two gigs, a pub in Norwich and a festival in Yarmouth were my baptism. It was also time and evident to have another change on the drum stool. The word went out. A couple of folks applied; auditioned. One was reasonably local (to the band) and came recommended by the person who taught him, Malaya Blue's old drummer Simon Dring. Welcome aboard Matt Furness. The line-up was complete and for the next three and a half years this was the band that gigged as the MoJo Preachers. However, during this time the whole music business in general went on an eighteen-month sabbatical due to Coronavirus. My 'Little Black Book' of gigs was sorely tested, but the view, the goal, was to up the ante, attempt to do only 'ticketed' gigs, the bigger and better. My good friend Stephen Stanley, of Solid Entertainments played a huge supporting role. I

Sky Trails & Pie Tales . . .

personally owe him one, over the many, many years we've known each other and worked together. He and my wife get on like a house on fire too and have much merriment, usually at my expense. I don't mind. The MoJo's played London's 100 Club three times, once headlining, as well as many theatres and festivals. These ranged from supporting the very well known, those not so and like the MoJo's, the up and coming. 2020 was going to be the 'make or break' year. I'd secured a run of mostly high-profile gigs and festivals for this year. January started off well with the annual Skegness weekend of Rock & Blues followed by the 100 Club, the band had started to hit its stride. Then came the tsunami of Covid19. The whole worldwide music business, regardless of level and standing within, came to a grinding Locked Down halt. All the gigs we'd got booked were either cancelled outright, or were postponed, some many times as the business stuttered back into life. We missed out on supporting Chris Farlow. We missed out on supporting Focus at their only London date of their UK tour. However, the Focus reason of drop out could be attributed somewhat to the band and passively to the virus. We missed out on a main stage slot at the annual GB R&B festival in Colne. The whole festival was cancelled. Not for this book, this story, but the time and effort, and probably money, that Paddy & Jenna Maguire and Jason Elliot had put into bringing the Colne festival kicking and screaming into the 21st century was cruelly ruined by recent events. For me, the heart and soul has been ripped out (musically) but will always be a good August Bank Holiday Weekend for those wishing to have the excuse to get up the following morning with a raging hangover. A little plaudit goes to the Maguires and Jason for past support. I've played this festival many times over the years, with many bands and always an enjoyable and worthwhile event. Maybe another thing, due to Lockdown, that has changed. Throughout writing this book I'm feeling there's a trend appearing. There's

Sky Trails & Pie Tales . . .

the Music BiZ Pre-Virus, then there's the Music BiZ post Virus. Never the twain shall meet.

The band successfully recorded a follow up album to the band's debut 'Confessions'. After much discussion the title and lead in track was to be 'Man Made Monster'. The backing and most of the vocals were recorded at Rooks Yard Studios in Essex split over two sessions. Twelve brand new tracks and one, you could call it a bonus track, revised and rearranged from their debut album. I'd worked with both Pete Crisp and Tim Aves at their previous studio built as part of a school department for local broadcasting. This studio was also used for local radio programmes. On a couple of occasions, I've been invited to sit in as guest on the more Blues related ones. Local musician and most knowledgeable about the subject was Tim Aves. He had a regular weekly show. When Tim was occasionally otherwise occupied Mike Lightfoot used to sit in. I recall one show in which he and I sat in the same studio, I never laughed so much. We just both hoped the studio mic was off at the time. I'd have never worked again if it had been left on. I'm sure some ears were burning. I liked Mike, a great character, he loved his music and was always kind and respectful. He was very supportive of me, very supportive of many in Essex and could be seen hiding in the shadows at many gigs in the area, most nights, not just weekends. Not many people probably knew he had a speech impediment and it occasionally surfaced. So, to take on the role of radio presenter was the mark of the man. We took no notice. I miss him. When the school studio closed Tim and Pete made the decision to start their own, becoming Rooks Yard. Pete had a good ear for mixing and production so was one less thing to worry about. All twelve songs were written between, or by Andy & Carleton, with the lyrics provided by Sophie. The band arranged. As I say the main bulk was recorded over two, two-day sessions either side of a three-week trip around the world by the bass player and his wife. On the way out I had the takes of the first session to listen to on the many long-haul flights we had, plus the demos of the remaining songs we were to record on my return. A couple were missing bass lines. One in particular, the bass line for 'Move', was written on a flight at thirty thousand feet and notation produced. When we got to the session to record this song it was the first time the band had heard it and the first time I'd played it with them. Sophie came rushing out of the vocal booth exclaiming she can't sing over this bass melody. I said I'm not changing it and thought she ought to persist. What she came up with was much better, in my opinion, and one of my favourite tracks on this album. 'Move' was a classic go to track, for me at least, as an example of my own playing. Must have been the rarefied air at thirty thousand feet, or the free bar. I've been accused of 'not playing the song' occasionally, over the years. I'm probably not your typical, run of the mill, root-note, keep it simple bass player. When called upon I can and will oblige but given half a chance I'll flit between the rhythm and the melody, occasionally supplying a counter melody to the one that's going on. Keeps it interesting. Some folks I know hate it. I don't see them much these days! The two sessions produced the quality of the backing required. Over the next couple of weeks both Andy and Carleton, from their own home studios, fired in re-recorded parts for replacement and often additional over dubs and solos and tweaks. One track has five tracks of layered guitar and another, 'Heartbroken Sailor' much synth from Carleton in the audio range of whale chatter. The whales disappeared into the distance but can still be heard as sonar blips in a less over demanding way. Too much was overly distracting. Subtle is a good word. Pete produced wisely from the view of the listener and mixed the final product whittling down the fixes over a period of two evening sessions. I sat in the background to ensure all was well. Mastering and artwork ensued, production run occurred, bills were paid, delivery taken. Job done. I may have mentioned how much I loved the

Sky Trails & Pie Tales . . .

music this band created, a complete fit for my style of playing, perfect and the missing piece of the puzzle. The album was a prime example of this. The album was formally released on 28th June 2019 at the launch gig hosted by the New Crawdaddy Blues Club in Essex. I hasten to add the turnout was remarkable despite another gig in the locality being hosted the same night, which unfortunately drew some supporters of the band away. 'Man Made Monster' was very well received. The reviews in the press substantiated this, as did the airplay, UK and worldwide. The album crept up the IBBA radio play charts over the following months; number 36, number 5, finally residing at number 2, in July 2019, before the slide down the top forty most played album in a month chart. We were stopped by The Allman Betts Band in hitting the number one slot. I don't mind. Worthy, plus the Allman legacy has slightly more weight, I suppose. At the end of the year all the months 'play tally' were added up and 'Man Made Monster' secured number 15 in the top forty chart of 'Most Played Albums' in 2019. No mean feat considering it was only in vogue for four to five months of that year. Would it have got higher if we had released earlier? Couldn't have done anyway, the craft and the creation were prime. Personally, an album I'm most proud of and one I occasionally still listen too. There are not many albums I've made over the years I actually go back and relisten. Some I can't as the (disappointing) memories evoked are still too strong. One day, maybe? 'Cherish Ever' is an album that I do listen to, a lot. It has much longevity, seems like that, as I keep getting the occasional airplay. The odd track still gets played on the airwaves, read the next chapter. The press coverage for 'Man Made Monster' came rolling in. From the magazines, a two-page full feature in Blues in Britain, a one-page feature in Blues Matters, in two issues of 'RnR', one on the covermount CD and a lovely seven out of ten score and review in Classic Rock. There were many other reviews, some worldwide, such was its appeal. One reviewer even quoted the album as being 'Cerebral'. Do for me, in one succinct word. We ended 2019 on a bit of high, on a roll no less. However . . .

I have to mention the 'Tuna Man' at this point. During the life of the band proper, rehearsals were always held at Blue Shed Studios, Newmarket. These were selected as a half-way house between Norwich and London as the band were spread over both locations. Fair enough it was me that lived in London. It helped no end and halved the round trip for me. We chose Blue Shed as they were used for the occasional Malaya Blue Rehearsals, so a known quantity. Very much spacious, comfy sofa's and the usual one wall of mirrors. PA and mixer provided. This 'mirror wall' was completely wasted on me. No way did I manage to hone all the dance moves and shapes needed for 'Pan's People' (and yes, I date myself here). I played with my back to the mirror to avoid catching a reflection. 'Tuna Man' came in the shape and form of drummer Matt Furness. Little in stature, big in beat, but he was rather partial to tuna and sweet corn. The rest of the band used to stop and buy, expensive, fodder (read sandwiches) and drinks from the petrol stations on the way. Matt didn't. He was supplied with a big bag, containing the biggest Tupperware containers known to man. Inside could be anything, but always the main ingredients were tuna and sweet corn. A fork was often provided. These two basic ingredients could be twinned with pasta, bread, salad and all manner of combinations. Boy did he get through a lot, to the point it became a highlight to guess as to what was in his lunchbox. Tuna maybe? On opening the lid, it became apparent, for those whose smelling faculties hadn't been ruined by Covid. Sometimes the virus had its positive benefits, rather than promoting a 'positive test'. Much jollity was had at break time and Matt took it all in good faith. Must admit on a couple of the overnight stays and meals the band did, between consecutive gigs, the chef's skills were put to the test, but always came up trumps to appease this drummer's palate.

Whilst on amusing stories, one gig was too; there were others. Held in the town centre of Norwich on one September's evening in 2018 as part of the towns annual 'entertain the folks going home festival'. The idea was to set up various gazebos around the city and invite the local bands to play three short sets as folks wandered past on their way home. Sounds like fun. The MoJo's were deemed as local. The day, on my drive up was quite sunny, a nice day I thought. My heart sank when I saw the so-called performance area. A garden gazebo had been set up, just a flimsy roof, no sides, just big enough to house one single deck chair. I called up the weather app on my phone. Rain due later, oh really! We set up; sound checked; played one short set, then the heavens opened. You've never seen a bunch of musicians pack up so quickly. Damage limitation. The event that day was cancelled; I drove home. I made a note not to do these sorts of things again, till the following year. The same happened the following year, the same event. At least it was a different location, and the 'tent' was bigger and better, plus the sun shone, it was really quite nice, dancing in the street ensued.

It also just happened that the MoJo's were the band I was to play with on my 365th gig of recent times. Yes, I'd done one years' worth of gigs; albeit spread over a few years. I hoped it would be a good one. It was a tiny pub in Sandwich, Kent. A village full of roads wide enough to accommodate just one small car. The stage and the attracted audience matched. Tiny. Where were the posters I'd sent? Destiny has asked me many times why we accepted this. I don't have the answer. In the end it was one of those gig's and I'm sure we all do them at some point or another, the phrase 'paid rehearsal' springs to mind. This was a classic. All of us rushing through the set list only to mutter 'last song' under our

Sky Trails & Pie Tales . . .

breaths. There's some unwritten rule amongst bands. Honour the gig, be professional, don't moan. Keep the moaning until you get in the car to drive home and make a mental note to scrub this one off the list. Sometimes laughter helps to dull the experience. Some folks call it 'paying your dues'. We all have them, even the Beatles did.

We did do some great gigs though. One night at The Murderers (a pub with music) in Norwich was, for all of us, one of those nights that was perfect. A good sound: We could all hear each other and an interactive audience. It was one of those nights that if you could bottle the musical essence then this was it. A night that any band strives for, I'm sure. The Apex Theatre in Bury St Edmonds was another gig that came this close. Big stage, professional mix, attentive audience. I could go on . . . As an aside, no idea how and for some strange reason, the MoJo's had come to the awareness of a fairly major UK based booking agency. I was besieged by their daily contacts. Having dealt with contracts in a previous day job, I took a softly, softly approach. Discussions were all heading in the right direction, until one day it was like a door had slammed shut; a patch had been soiled; mine and the bands. From over keenness to death knell in the click of someone else's fingers. From a raging river to a dried-up old bed in an instant. Over time we had our thoughts as to who, why and how their interest may have suddenly waned. As I write I now, it has been revealed and I have the answer, the reasons, and the 'plot'. How many times have I said this is the music business, it comes with the territory. Many times it's about those who you know rather than what you know, or, in this instance, those who you don't really want to know, especially those with 'a monkey' still on their back. I love it . . . most amusing now.

Our last gig was to be memorable, probably for all the wrong reasons. For a long time, I secretly wanted to

Sky Trails & Pie Tales . . .

break into the lucrative HRH franchise, but had got lucky, pre Covid, with a slot at the Great Yarmouth HRH Blues festival. Again, due to the viral issues this had got moved a couple of years, ending up on Saturday 13th November 2021. It was a 'do well at this' opportunity type of gig. An early evening slot. I must say it was very well organised, a one in, one out, affair. I thought we played well, the room was full enough, despite one person calling out my name incessantly during the breaks. Good job one or two songs segued into each other. It was one of those gigs; a five-minute change over, no sound check, back line supplied, get on with it type of performances. We met our start/finish times perfectly. All was a bit of a blur musically, but was appreciated, not only by the band but by those in front of us. The last note rang out, we rushed off, didn't hang around and then went home. Little did we know that this would be the very last time the MoJo's would perform. The only sour grapes, and I never got to the bottom of it, but the bands mediocre fee was paid in Euro's rather than the contracted UK Pounds, even more mediocre after the exchange rate/fee had been applied, but in hindsight, it didn't matter, it was the last pay day and just about covered our expenses. For me it had achieved the aim with a view to possibly developing the bands relationship with HRH. Not to be. Why?

Well, winding the clock back a few gigs, back in October of that year, the band had been booked, yet another set of postponed festival dates, two gigs on either coast of England. One on the East coast, then the other, the following day, on the West Coast. Both were run by the same promoter and company. My wife and I decided to make a weekend out it and we based ourselves mid-way between both venues, arriving the night before the first gig. The rest of the band were either travelling up on the day or had done the same as us. On the Saturday morning of the first gig, I'm sitting having a leisurely breakfast musing on the day to come when my mobile rang. Covid had invaded the band. The decision was made there and then to pull both gigs. I agreed to call the promoter and stall the rest of the band traveling up on the day. So, I'm sitting in the middle of a restaurant, gently and unemotionally letting the promoter know of the situation. Personally, and something I've learnt to manage better in my later years (nearly), was to keep a rein on my emotions. It was disappointing, but thankfully the promoter was understanding. We weren't the first band that had let them down due to a positive test. They were able to manage both running orders over both days. Everyone got a longer set and probably a little bit more in their fees. The MoJo's took the financial knock in having to return our pre-paid fees to the promoter. I finished breakfast, packed up and drove home. The journey home was a quiet affair. I lost the use of a second pre-paid hotel night's accommodation too.

The next gig was at the 100 Club, with the enforced ten-day Covid quarantine period running out the day before the gig. We all were hoping that the previous two in a row gigs, now unable to do, would have given the band an edge for this London date. Plus, we were unable to squeeze in a rehearsal either. Most of the 100 Club gigs I've done are granted with the understanding that each band will pull in a certain amount from their fanbase, selling their own allocation of tickets. All the collected revenue is shared, for all involved, bands and promoter alike. This was no different. I'd personally done well exceeding the required quota. It took lot of work, cajoling, and encouragement, some from my family members and friends. As the band's Covid 'Positive' Test Line over the days leading up to the gig became fainter I must admit I did offer up a few silent prayers as I didn't wish to let the same promoter down again, plus having to refund all the money collected to those that I'd sold tickets to was daunting and something I had no desire to do. The other thing, if this had happened, then the fanbase would be less likely to pull together the next time. It was also starting to affect my long-term personal relationship with the promoter. In the end a negative test came through and we all turned up at the 100 Club at 5:30 to sound check. You could hear the sense of relief as we walked though the door. This night was special as we were supporting another good friend of mine from the Midlands, Rebecca Downes and her band. There was a standard policy with these nights, most nights really. The main headline band set up and sound checked first, followed by the second on band; the MoJo's in this instance, with the first band on sound checking last. An hour and a half to sound check three bands at this club is plenty of time, especially when drums and odd bits of back line are shared. However, tonight was grossly marred by the club employing an inexperienced sound engineer. He tried his best but was struggling with the PA set up and location of certain items and protocol. I heard, unconfirmed, that this was his first gig, at the club? We all sat and watched Rebecca and her band sound check, it took an inordinate amount of time and sensed the frustration as in-ear monitor systems were rendered useless and discarded. The on stage foldback disappeared then returned, voices were raised, heads were held, a groove worn in the floor of the club from the stage to the mixing desk. The guy tried his best. It was then our turn . . . the doors were due to be opened in a few minutes!

We did our best in the ten to fifteen minutes it took for us to sound check. Most of the time was spent by the sound engineer in finding other leads and mikes for our amps. He'd assumed we would be sharing Rebecca's bands gear. Wrong. Yes drums, but that was all. Keys were directly injected into the PA. There was nothing in the monitors. It was a shambles, but we vacated telling him what was needed in the monitors and were assured. By now the promoter had the door held to 7:30. The restless folks queuing outside were missing out on valuable drinking time. The last band on quickly set up

Sky Trails & Pie Tales . . .

and were still getting balances as best as they could when folks started to pour in. It must have been odd as there was no discernible difference between their sound check and when they started. They ploughed on, drinks were ordered, and enjoyment galvanised. Next . . .

The MoJo's were on stage at 8:30. The first two numbers we played could have been part of the preliminaries. The sound onstage was incomprehensible. Sure, I could hear the keys, it was all I could hear. No vocals and guitar, I watched drummer Matt with close intent. I thought if we're both together then we'll be OK. Frantic waving to the sound engineer to drop the keys in the monitors proved wasted as getting a good sound and mix was high on his agenda. This night was also being filmed and there's some really bizarre video on YouTube of our set. Evidence of mixing on the hoof, sound and colour clashing as the evening presented itself. I do recall words were said and the sound and the mix got a bit better. Most folks, out front said it sounded great. A relief, but to us musicians, thankfully, visual clues and intimate knowledge of fingers on frets and keys assisted no end. We got to the end. Took our bow. That first post gig pint never touched the sides.

As an aside whoever was to blame I can't, but at a club with such a powerful legacy and a prime location in London's gig going calendar a little more professionalism and duty of care should have been in the house that night. Regardless of who's playing. At the end of the day all three bands on this night acted in their own best interest, professionally, to cater for adversity to give the paying punter a night to remember. For me, memorable for possibly all the wrong reasons, but will never dim the joy and thrill of playing at this iconic venue. The boards that many before me have trod will endear me to their legacies, and to the memories I covet. I've played at the 100 Club many, many times, but didn't want this to be the way I remember the last time I played here. As I write this is likely to be the case.

There were two more gigs after this 100 Club one, culminating in the HRH one as mentioned, which was the actual last one. There was to be one more. I'd secured a support for the MoJo's to Focus, pre pandemic. The intention was that we were going to put a very Prog orientated set together, of which we had enough material. It was an opportunity to gauge how well the band would fare in front of a wholly Prog audience. Maybe it would dictate the future direction for the band, who knows? We were never to find out. The gig was Focus's only London Date on their 50th Anniversary Tour, which was two years late, once the Covid restrictions were lifted, at Chelsea's premier venue, Under The Bridge. This was also a venue on my bucket list to play. Very state of the art, big stage very well set out and all part of Chelsea's Football Club Stadium complex. The Band had missed out playing this venue here some months earlier as part of a day long bill with Chris Farlowe headlining. The reason is that this one had been 'Covid' moved to a date that clashed with a festival date we were already committed to but were promised by the promoter we'd be on the 2022 line-up for this annual event. Back to the Focus booking. Eleven days before the actual gig, which just so happened to be the last day in November the news came in that another positive Covid test in the band had been discovered. However, the band needed a prior rehearsal to refresh the Prog material we hadn't played for a year, or so. We were unable to rehearse again as the Covid quarantine squashed that option. The Focus gig was high value. A poor, slightly less confident performance would have been disastrous and probably another opportunity like this may not have presented itself. We took the unenviable decision again to let the promoter know and pulled.

Sky Trails & Pie Tales . . .

Hindsight can work in one's favour and it can also work against as well. This gig did. Thijs van Leer, Focus's aging keyboard player was taken ill shortly after the MoJo's decision and whilst he was in hospital, contracted Covid. You can't write this stuff. He got better and the end of Novembers 2021 gig had to be moved yet again to a new date in March 2022, due to Thijs's positive test. If we'd have waited a couple days, then it would have been solely down to Focus to postpone rather than a combination of both bands. The night of what was supposed to be the actual Focus gig I went to the 100 Club, just for a night out and to catch up with a few people I'd know were going to be there, the promoter of the Focus gig for one. On my way down the stairs, I was taken to one side by the promoter who told me the new date of the rescheduled Focus gig, but the MoJo's had been dropped. Keeping my emotions in check I was told that the band had become too much of a risk to book. We'd let him down three times recently (could have been four; re the previous 100 Club gig) and they didn't wish to take the risk. Frankly, I had mixed emotions, disappointment and the other one. At the end of the day, it's not the band's decision but I felt it could have been down to the fact of venue and promoter policy at the time of this period of UK Covid control and was assured that personal views were no part of this decision. At the end of the day being a promoter is a risky business under 'normal' circumstances, but this wasn't normal. I understood the promoter's decision to swap out and if it had been me, my business, my livelihood, I would have made the same choice. Rationale of "support me and I'll support you" was strong and right in this instance. Yes, I missed out on two ticked boxes: supporting Focus and playing at Under The Bridge but this proved to be key as to what followed.

It wasn't well received in the MoJo fold, but we cracked on. It opened many weekends to knock the songs into shape that had been written since the last album, in order to record the follow up to Man Made Monster. Some rehearsal days were agreed and provisionally booked into 2022. It was about time. As November turned into December a couple of the gigs booked for the band got twitchy and agreed to revise their calendars. I suspect the grapevine had been active. No evidence: sixth sense was strong. One agreed to cancel outright, the other said to come back once we've done the album and agree a revised date to dovetail into album release PR. Not a problem, I thought. There were two crucial events that in effect put the last nail in the MoJo's coffin. One was, if you recall, the offer to rebook the band on the 2022 annual gig that we were unable to do in 2021, the Chris Farlowe one. I was contacted by another band, who shall remain nameless, who'd been in effect offered our slot for 2022. Not a problem there I thought and were pleased for them, a great opportunity. Their contact with me was to pick my brains as to the process as they were unsure. I helped them, they're my pals. Following on I dropped a line to the promoter tentatively asking about the promised MoJo slot and reminding them. The band aren't booked. OK. The other event I got wind of was that during the constant quest in looking for gigs it transpires that nervousness was rife as regards booking the band. One even told me that, in their opinion, the MoJo's had become 'unbookable'. Oh right.

This started to paint a different picture in my mind. Bridges burnt? Ways forward stilted? These promoters/bookers are not the pubs, but the bigger Blues circuit in general. Very much oil on water. Was it even worth recording a new album? The time, effort and cost when the opportunities to promote were limited, or non-existent? I had some thoughts rattling around in my head, most didn't involve the band, this band. Late in December Carleton and I had what you could call a difficult conversation. I had things to say, he had things to say, but neither of us wanted to be the first to say them. I can't recall who went first, but the 'MoJo monkeys' (read issues/problems) on our backs had to be removed first. My monkey problem was . . . and Carleton's monkey was . . . Each monkey had similar issues but Carleton's and mine each had a different personal reason. Putting them together it was apparent as to the solution. Once we'd seen this solution present itself the decision was clear. We both would leave the band and pursue a new goal, a new venture, a new genre completely. But first, notices to the rest of the band had to be tendered. Both Carleton and I did not take this decision easily and lightly. We carefully thought it through and lived with the idea over Christmas. Sure, the other two new members of what was round the corner were sounded out. "If this were to happen, would you be interested?" Inevitable there would be fall out, always is, we'd both seen it happen in the past. Managing it was key.

Early in January I received an E-Mail from Carleton pretty much outlining his tendering of MoJo notice. I'd already written mine separately and with a slight rewrite tacked it onto the end of Carleton's E-Mail. It was posted at 1PM on Friday 7th January 2022. The band that was to become the Random Earth Project flickered into life.

I suppose you'd like to know what both Carleton's and my reasons were? OK. Carleton's were musical. Can't say musical differences. Like me with 'Cherish Ever', a side project to the MoJo's, Carleton also had one too. His was very Prog Rock based, writing music in this vein and genre, some in collaboration with others. One of the others was me, especially during the period of Covid Lockdown. We both are influenced by this genre and seemed natural to pursue this avenue, both creatively and playing wise. Some of these songs were presented at MoJo rehearsals but failed to ignite and subsequently became side tracked. Many of these were developed outside of the MoJo's and took on another promising life. The resulting recordings were collated and mixed remotely, all from home studios and proved the process viable. At the time it wasn't the intention to forge ahead but given the 'lost' MoJo gigs and potential of difficult times to get booked in the future, there was a readymade building block.

For me, the overriding 'issue' was the growing reputation of the band becoming 'unbookable'. It had got to the point, and I'll be brutally honest here, my fifteen-to-twenty-year (good) reputation with a handful of promoters, bookers and venue owners I could see becoming tarnished. I wasn't going to let that happen and my 'personal' decision overrode anything musical. From the day I joined the MoJo Preachers it was musically the right band for me, without a shadow of a doubt. The Prog overtones, mostly from Carleton, just made it a complete and utter joy to play music with this band. Their style suited me and my style of playing suited them. I'd even gone to say on record that if anything happened to the MoJo's that would be the end of my days, musically. However, the Random Earth Project has again eclipsed this, for all the reasons in the chapter that follows. Ever since the days of Still, I must admit, I was looking for something similar musically, the MoJo's came very close, but what came next surpassed. Despite all of this, including the stress and anxiety of securing gigs over the years had taken its toll. In recent years the market has changed, the familiar faces have disappeared, the effort of building new and trusted relationships became tiring and, in some cases, draining. Lockdown and Covid has spawned yet another breed of promoter, booker and venue owner. Some have developed and come with a ready made 'family', a new 'clique', some I wasn't part of, some I wasn't prepared to make the effort to join, some I was excluded from, with one or two making it plainly obvious to me. Some were more outspoken; driven you could say. As the pool of bands, artistes and session musicians became full, then overly saturated, there was always someone to fill a place should these new promoters, bookers and venue owners upset other musicians along the way. The event of the decline of the record contract and the rise of the home spun, cottage industry, has made things easier for those that book, gave them a voice, even to the point that some dominate and, in some cases, 'control' the music industry. These self-called tastemakers greatly influence what they deem is good, what is the new trend etc. Careers are built; careers are destroyed, some in an instant. The promoter has become King. Over two decades my experience has been mostly on the so called 'Blues' circuit and I've seen this change. With the demise of the MoJo's, for me, the opportunity to jump out of the 'Blues Pond' into another completely different genre has been cathartic. So much so, that subconsciously this was another reason to terminate my MoJo tenure. The Prog Rock circuit will never cross over into any other genre, period, never has and never will. I'm not overly religious but my decision was like being baptised by another church, an epiphany no less, embracing another sect. Prog is very different musically, very different personnel wise, almost devoid of age and time, where those who make the music are a little bit more respected, with and by those that enjoy this genre. The musician is King. To me, ever since I first picked up a guitar, it has taken me a long old journey to realise this. Comfortable is a good word. Random and Earth and Project are also other good words.

The MoJo's will be remembered with fondness, with respect. Sophie came up with some bizarre lyrics, but all meant something, quirky, or not. As an artist (proper art); her creative force was strong, as so were her views on the world and life in general. I really can't recall any arguments, any major fallouts in the band, mind, for half of the bands existence we were sitting at home under Covid Lockdown conditions. Zoom sessions never appealed to me. Some bands, some duo's, some married couples even made careers on the back of the viral conditions. It was digital marketing persons' dream. The MoJo's were essentially a band to experience live and shied away from this fractious Zoom technology. It might be better now, who knows?

16   Cherish Ever

'Cherish Ever' is the title of my so-called legacy album. It came about because of the book you are now reading. The initial writings have grown over time. I have no idea how the seed was sown, but at some point, in 2019 I had the bright idea of what if there were a CD, a physical disc to accompany this book, then at certain points along the way in the story you can pause, put the CD on and listen to the music of which I relate to and write about. At the time this book was only half written and would have taken me many months to complete. The focus then moved from being an accompaniment to this book to a stand alone release on its own merit. It wasn't too far removed from that seed that the idea to supplement the CD with a booklet of its own came to fruition. The first thought was to have a digipak CD with a booklet which would fit neatly into this format. Great idea but it didn't last long. The first thing I drew up was a list of the bands I'd played in from early 1970's to the present. There were many. I picked a track to represent each band, something linked, something tangible, hopefully written by the band at the time, make it wholly relatable, a memory jogger no less. After the first sweep it was obvious, I'd be looking at a double, possibly triple CD release. My first thought here was cost and who'll manage to maintain listening concentration. Quality over quantity became the driver. A standard audio digital CD can fit in eighty minutes of material, but anything over seventy-four minutes can't be guaranteed to remain error free in production and listening. I stuck to the maximum of seventy-four minutes as the limit, keeping the quality issue in mind. A long story short - I whittled it down to twelve tracks covering ten to twelve bands, each with an interesting story to tell. Each song chosen with a strong relevance to the band with which it was associated. I had to drop one song that I particularly

Sky Trails & Pie Tales . . .

wanted to do. I'd approached Connie Lush for her approval to record as it was one of hers. A lovely lady, she said yes without a doubt. I had it in my back pocket, but never managed to get it recorded, maybe one day. Lovely that she'd granted me usage all the same. The chosen were a mixture of the interpretational and the self-written. The interpretational were easy to select. Some needed charts and arranging. Another challenge, but over time I managed to score and achieve. Initially this CD, this album, was only going to be a very small run, for family and close friends that were either involved directly, or indelibly linked with my journey over the fifty years, hence the words private and personal would crop up often and all the way through from the start of this project to the point of selling out.

With this list in mind, I started to draft out the booklet, cum liner notes to tie in with each track. I'd already had the seeds of the stories from what I'd written for this book, but heavily précised. Easy. The bits missing weren't too far behind. However, it dawned on me pretty quickly that what I wanted to regale, needed to say, would have rendered the CD Digipak Booklet too bulky to actually fit the sleeve. Instigate Plan 'B'. One evening I was idly browsing a few new albums I'd had recently and was reminded by a release from Half Deaf Clatch 'Crow Soul'. This was a so-called Blues Concept Album consisting of just two tracks, but . . . it came with an A5 sized booklet of the story relating to the concept. A 'light bulb moment' if there ever was one. I subsequently found out where this booklet was manufactured and got the template loaded up. This proved a key moment as it became so apparent for the look and feel of what was to become 'Cherish Ever'. The stories and the format were easy after this. A page for each track, pictures too, plus the necessary and additional preface, postscript, lists and thank you's drove the booklet to twenty-four pages. I'd pretty much completed this booklet and had a

Sky Trails & Pie Tales . . .

working format even before anything was recorded. The right way to go. Who knows?

How did the title of the album 'Cherish Ever' manifest? The booklet at this point had a blank inner last page. A shame to leave it so. One of the tracks, 'House on the Hill' was a very old song from the days of 'Still' and selected to represent this band and this era. An original piece written by Larry Homer with lyrics provided by the singer Rob Lake. It was decided to re-record this song in order to bring it up to date as regards arrangement. Larry did this from his home studio, playing all the instrumentation, except bass (me) and lead vocal line, Yve Mary Barwood. The lyric Rob had written for 'House' were lost to time and acts of emotion. Rob had, at one point, before he died in 2006, destroyed all his lyrics in a fit of despair and lack of self-esteem. He was never a well lad at the best of times, but that's another story and not really for this book. Both Larry and I will always retain fond memories of Rob despite the trail of devastation he would cause in his wake and often be cleaned up, by others. All Larry and I had was the tape of 'House on the Hill', recorded and subsequently recovered from the studio session the morning after the building had burnt down overnight. (Not guilty.) I'd transferred this to cassette then digitised. Over time the quality had degraded, as had the performances. We both wrote down our own versions of what Rob sang. Larry's and my versions were close, but not close enough. As Larry was the main song writer, we decided to go with his version, with a very subtle twenty first century tweak. I wanted to keep these lyrics pretty much as how Rob had originally sung them, purely as our legacy and testament to Rob. These lyrics are printed in the booklet and filled this then blank, penultimate page. Whilst typing these lyrics there's a line, just before the building outro, that goes:

Sky Trails & Pie Tales . . .

> Cherish ever the house on the hill.
> Forget never the dream on the hill.

Boom! Right before my eyes was the title. The album was known as 'Cherish Ever' from this point on. A fitting title I thought and an epilogue for Rob. And so, it was . . . With the new version and arrangement presenting itself, it was my wife that had the bright idea to use both a male and a female voice to sing the lyrics. Rob wrote the lyrics from inspiration of a small plaster cast artwork that hung in their flat, that his then wife, Jenny, had made at school. This artwork was a hand painted house on a hill no less. It was also Rob's and Jenny's little dream to own such a house one day, but not to be. The lyrics sort of leant towards a call and response. We wanted Yve Mary Barwood to sing anyway and thought it would be a good idea to get another young male voice to compliment. But who? For all of the music on this album, one constraint I'd made is that it all should be played by musicians I've actually played with over the fifty odd years, either as part of a band, or another fleeting occasion. This limited the choice of who to pick. It was quite obvious to choose Joe Anderton. In the end two versions were recorded of the song, one by Yve and the other by Joe. The idea was for Larry to pick and choose a line from each and mould it together in his studio. Both versions were recorded during the constraints of Covid Lockdown, so the element of face-to-face orchestration was missing and difficult to convey otherwise. In the end Larry struggled to make the melded piece work and we took the decision to drop one voice. It is Yve who can be heard on the finished piece. Sorry Joe. Both had sung it immaculately, but each personal phrasing and their own interpretations never dovetailed.

At this point I'd got the booklet 95% complete, the title of the album, but no artwork for the CD and the booklet. Most other recordings I'd done with other musicians it was the recording that came first followed by the design

Sky Trails & Pie Tales . . .

of the artwork. With 'Cherish' it was the reverse process, and with hindsight, the right way round. Throughout the years of playing and listening to music there was always one constant: King Crimson. Over the years their music was just as inspirational as the artwork on some of their album and CD covers. I would suggest that anyone with a bit interest in music, especially if from the era I grew up, would be aware of the artwork of King Crimsons eponymous debut album, 'In The Court Of The Crimson King', by Barry Godber. Barry sadly died a year after this release. During these so called 'Golden Years' some artists album covers were more well known than the music they housed. Look at Blind Faith's debut, great music, but an even more memorable cover. How many teenagers of the time would buy this and secretly hide from their parents? Some may not have been able to muster up the courage to ask for a copy at their local record emporium. I wanted, for 'Cherish Ever', something fitting, something relatable to my years of enthusiasm of Prog Rock. In the ideal world it would have been something along the lines of those epic covers by Roger Dean, or Barry Godber. In later years King Crimson chose to use the talents of artist PJ Crook MBE. Her particular style I was pretty much drawn to in an instant. Over the years we've become friends, from the initial sporadic "Hello, I really admire your work" to ownership of her original paintings, and "Would you like to buy my next piece, I think it may appeal?". The very first piece I bought was called 'The Enlightenment' having had the pre-show catalogue from the private art gallery that was hosting her exhibition over two weeks in September 2019. I was invited, and of course I had to attend the private showing the night before the opening to the public. I found it most compelling (nerve racking too) standing and talking to the artist who had painted this original, now mine, complete with the 'SOLD' red dot sticker, hanging for all to see in the gallery. PJ was most gracious and what she said to me that night was to prove the final piece of the jigsaw for 'Cherish'. "I'd be

Sky Trails & Pie Tales . . .

willing to let you use my painting, The Enlightenment if you wish for anything you create." She knew I was a musician. I owe a great deal to PJ, a most kind-hearted gracious person you would ever have the chance to meet, as is her husband, Richard. As I left the gallery, with my daughter, who I'd taken for moral support, it became apparent that I was able to use PJ's painting as the cover for my legacy album. I smiled a lot that night and for quite awhile after. All the physical pieces were in place. Just the actual music to record.

As I'd decided to only use musicians I'd actually played with for this recording, over the fifty odd years I've been active, I drew up a list from those in the bands, those from the odd drop of depping I'd done and those from the odd jam, or acquaintance. It was quite a comprehensive list, of the known, the not so well known and the unknown. In the end it was about twenty people, whittled down to about fifteen, purely for the recording of the new versions of the songs I'd chosen. One or two couldn't squeeze me into their busy schedules, Will Johns and Nick Magnus. One could but Covid Lockdown prevented a recording session to be mutually arranged, another time John Altman. One never materialised, due to location and practicalities, John Wilson. One I couldn't get hold of, Simon Dring and one that declined my invitation (the reason remains with her), singer Helen Turner-Black. In the end it was thirteen musicians I had to play with and juggle, over two single day recording sessions. These were:

First Session:
Singer/Guitarist – Joe Anderton, Singer/Guitarist – Connor Selby, Drummer – Matt Furness.

Second Session:
Singer/Guitarist – Yve Mary Barwood, Guitarist – Mark Howes, Drummer – Glen 'Bo' Buck.

Sky Trails & Pie Tales . . .

The two sessions spawned the backing tracks for six of the new tracks. These six were embellished by other musicians from their home studios. Remember it's still Lockdown. I was actually limited to a maximum of six people in the studio at one time, including myself, Tim Aves and Pete Crisp of Rooks Yard Recording Studios. No mean feat to get the people balance right to record usable tracks with enough discernible variety. I think it was achieved; you'd never know listening to the final album. Those that added their gloss, their overdubs, were:

Additional Remote Sessions:
Singer – Lauren Dove, Guitarists – John Verity & Andy Walker, Keyboards – Carleton Van Selman & Andy Cooper, Saxophonist – Phil Marshall, Harmonica – Tim Aves.

There was an interim session at Phil Marshall's studio where Lauren Dove recorded her lead and backing vocals for three tracks. A fourth was sent via the ether to Larry for one of his. This additional track, that Lauren provided the lead line for, was King Crimson's eponymous track 'Starless'. Apart from her voice and my bass, the rest you hear is Larry. This track and this particular version resonates strongly. It's fittingly the last track on the album and stops short of the 13/4 King Crimson version ending, thus making it more complete, than like the original i.e. two pieces joined together.

In addition to these six Rooks Yard tracks another two brand new tracks were arranged, recorded, and assembled by Larry Homer at his own studio. I went there for a one-day session to record the bass lines, making it a bit of a weekend back in the Midlands with much pleasant company. Another two tracks were re-mixed and re-produced at Andy Walker's studio, having been captured during a couple of MoJo Preacher studio rehearsals. These were excellent quality demo's but very

Sky Trails & Pie Tales . . .

much usable in their own right. Again, you'd never know when compared with all the other tracks. The last two were archive recordings being lifted off past studio sessions, one never being released, until this album. For these last two I sought, and obtained, the agreement and acceptance that I could use these from the respective songwriters. The original source recording was unfounded, lost, so we had to accept the mix at the time of the recording. Both were recorded at quality, high-end studios anyway so no real cause for concern. These took on a remarkable gloss after mastering. I had twelve tracks, ten of which were freshly recorded in 2020 and all fitted within the golden quality audio running time window of seventy-four minutes. I had four minutes spare. Quality, not quantity.

All the finished tracks were assembled at Rooks Yard Studios and the six specifically recorded there were mixed and produced by Pete Crisp. High end mastering was by Hiltongrove who I'd sourced and specifically used on previous albums. Glossy, glossy ensued, as was the booklet. The initial concept of this release was really only for my record, my pride and to circulate between my family, a few close friends, plus including all the musicians and cast involved in creating 'Cherish Ever'. Word got out, inevitably. In the end, I can't recall by whom, maybe there was a general outcry, but I was persuaded to offer this to a slightly wider remit. The one hundred limited edition was born and formally released on Monday 8th February 2021. These one hundred I would individually number by hand and send out complete with the twenty-four-page booklet. It was the booklet that was the limiting factor, being the hand numbered component. Each copy was shrink-wrapped and placed in its own cellophane bag, ready for its journey to a new home. Have to say I never made any money out of this, I knew I'd run at a loss, but as one radio presenter said it was a 'Labour of Love'. I tend to agree. A money-making project this was never to be.

Sky Trails & Pie Tales . . .

The time and the effort paid dividends for me and 'Cherish' is still doing it. In the end I had two hundred pressed, both CD digipak and booklet. One hundred went as the Limited Edition. About thirty to forty went as complimentary copies to family, close friends and those directly involved. However, one copy on the list of 'those not directly involved' was never taken up. I never had a reply, despite the kindness of my offer. They played a big role in the craft of not only of me, but those in the bands at the time I was with them. I find it disappointing and difficult to understand that their respect (and part of this album was their legacy too) and the pleasure of making music should have no boundaries, no issues, but then again, I don't have their problems and my perceived issues of those that they may have. One word, OK two. A shame: then again this is the music business we are dealing with. You can never please everyone, it runs rife. A perfect example. Fifty copies went as a 're-run' version after the one hundred 'Limited's' disappeared in less than two weeks. These fifty were not numbered. Have to mention one was ordered from Abu Dhabi. The recipient never received it. Many weeks later it reappeared in my daily post, a bit worse for wear and the journey, obviously opened. The purchaser did eventually receive a copy, on one of their occasional trips back to the UK, I'd left it with a member of their family. The very last one I posted out abroad was to a local musician in Moscow, Russia. Like the Abu Dhabi one, it took an eternity to arrive but eventually reached the new owner. Shortly after receipt things went a bit awry with Russia's placement in the world of 'goodwill to all people'. When this page eventually gets read a lot of water is likely to have gone under the bridges of the world and I have no idea as to what the circumstances will be in Ukraine at the time of you reading this. We could all be dead but hope that sense and sensibility have survived, and we all live to see another day. I find it sad that the last ever recipient of my album was never allowed to send me their thoughts. This is no political rhetoric, but social media and contact with the world in general outside of this huge land mass was cut short, not encouraged, sometimes punished. I've disappointedly and completely lost touch now. After all of this I still have a very small stock, somewhat unique now. These I use to embellish my recording portfolio when asked for samples of my past work. Very much like an aural Curriculum Vitae, a CV-CD! I have to say it worked rather well with Amanda Lehmann. She'd left me a copy of her album 'Innocence and Illusion' on the merchandise stall at the third and last Steve Hackett gig at the Palladium in 2021. I'd been to the previous two nights. Amanda always played the first set with Steve. Have to say it was rather spooky to be receiving texts from her, from the dressing room, during Steve's second set whilst listening to 'Supper's Ready' for the third night in a row. An address was one text. I sent her a copy of 'Cherish Ever' the next day. It had much positivity in the reaction stakes. The story as to what percolated is in the next chapter about the Random Earth Project. Not wishing to blow my own trumpet, but would be absolutely useless should I have one, but playing with these musicians on this album certainly brings out the best, not only in me, but in others too. Most pleasing, and a measure of my personal standing and self-esteem. Before you ask, no . . . I'm not having any more manufactured.

I'd like to think that my ego has diminished with age. I dispute the fact that you can't not have an ego and be a musician at the same time. Both are indelibly linked, and it comes with the territory. It's just a degree thing. Big egos are bigger targets, in my view. They just have further to fall or have a good safety net. However, have to say though 'Cherish' had some great airplay, all around the world in fact. It even ended up 'mid table' for one month at number twenty in the top forty of a UK chart. One specific instance was, and hopefully is still occurring, being played on the on-boat sound systems of

Sky Trails & Pie Tales . . .

the river taxis that ply their trade up and down the Mekong River in Laos. Very much 'Apocalypse Now' inducing. The printed reviews and magazine features were kind too. Eight out of ten stars in Classic Rock Magazine put the smile back on my face, was just one of many, but this book is not a PR exercise. Mind you, BBC's Cerys Matthews received a physical copy, but it probably still remains at the bottom of a big, and growing pile on a desk somewhere in the depths of Radio Two. I never made the national blues airwaves. However, it ticked all my boxes, achieved the aim, and some more. I for one will cherish this collection, for ever.

Addendum One:

I thought I'd add this, mostly for completeness. These are the liner notes for each song and the band I played in, to which it relates, as it appears in the booklet. If you haven't a copy of one of the 100/150 physical private and personal release of 'Cherish', then as you've bought a copy of the book you are now reading, all that's missing is the audio. If you can find a copy of the audio, then together with this book you're pretty much there. Some may end up with all three; CD, A5 booklet and this book; you lucky people. These songs are not in track order, but more chronological as regards inhabitancy. The musicians listed are those that appear the recorded tracks on 'Cherish Ever'.

Love That Burns > 'Ginger/Labyrinthus' (Track 4)
(Greenbaum/Adams)

Musicians: Connor Selby, guitar/vocals. Joe Anderton, guitar. Phil Marshall, saxophone. Matt Furness, drums. Trev Turley, bass.

I've picked this song purely on the basis that the genre was a starting point for many, the blues and early Fleetwood Mac in general. The British Blues Boom was in full swing, with this tune being written in 1968, so even more apt. I heard Connor play this as a tribute to Pete Green who sadly died in 2020. His version was so synonymous and echoed the way my first two bands felt and plundered the genre, my choice to represent Ginger and Labyrinthus was easy. Recorded at Rooks Yard.

I have another, very tenuous, link with (v. early) Fleetwood Mac. This was through their original bass player, Bob Brunning. A few years before he died Bob ran a blues club in Merton, London; BB's Blues Club. We struck up a familiar friendship and he booked both 3am and BBBB into BB's. Also, sax player John Altman, with whom I have played alongside a couple of times, most notably with John Verity and in Malaya Blue's band has also played with Peter Green and Bob Brunning. So, these are more reasons why I chose 'Love That Burns'; like I say, a very easy choice.

Ginger, morphed into a three piece and became Labyrinthus, they rehearsed and practiced a lot. So much so we only did one gig. Labyrinthus did less, only half a gig. The plug was pulled. It was years before noise limiters. Small venue, stadium sized PA and back-line wasn't really appreciated in the leafy suburbs of Solihull, Birmingham. We all moved on.

House on the Hill > 'Still' (Track 2)
(Homer/Lake)

Musicians: Larry Homer, all instruments, backing vocals; except bass. Yve Mary Barwood, vocals. Trev Turley, bass.

Written back in the early 1970's this was integral to Still Mk1's material. Inspiration for the lyrics were borne from a piece of plaster cast artwork (the original lyrics follow) made in school art class during the 60's. I learnt 'Hill' for the audition after a chance introduction to Larry on one debauched night at Dudley's infamous club JB's. This song was captured on tape at one late night recording session in the Midlands. Sadly, the studio burnt down in the early hours of the morning after we'd left, but the original tape remained unscathed. From this version Larry has rearranged the song and is the version on the album, recorded and mixed in his studio in 2020 and brought back to life.

Original Still vocalist, Rob Lake, wrote the lyrics, but over time these have been lost to emotional acts and time. Rob died in 2006. The words here are close to the original and embody his muse. Both Larry and I had similar versions of lyrics, but it was Larry who cast his mind back nearly 50 years to correct mine. Larry wrote the melody plus the rest of the music and has arranged and produced this Twenty First Century version. For this I'm truly grateful as it evokes so many memories, musical & personal and this is the reason why this song is included; it means that much to me.

Still was my first 'proper' band, with, at the time, the talent and ethos to make a mark. I was 20 at the time of joining, the vision was 'Symphonic Progressive Rock', and it truly was. The band wrote some glorious material, including an epic 24-minute piece, as was expected back in the day. I still have an audio copy but transferring from reel to reel and all formats in between has lost its edge and gloss.

Sky Trails & Pie Tales . . .

Lyrics:

Looking with eyes fresh opened,
with heart, to see.
Open the gate ascend the endless stairway,
open your heart within the dream.

Just like the joy of seeing a cloud.
Its blossom's blessed with timeless beauty.
It has time to be enjoyed.

Misshapen though you may be,
oh, great beauty, it lies within.
It seems as if among the laughter, music, oh the dancing,
our game begins.

Just like the joy of seeing a low cloud.
Its blossom's blessed with timeless beauty,
It has time to be.

Cherish ever the house on the hill.
Forget never the dream on the hill.

La La La La – La La La La

Rob Lake 1953 - 2006

NO Track > 'Ferret'

I have to mention a couple of bands that are not represented in music on this collection. One is this fleeting band and very key in my musical education. A complete instrumental band, born out of a jam one night at Birmingham University. We had beginnings and ends, but the middles went where we took them, depending upon what was on offer on the night! 'Ferret' was where I learnt how to 'wing it'. There were some 'train wrecks', but equally some magical transcendent moments, the

Sky Trails & Pie Tales . . .

sort where you all play something and then look at each other with such great disbelief and joy that all the musical lay lines joined as one for a brief moment.

With sax in the line-up the music was very Avant Gard, wayward at times, atonal. A great opportunity to learn the craft whilst hiding behind the 'Jazz' genre, but we got away with murder in those days. At the time we were unaware of the bands draw; apparently it was the appeal of the dangerous musical line that we trod. Every gig was not only a journey for us but a journey for those that followed us. 'Ferret' quickly started to build a 'word of mouth' cult following, but sadly once the word got out other bands came calling. 'Ferret Poaching' are good words. Probably the most uncommercial band I have ever played in but given the youthful drive and the era (1973) we all thought it was marvellous. Did wonders to one's musical self-belief and confidence.

NO Track > 'Nick and the Dogs'

The other band that needs a mention is this six piece 'funky' line-up and exposed me to another musical facet. My tenure was brief. We played extensively in and around the Birmingham area and one momentous support slot at Essex University. Usual on the road shenanigans, sleeping in the back of the van on the PA bass bins etc, dropped off at work at 6am the following morning, slept in the toilets during the day, gig that night. Band broke up. I moved to London. It was 1979.

(John Wilson's brother Bob was in the first incarnation of the Steve Gibbons Band. Both brothers circulated and were heavily involved in the BrumBeat scene of the day.)

NO Track > 'Free Spirits'

A quick mention about this 'One Night Only' Band. It was the sixtieth birthday of an old Midlands friend, Geoff

Tristram. To celebrate he put this band together playing the music of Free and Bad Co. The five of us never rehearsed together, I drove up from London, we all assembled and played. I, and I presume all the others, familiarised themselves with the material beforehand. I had a couple of interesting phone calls with Geoff, both of us trying to explain to each other the nuances of Andy Fraser over the ether; it must have worked. It was an exceptional highlight, a momentous evening. To cap it all, apart from rekindling old friends whom I hadn't seen for years, it was the first time, since the days of 'Still', that I'd played with Larry Homer. 'Little Acre's' Johnny Bryant also got up to sing at one point. (It was Johnny who lent his initials to Dudley's infamous club, JB's, where all of this story sort of started, another full circle.)

Red Hot and Blue > '3am' (Track 9)
(Renton)

Musicians: Tim Renton, guitar. Chris Parren, keys. Helen Turner-Black, vocals. Iain Black, guitar. Andy Renton, drums. Trev Turley, bass.

This song is so indicative of the band and was recorded way back in 2008 at Bill Gautier's studio as part of a session for a new album, which never saw the light of day, until now. Tim Renton wrote this following an evening at a 'Tex-Mex' bar in Prague. The reference to the 'Paradise Bar' is a wine bar in Richmond and also muses on the gigs he went to, with his children, down Charing Cross Road, London.

'Red Hot & Blue' heavily features keyboard player Chris Parren's 'brass' work and for me is the epitome. 3am was a band of many influences, mix of genres and a unique song writing palette, this song here is atypical. The band drew upon many past dalliances, e.g.: with 'Reign', a band with Robin LeMesurier (his dad was John, of 'Dad's Army fame and his mum Hattie Jacques, of the

'Carry On' films fame); Chris's session work (George Michael's 'Careless Whisper' for one) and the Wombles; another story. (Oh OK, the brothers Renton went to school/college with Mike Batt, and it is them in the furry suits you see at the Eurovision's, the year ABBA won and many 'Top of the Pop's'.) Helen replaced Kat Pearson in the Mk2 line-up, in response to my advert for a singer. 'Red Hot & Blue' is a suitable and indicative reminder, previously unreleased.

During the five years this line-up was active we gigged a lot, most weekends, occasionally twice in a day! Recalling the previous line-up, with Kat, sadly, we never gigged and that is one regret. Kat has gone on to do some fabulous things since.

The track was lifted directly from the 'Listening Copy' CD (1-9-2008), as recorded and fully mixed by Bill Gautier at the time and imported into the album by Rooks Yard. (Thanks to Tim Renton for release and use of the copyright of the song and the recording in particular.)

Black Coffee > 'Bare Bones Boogie Band' (Track 1)
(Turner)

Musicians: Joe Anderton guitar/vocals. Connor Selby, guitar. Matt Furness, drums. Trev Turley, bass. Tim Aves, harmonica. Glen Bo, percussion.

I chose this track for two reasons. One because it's my all-time favourite song sung by Stevie Marriott, as made memorable by Humble Pie's rendition on the Old Grey Whistle Test (a BBC 70's late night music programme), and two because the BBBB used to do a version of this live, later featured on our last album 'Tattered & Torn'.

I decided to re-record this, at Rooks Yard, with a new set of musicians rather than just lift the BBBB version off the album, mainly to add a new slant and give it a youthful polish up for longevity's sake. However, 'Black Coffee' is a fine and fitting reminder of the BBBB, evoking the right memories. The Turner writer of this song is the Tina variety.

On this version it was the first take, including the vocals; all four of us in the room; complete eye contact. Prior to this, Joe disappeared, steeled himself and gave this performance. I have purposely left in all his vocal nuances, as it adds to the rawness and the genuine live feel. Pay attention.

As a postscript: After the demise of this band, I was nominated as one of six finalists in the Bass Player Category of the 2014 British Blues Awards and shortly before that 'Tattered & Torn' featured in the top 50 best album chart of 2013 in Classic Rock/Blues magazine, a culmination of five years growth.

Let's Reinvent Love > 'Malaya Blue Band' (Track 10)
(Marshall/Blue)

Musicians: Malaya Blue, vocals. Andy Walker, guitar. Andy Cooper, keys. Phil Marshall, saxophone. Simon Dring, drums. Trev Turley, bass. Graham Pettican, piano.

This song was recorded in 2015, during my nine-month tenure; at The Grange, Norfolk along with another tune, 'Hope' and both featured as a Double 'A' side single. For me, an easy choice to represent this period & line-up. Paul Long mixed and produced the track and is so indicative of the sultry, smooth, even jazzy performances of this band. During the first eight months of 2015 the band gigged heavily and gelled very quickly into something that this song is wholly representative.

'Let's Reinvent Love' was pretty much put to the band on the day of the recording. Drummer Simon Dring hadn't heard it at all! However, it didn't take long for this group of musicians to seek out and settle on the laid-back groove. From memory this was second, or maybe third, take. Saxophonist Phil Marshall breezed in mid-session and perfectly dovetailed his contribution, and yes, Phil has a rather well-known uncle. Uncle Jim's surname graces the front of many amps and cabinets around the world. I'm sure we've all had a Marshall. I certainly have in the past.

It was more about the simplicity, the notes you don't play. At the time this genre of music and style of playing was something that I really hadn't explored much, until then. Listening back during this compilation it's so apparent, I'm very proud and pleased.

This track is lifted directly from the single, as recorded, mixed and produced by Paul Long and imported into the album by Rooks Yard.
(Thanks to Malaya Blue for release and use of the copyright of this song and this recording in particular.)

Down by the River > 'Joe Anderton Band' (Track 7)
(Young)

Musicians: Joe Anderton guitar/vocals. Connor Selby, guitar/backing vocals. Andy Cooper, Hammond. Matt Furness, drums. Trev Turley, bass.

This band came about after the day long BB King event held close after his passing. I was in the house band, along with Glen Bo, playing with a whole raft of ever-changing musicians. The professional and the not so professional, but two young musicians stood out and stuck in my mind. It was also the first time that Joe Anderton and Connor Selby had ever played together. A mental note was forged. After the Malaya Blue Band, I sought out Joe and we formed the Joe Anderton Band, more lovingly known as 'The JAB', and why not?

Joe is a prolific songwriter, and a set of useable material was quickly compiled. He's a big admirer of Neil Young and 'Down by the River' was added to the set pretty much from the start. It became very much a synonymous tune for the JAB. It got longer each time we played it. The band hit its stride one evening with 'River'. It was Joe's debut at the 100 Club, London. The often jammed, two instrumental sections were a musician's delight. There always was some sort of structure, but where it ended up was no one's idea. For me, thankfully, the days of the 'Ferret Experience' came flooding back. The version, recorded at Rooks Yard, attempts to show the fluidity and calibre needed to work within a loose framework.

The Thrill is Gone > 'TT&F' (Track 6)
(Hawkins/Darnell)

Musicians: Lauren Dove, vocals. John Verity, Mark Howes & Andy Walker, guitar. Carleton Van Selman, Rhodes/keys. Phil Marshall, saxophone. Glen Bo, drums. Trev Turley, bass. Yve Mary Barwood, 'Punctuation/Introduction'.

At the same time as the Joe Anderton Band, I put together what in effect was my own band, TT&F (Trev Turley & Friends), only because the collective couldn't agree on a joint name! We were pretty much the core band that gigged in Jan - Aug 2015 as Malaya Blue's backing band, but we had an intuitive chemistry and bond, so much so that we needed the outlet to musically express ourselves and 'The Thrill is Gone' is such an obvious choice. The original live version we did was funky and spontaneous, but I wanted to get a slicker version; this being recorded at Rooks Yard with the 'kitchen sink' thrown at & applied. John Verity featured here too. I played alongside John as part of the BB King event, mentioned on the previous page, and as John was also on the same record label as BB King, another reason to include.

'The Thrill Is Gone' had also raised its head in one, or two of my past bands, jams and rehearsal throw-abouts over time, so always there to be pulled back into life. Very much like an old friend.

Also, with a slight digression, and another tenuous link to BB King, I actually played at one of his clubs, (1-9-2009), in New York one night. It all came about towards the end of a US holiday with my wife. We'd gone to BB Kings club one evening to eat and catch the ambience. During the bands break my wife struck up a conversation at the bar with an English chap who happened to notice her accent. It was the drummer in the house band. My wife mentioned I play bass etc etc. Next minute I find myself jamming blues with these guys, at BB Kings Club, NYC! Prior to this my wife had asked who the drummer plays/ed with, "Oh you might have heard of a band called Wings." I'm forever indebted to Steve Holley.

An additional bit, not in the booklet, I must be thankful to bass player Amy Madden as it was her bass I borrowed on the night. New York born and bred she was obviously concerned that some unknown bloke from over the 'Pond' would inflict untold damage on her instrument. I assured her my hands were not greasy and I'd not trash all un-sundry a la 'Who'. I don't think she got my strange sense of English humour. Bear in mind at this point I'd had a couple of beers, probably much needed 'Dutch Courage'. As for the songs I played I have no recollection given the circumstances of drummer and location. When I got back to our hotel that night, I'm on the Social exuding what I'd just done. The sad part about it is that most of the UK were asleep, how dare they. I didn't sleep much myself either that night. I do recall I was given a solo that night. All the bells in my head are going "Don't give me a solo", but appreciation was in order, so I must have passed the exam.

Can't Find my Way Home > 'TT&F' (Track 11)
(Winwood)

Musicians: Lauren Dove, vocals. Andy Walker & Mark Howes, guitar. Andy Cooper, Hammond/keys. Glen Bo, drums. Trev Turley, bass.

This is another TT&F classic and a long-time personal favourite. I just love the touch that bass player Nathan East brings to this song, plus Steve Winwood went to the school just behind the house where I lived whilst in Great Barr, Birmingham, but these are not the reasons why 'Home' was included. The real reason is due to a close friend, Mike Lightfoot.

Mike was well known throughout Essex, mostly at the New Crawdaddy Club. He died very suddenly in December 2018, only 56. The very first gig that TT&F did at the club was posthumously recorded and released as a live album. The last gig we did there was also recorded but never released. This last unedited gig contains all my introductions. Mike introduced the band on the night and the first number we did was 'Can't Find my Way Home'. As a tribute to Mike, club promoter Paul Dean and I decided to release the live version from the recording, as it was of good enough quality to do so, with all the sales going to charity. The release featured Mike's introduction and his evenings 'goodnight', probably the last known recording of him, as within a couple of weeks . . .

I'd decided to record 'Can't Find my Way Home' properly at Rooks Yard with as much of the band personnel that night and appeared on the album, more with Mike in mind, but again just a good example of the musical chemistry.

Sky Trails & Pie Tales . . .

Addendum: In addition to this charity single, now a rarity, all the money raised was sent to the British Heart Foundation and supplemented the funds that were also raised from a one day, one off, event, held locally to the New Crawdaddy Blues Club, where bands and artists that knew Mike played for free. Local Essex promoters Paul Dean and Nick Garner were generous without fault. Mike died suddenly following a heart attack, so the chosen charity was relevant and very worthy. His funeral was memorable, fitting and wholly musical too.

Bell Bottom Blues > 'TT&F' (Track 8)
(Clapton/Whitlock)

Musicians: Yve Mary Barwood, vocals. Lauren Dove, harmonies. Mark Howes, guitar. Andy Cooper, Hammond/keys. Glen Bo, drums. Trev Turley, bass.

Another example and reminder of this band. Within TT&F there was a lot of love and passion for Eric Clapton, so it wasn't surprising that we played a fair chunk of EC. We always tried to put our own spin on proceedings rather than play it straight. 'Bell Bottom Blues' is a good example. I'd actually heard Yve do this as a solo piece with just voice and guitar and it was her twist and arrangement on the original that appealed so much to me that I had to include this version, again recorded at Rooks Yard. Yve and I have also collaborated on other material outside of this track and through her, Yve has opened my eyes and ears to other musical avenues I thought I would have never visited.

Glen Bo, who appears on the TT&F recordings here, and I played a couple of times together over the years, most notably in the house band when Connor Selby and Joe Anderton played together the first time. (See 'Down By The River'.)

Change Everything > 'MoJo Preachers' (Track 3)
(Van Selman/Hammerton)

Musicians: Sophie Lindsay Hammerton, vocals. Carleton Van Selman, keys. Andy Walker, guitar. Matt Furness, drums. Trev Turley, bass.

'Change Everything' started life out as 'Cave and a King'. Cave/King was released on the Mojo Preachers 2019 album 'Man Made Monster'. In 2020 the world fell foul of a deadly virus (Covid 19) and in March the term 'Lockdown' became widely used. During the inactive months that followed, of cancelled gigs, no live music etc, the world/UK turned to other musical means and outlets. This song was just an example. The lyrics were revised by Sophie and the whole instrumentation solitarily re-recorded. This version is like an old style 'Re-Mix' but under Lockdown constraints.

There's an associated YouTube video for this track which instils the starkness of this period under viral control.

This band and the musicians therein appealed no end to my love of Progressive Rock, even to the point we thought about 'Progressive Blues' as the genre to embellish and pigeon-hole us. What appeals to me is the very broad-brush stroke of style of music that this band writes, creates and plays, not just tied to one specific genre: and why not? 'Change Everything' was just as close as it got to a MoJo-Calling-Card.

'Change Everything' was mixed and produced remotely by Andy Walker and supplied to Rooks Yard as a complete, mixed entity.

White Rabbit > 'MoJo Preachers' (Track 5)
(Slick)

Musicians: Sophie Lindsay Hammerton, vocals. Carleton Van Selman, keys. Andy Walker, guitar. Matt Furness, drums. Trev Turley, bass.

The Mojo's had talked about doing this song, ever since the day I was asked to join the band back in May 2018. The version was recorded at a full band rehearsal studio session, in one take, with no overdubs. This particular day was the first time the band had actually played this song all together. There was one unrecorded run through, an aborted first take, then the final recorded version. The Mojo's doubled up on the original song structure and introduced a Jefferson Airplane influenced guitar solo, sandwiched in between.

It could be classed as a 'Warts n' All' performance, but this captured, succinctly, the very essence of the band, the song, the day and was the sole reason for inclusion. A prime example of the 'Performance-Spark', the 'Crackle', that we all strive for each time we play. Even on the recording there's evidence of the band hunting for a new and unique groove, looking for that elusive 'let's make it different'. There was no initial intention to use the take, but overall, it turned out better than expected. Even rehearsals can yield something special, this certainly has it, and the lesson here was to keep the "Tape Rolling . . . "

As with 'Change Everything', 'White Rabbit' was remotely mixed and produced by Andy Walker and supplied to Rooks Yard as a complete, mixed track.

Sky Trails & Pie Tales . . .

Starless > 'Autumn' (Track 12)
(Bruford/Cross/Fripp/Wetton/Palmer-James)

Musicians: Larry Homer, all instruments, backing vocals; except bass. Lauren Dove, vocals. Trev Turley, bass.

For me this piece has always been the defining, classic King Crimson motif. I never tire of listening to it, so it seemed right to include here.

Back in 1977, I applied to a 'Muso Wanted Ad' in the back of the Melody Maker (one of just a handful of four weekly music papers, pre internet). I was selected to audition. I did and spent a very memorable weekend in a tiny cottage in Rowlands Castle and this is the reason for this band to be included and mentioned. The band was instrumental and very 'Prog'. I didn't join. With the event of Punk at the time, giving up my day job and moving 150 miles from the Midlands were the main (risky?) drivers. However, I have since kept in touch with Nick Magnus. Keyboard player Nick had just left The Enid at the time and has since gone on to greater notoriety with Steve Hackett (Genesis) and a burgeoning solo career. We both spoke about doing a version of 'Starless' but it never materialised. The day jobs got in the way.

This version is solely Larry, playing everything, bar bass and vocals. Over time it has matured into something exceeding my expectations. Hugely epic and grandiose. This version is the beginning section only stopping short of the 13/4 end, for those that know the original. The slightly modified end made it more of a single and complete piece with Lauren bringing a soft and delicate touch to the vocal line.

Not only with a tangible link to what might have been, but on a slightly morbid note this is what I intend to use when I do the 'Mortal Coil Shuffle', hence it was the last track.

Sky Trails & Pie Tales . . .

Preface & Postscript:
For those wishing for compete completeness, here's both.

What you now hold in your hands (the CD) took a long time to assemble, a long time to gather and a long time to gestate. Is a collection of songs that reflect the 50 years I have been playing music, always the bass the guitar, ever since 1968 when I first picked it up.

I wanted to create something a little more lasting, a little more tangible, something to pass onto my children and their children's children and would answer the question "What did your (Grand) Dad do?" This was very much a private release, call it a labour of love and very much limited to 100 copies. So, this was it, take it out, play the album, read this and you'll get a pretty good idea, especially when I'm not around anymore. Ever since the fateful day I acquired my first bass guitar I would say that there hasn't been a day since that I haven't listened to music, or at worst thought about it; still doing it.

What I've tried to create is a good broad-brush stroke of the bands and the genre of music I've played over the years. Pretty much from the off I was heavily influenced by the Progressive Rock era of which I became instantly drawn to for some strange reason and which kicked off in earnest in 1969 with the release of the first King Crimson album 'In The Court of the Crimson King'.

I haven't listed and religiously categorised each band and step along the way, there have been too many, I'd have been here a long time, therefore all the bands and artistes I've depped with and guested 'For One Night Only' I've omitted (on the CD), purely for this reason. Each song is relative to a particular band and a period. Some are just one song, there are a couple interrelated. The tracks on the CD were not chronological, they intended to run like a normal album. Due to the available digital space on the format, I mainly concentrated on those bands with whom I'd done more than a handful of gigs.

Each song featured me, on bass guitar. All the other musicians you hear I have played with at some point in time over the years. These were the only two criteria I adhered to. All the songs, bar two, have been recorded new and fresh. The two that hadn't have been re-recorded and lifted off the original studio master tapes and brought into digital clarity here. All versions are unreleased and were not available in this form anywhere else.

Ever since my days of 'Still' in the mid 70's and the journey taken I've covered many genres and styles, but my one overarching musical passion, Progressive Rock, had never deserted me. The Mojo Preachers touch(ed) on this genre a lot and is a joy for me to express fifty years of collation and collection. However, at the end of the day it comes down to the general music loving public and their support, without whom it would be a dull old world and none of this would have been possible. Applies to all of us, not just me, but also for all the bands I've inhabited, it's very much appreciated, as without you it would be a dull old world. Full circle came to mind as I initially wrote this, a fitting end came pretty close too.

I hope you enjoy delving into this as much as I've had in creating it together with the musical arrangement. Plus, I can put my hand on my heart and claim it is my unique legacy, all true and would be a bit of a shame to let it slip, wouldn't it?

Finally, there are too many to mention, but you know who you are, I always appreciate the pleasure and enjoyment of playing music over the 50 odd years and the good luck and temerity to do so. Music is a joyous participation but can be marred occasionally by 'humans' within and occasionally outside of this experience. What I'd put together is all joy and highlights in equal amounts, for many different reasons. I'm quite humbled and amazed that its lasted this long. I was never going to be well known, notoriety never came calling, but it was a whole lot of fun. We can all dream and continue to dream. This is mine, all 50 years of it.

Addendum Two:

You thought that was it? During writing this book and going through the various bands I've actually played with I thought about all the songs I've graced too. At one point I considered a small note, a commentary, on all the music I've committed to posterity in the public eye, on CD etc, but I couldn't find any decent interesting stories, or facts. There are a few, but not many, and those that did cross my mind I've already mentioned. I'm not a great lover of books that list the material of all the recorded output of an artiste, together with a concocted story behind each one. After a time, I find myself looking out of the window as each one starts to become similar. Great if you're interested, but not for me. As with my own contributions it would be boring, both to you and to me. However, I have inserted over the previous few pages the album booklet notes for each track off 'Cherish Ever' and as mentioned only for completeness. Then I had the idea that I'd use someone else's view, a third party no less. At least one 'independent' nod to some of the songs of my craft, another soupcon, and a flavour. Of all the reviews I've had written over the years I pick the one that follows. It was written as part of an on-line magazine and was for 'Cherish Ever' and is the sole reason I include here. The thoughts and musings are not mine and are much less positively tainted. In the end if you wish to investigate the actual music, to make up your own opinion, all the released music is out there, somewhere. Most could be still in my attic, or on some digital platform, who knows?

The other reason I chose this review is because the author also made his own bass guitar at home, he too in his dad's shed. I'm not the only one then and have a degree of empathy and understanding for his reasons. I also feel somewhat relived, thank you. I made two, but his solitary creation was crafted from something that did resemble a proper guitar in the first place. The story behind his 'craft' follows, and so does the review of 'Cherish Ever'.

"*Trev Turley shares those he will Cherish Ever:*"

"Are you sitting comfortably? Then let me tell you a true story about a would-be guitarist who possessed a Kay's Catalogue Telecaster copy who, at the age of fifteen, was asked to be a bass player in a local band. This youngster took up the challenge and, using a photograph of Roger Glover with his Fender Precision Bass, worked out a scale to create the neck and fret distances, yes, really. In his dad's shed he sculpted a bass neck, adjusted the bridge for four strings, sawed off two of the six machine heads, marked the inlays with pencil (renewed each night) and used it to wow the audiences at various North Eastern working men's clubs. This 'Frankenbass' used to scare, horrify and shock the pre-bingo, blue rinse audiences but also used to entertain the younger, more music minded imbibers of cheap beer.

That completely true story shows my credentials: I understand the intricacies of the instrument and the importance of the bass (and drums) to the sound and 'completeness' of a band, despite (usually) being out of the spotlight in every sense. So, as I listen and write about a fellow bass player who has entertained far more, far bigger audiences and done it with far more skill and ability than I ever have, I can appreciate the complexities and, perhaps, why he chose these songs.

Sky Trails & Pie Tales . . .

My encounters with Trev's playing are from the rather lovely Mojo Preachers ('Man Made Monster' is reviewed on the Bluesdoodles site) and I said then that "The bass, the drums, the guitar, and the keys need to be isolated and listened to, then you will truly appreciate what a sonic landscape awaits the listener." Also in my collection is his work with Malaya Blue where he once again underpinned her sound with rock steady but imaginative bass playing.

Now the bad news: this release, called 'Cherish Ever', is limited to 100 numbered physical copies, and a few additional un-numbered ones. Some of his previous recordings with the various bands named will provide the originals.

To the music, and Trev has essentially written his autobiography with tracks from his fifty years treading the musical boards. Track one, 'Black Coffee' is from Trev's Bare Bones Boogie Band days, albeit freshly recorded, and it is their take on the Ike and Tina Turner composition but inspired by the brilliant Humble Pie version. I have to say that this is the next best thing to Steve Marriott's version. Joe Anderton does a great job on the vocals and the band are sparse, yet weighty, giving a rock-solid base for the song to develop. The next track, 'House on the Hill' was one of Trev's earlier bands known as 'Still'. With the original member, Larry Homer and the delightful vocals of Yve Mary Barwood we get an acoustic ballad structure, a lovely electric guitar and a piano solo to make this a laid back, yet powerful song of beauty. Trev's bass, by the way, is so wide ranging, skilful and suitable I am full of envy. (My Frankenbass never sounded like that!) Next up is a Mojo Preachers song, 'Change Everything (Cave and a King)' but with revised lyrics from Sophie (hence the title) to reflect what the world is going through with the damnable pandemic. The blues/prog mix is still there and retains the essence of the original with Sophie sounding as if she is talking only to you, there's a bit more weight to the chord work but preserving the original song. 'Love That Burns' is a Peter Green composition and is a song that Trev played with his first bands, Ginger and Labyrinthus (it was the early 70s!) A neat reading of the master on a song from 1968 on Mac's 'Mr Wonderful' album; the sax is a little higher and Connor Selby does an amazing and empathetic solo that is fitting and wonderful in equal measure. 'White Rabbit (Rehearsal Take)' is my favourite. The Grace Slick composition is from a Mojo Preachers rehearsal and is the second, warts and all take, from the band just being natural, feeding off each other in the studio. It has the same atmosphere from bass, then guitar, then snare and keys. The vocals are all Sophie but with such an awareness and composure. 'The Thrill Is Gone' is so well-known and Trev's collective (Trev Turley & Friends or TT&F) who took the funk they put into their live version, polished it in the studio (with none other than John Verity as guest) and with professional singing tutor Lauren Dove showing why, the whole band put in a stellar performance and, if you only know BB King's, or Gary Moore's version, then listen to Roy Hawkins' 1951 recording, then this one, and be in awe, it is that good. We've heard the 'chops', as they say, of guitar/vocalist Joe Anderton, now from his own band is a Neil Young song, 'Down by the River'. Young is a gifted composer, but one I find impossible to listen to and yet love his songs covered by people with tone in their voice and guitar (ooh! controversial). Well, here is another one that proves, to my mind, that very point throughout the entire eleven minutes, enough said. (Nice nearly bass solo from Trev too.) Clapton is the source of the next song, 'Bell Bottom Blues', in the hands of TT&F again. Yve is back on vocals and Lauren on harmonies, and they bring a whole new dimension to a classic. It's lovely the way Yve has developed the melodies into a countrified blues feel and the band do a cracking job too. Any perceived difficulty in 'doing an EC' on the solo is quickly dispelled. It does nod to 'Slowhand' but is original (and too short by the way Mark.) Another of Trev's bands is responsible for 'Red Hot and Blue'. 3am was the band and guitar man Tim Renton penned this smoky jazz/blues/rock hybrid that has never been released until now and sung with feeling by Helen Turner, it has all keys brass but a feel of blues as it used to be. 'Let's Reinvent Love' is from the Malaya Blue Band and the 2015 single. It is one of those slow, soulful blues songs that shows how every instrument can benefit from 'just the right number of notes in the right place' (I do not address that to Andrew Preview!) Add into this the sensitivity of Malaya's superb vocal, and it is the epitome of soulful blues. Back to TT&F and a Steve Winwood cover. 'Can't Find My Way Home' first appeared on the Blind Faith album in 1969 and with Winwood and Clapton's unique guitar work and Ginger Baker's even more unique percussion, this is one hard act to follow. Having Lauren on vocals means it starts very strong and, instrumentally, the band interprets sensitively but with their own characters showing through. In other words, they took a classic, made it their own and essential listening. Now, to wrap it up, how about some proper prog? Well, a long-time favourite of Trev's has always been King Crimson's 'Starless', having been required listening for many, many years. This new version may be half the running time of the original, but Larry does such a fine job, and the concatenation actually makes it more immediate and accessible. Lauren does a fabulous job again. This may sound strange but, while listening to her on this track for the umpteenth time, it occurred to me that she has the nous, the drama and the range that reminds me so much of Ronnie James Dio in his Sabbath days. Different tonally (and in most ways) but she has a presence that enthrals.

As this is a Trev Turley album, I could have gone in to great detail about the tone, the skin and the inherent feel he injects into every bass performance, but just take it read as that does indeed apply across every track. This is a rewarding album on every level. Variation in styles and genres but always with skill and deftness of touch. If you can find it, buy it!"

"A wonderful album that crosses styles and genres but always delivers quality."

© Tom Dixon (Reprinted with permission and first published by Liz Aiken in Bluesdoodles online magazine.)

17   Random Earth Project

As the MoJo Preachers died a passively related Covid death, petering out as explained, the Random Earth Project flickered into life before the embers had died. It was only the last week in December 2021 that both keyboard player Carleton Van Selman and I talked about this venture, so not really a covert operation behind the backs of the MoJo's. In all honesty, the REP (it shall be known as this from now on as I can't keep writing Random Earth Project all the time) punch and die were cast very specifically, from 1PM on Friday 7th January 2022, when Carleton and I cut the last MoJo Gossamer thread. Prior to this the other two core members, singer Kym Blackman and guitarist Larry Homer, had an inkling but no commitment, nothing tangible. Once the clock ticked past 1:01PM it was, let's get the binoculars out and look forwards. In the first few weeks. I did get the pangs of 'have I done the right thing' as regards the others in the MoJo's, but as the music of the REP progressed, I felt easier. Kym had been working with Carleton for some time now, writing and creating the pieces that were to become more familiar. One or two had been submitted to the MoJo's but never seemed to fit or create the spark needed to progress, so Carleton brought them back into what was to become the REP folder. With Kym and Larry now fully committed it was very much let's see what can be achieved. Carleton and I had been dabbling, mostly during Lockdown and Covid days, with some of this returned, un-MoJo-like material. Both he and I have a love, an appreciation no less, of the Prog Rock genre. Mine came from the days of the actual birth back in 1967-1968. Kym sang in his own interpretational (OK Prog Covers Band) for twelve years, 2000-2012, 'Hollow Earth'. You can see where the title of the REP has been living over the years, more to come. Initial contact between Kym and Carleton was in 2010, via another mutual musician and Carleton joined Kym's band for a while. They did a handful of gigs as a band called 'Random', then it fizzled out. The old Random name and the Earth of Hollow Earth seemed to be synonymous and right to call this project the Random Earth Project. The past felt right and real enough to use in the present, so we did. After the end of Random and over the following years they both kept in touch, on and off, each stuttering along to record Carleton's songs. Some worked, some didn't. Other commitments and musical tampering with the material often dictated that these forays resulted into stalling and shelving, until good old Covid came along. The virus and the time on our hands focused both mind and music. Larry and I had played in the symphonic prog band 'Still', as regurgitated in an earlier chapter, but both very much influenced by the genre from its beginning to current perception and all stops along the way. Despite the bands I've played in over the years Prog Rock has always been a close companion, something to return to, to re-listen, to re-percept. Larry and I jumped into the REP pool, with both feet.

The initial remit for the REP was for this to be very much a recording, 'lets make an album' band. At the time of writing the likelihood of it becoming a 'live venture' is remote, but you never know what's around the corner. The four of us agreed to make an albums worth of quality Progressive music, release it and go from there. Carleton had amassed a huge pot of suitable material, some of it with Kym's contribution and joint writing. Each of us have the ability to record from home, some of us have better studios than the other, but the output is the same. Larry has the better facility of us all and it became obvious that he would stitch all the stems (read tracks here, for the un-initiated) together, mix and take the production lead. The first track we tackled was something I'd lovingly known as 'Thing'. A couple of minutes of keyboard passage with theremin. Back in the dark days of Covid I'd added a brooding 'spooky' bass line, created a short video to accompany and we let it loose on social media. Both Carleton and I were, at this time, unaware that this was probably the point of germination of the REP. All very subliminal and in the subconscious. As an aside, during this time, we hadn't forgotten MoJo completely but both Carleton, MoJo Sophie and myself remotely recorded our version of Paul Weller's 'You Do Something To Me'. This followed the same process as 'Thing'. It's out there somewhere, with a video by Sophie, but I digress. With the formation of the REP we chose 'Thing', with another similar Carleton piece, as the first foray into creation. Over time these two parts were grafted together and became the track now known as 'Airwaves'. Without going into detail, this has set the standard, a benchmark. Each piece of 'Airwaves' was in a different key. No problem to the REP! In days of old this may not have even been considered. Whilst the collective were assembling the sections, the parts, all their own tracks etc for all the other material, 'Airwaves' went public, complete with a seven-minute film, commissioned by the REP, made by Director and Producer Ross Eaglesham. I'd come across his work via his father Martin Haggarty (Long Earth vocalist); still all very incestuous. Apart from Ross's solo work, he also has had other TV & film contributions. One of which was nominated for a 2021 BAFTA in conjunction with BBC Scotland with the company he's affiliated. They didn't win. The programme was 'The Dark Shadow of Murder'. Ross was an obvious choice to make something visual to accompany 'Airwaves'. He didn't disappoint. A very simple yet thoughtful film, with a moving and could be construed as a disturbing end. It fitted the music perfectly. The REP had entered the public eye and ear. Some have said that this music, coupled with the visual has "conjured up an immediate unique identity". Nice to hear at the time. 'Airwaves' accrued many thousands of views on social media and set a high benchmark for future material from the REP.

Sky Trails & Pie Tales . . .

In March 2021 I had plucked up the courage to buy a fretless bass. This has since proved fortuitous. I've not really played much fretted bass since. I've always shied away from fretless, a 'black art', well, to me. Many years ago, I'd tried a fretless in Manny's in New York, yes, the USA version. Manny's has since long gone so you can see how long ago it was. The shop was littered with memorabilia and evidence of the much richer and more famous than me trying out stuff in Manny's. I'm glad I went in to breath the influential air. I bought the tee shirt and touched a few basses in the department up the stairs. I took this Fender fretless down, caressed it for a short while expecting something magical to happen, it didn't so returnedMa to its showroom hanger. Roll on many years and this very well packaged box was delivered. Big investment for a trial! What if I still don't like it? What if I can't play it? I sat down and caressed it. I sat down and played it, on familiar songs. The logic was if I can play these known songs, with my known notes, then progress. It took about a week, with daily sessions and suddenly it kind of clicked. I felt that there's a certain manner, a certain way, a definitive approach. No plonking the fingers down at each fret, more like a laying on of the fingers, that vibrato you can get, even more so with a slight excess finger movement. It's like treating something with care, with love, a gentleness that the strings can almost talk, inviting to play another note. It has improved the technique no end and the need to be more precise, almost choosy, a 'what note deserves to be played next' scenario. The other thing I've found is that my playing has become more melodic, intertwining, and yes, there's notes I can play between the frets. All this time they've been hiding there! On the odd time I've picked up a fretted bass since it feels odd. Definitely different approaches to playing between the two. I'll persist. I've used fretless on pretty much of all of the REP material, brings its own identity, especially with my fingers on it. If you ask a Prog Rock devotee as to which bass is synonymous with

Sky Trails & Pie Tales . . .

the genre most will say 'Ricky', Rickenbacker to the uninitiated. This is the mostly, go-to instrument made more well-known by Chris Squire of Yes. I have a couple of Ricky's, with one REP track featuring said guitar. Had to, didn't I.

This chapter is likely to be open ended as I'm hoping this collaboration, the REP, will outlive the publication of 'Sky Trails & Pie Tales'. The intention of the Project is to utilise, invite, the additional musician as the recording process and the material develops. Even in its infancy the REP invited, and she accepted, Amanda Lehmann to contribute to a couple of pieces. She came on board after my attendances of all of the recent Steve Hackett gigs at the London Palladium and listening to my legacy album Cherish Ever. Two invites crossed over: I of her and she of me. "Be an honour and a joy for you to contribute to my new album." I accepted her request to me and visa versa. She sings and plays guitar on two pieces of the REP debut album, and her invite of me, on her follow up to her debut 'Innocence and Illusion' remains open as I write, waiting to be honoured. Amanda has that unenviable task of being a sister-in-law of the ex-Genesis guitarist Steve Hackett and occasionally has the opportunity to appear and work with him. Keeps it in the family. Amanda also works very closely with another long-time old friend of mine Nick Magnus. Nick and I were introduced via the 'Wanted's' from the Melody Maker back in 1977. The chapter headed Autumn reveals all. Nick produced Amanda's debut album, even appearing on there too. The incestuous-ness goes on and on. To have Amanda on board with the REP feels right and is just a treat all round. Maybe Nick will one day? Who knows? Two great keyboard players on one album, Carleton and Nick? Over the first three months of well-being within the REP, Larry has revisited his material from the days of 'Still'. One song 'Fame & Miss Fortune' from the old portfolio and very badly captured on cassette, by me, at an old 'Still'

Sky Trails & Pie Tales . . .

rehearsal has been given a refresh in the arrangement and technology stakes and brought to the project. For me, and probably for Larry, this is not only a nod to the past, but a full circle regeneration of how timeless music can be. Some forty odd years have past whilst this song has slumbered and now the legacy continues. Emotional. It just goes to show how tangible and fleeting things can be yet brought back to life in the wave of a hand. Plus, the REP is not just a vehicle for mostly one person's writing. Very much a collaboration, a continuum, a respectful amalgamation. In recent years Larry said he'd never join another band as long as he lived, but I'm glad he accepted my suggestion at the end of 2021. It's given him, and the rest of us, as part of the REP, a sense of purpose, a creative outlet, that might have otherwise been lost. I'm very much a believer of fate, things happen for a reason etc. You are unaware at the time but can be the key to future opportunities. This time if it wasn't for a worldwide virus then where would we be, no REP for starters.

As I write, the high pile of material is being religiously whittled down, one at a time, arranged, recorded, tampered, re-arranged, re-recorded, approved and completed. Next! Hopefully, when this book is published, we'll have had all the pieces mastered and released on both physical and digital formats. As for the working title, no idea, yet to be decided. I told you it was open ended.

Sky Trails & Pie Tales . . .

18   Epilogue: What's Left/Next?

This could be the shortest chapter in the book.

I'm not really sure to be honest of what is left and what is next. The previous chapter pretty much outlines, drives and generates the creative process for the short term, and hopefully if well received, the long term.

As an aside in 2022, I updated my home studio with the latest software, and hardware in order to be able to produce quality professional studio recordings. I also took the tentative step to offering my services to the wider world. The remit is supply me a 'bass-less' track and I'll supply you with the missing part, or parts, depending on what's needed. Armed with a new business card and postcard PR, these have been either posted, or thrust into other musician's hands at every available opportunity. One of the commissions was for multi musician Jon Farley for his Volume Two of 'Checking for Echo' project. A wholly charitable release, as was Volume One, for 'Support Angel Lynn's Recovery'. I never appeared on Volume One. Volume Two has been released with my contribution to one track. I'd done four other tracks but over time these have been embellished and taken on yet another different 'bass life', by Jon. Then there's Amanda Lehmann's follow up release. Amongst all of this there's a growing, yet manageable, portfolio and bunch of requests of contrlbution of which to add some bass. Saxophonist Phil Marshall can also be relied upon now and again, especially at seasonal junctures in the year.

All of the above is really dependent upon my hearing and how long it will last. It's been a bit of a double-edged sword, as it's probably the same for many musicians in this world. The music, or more than likely the volume of the music, has rendered the tools we use, our ears, and very much needed to ply our trade has been Catch Twenty Two'd rather neatly by the music itself. I've worn hearing aids since 2016. My grandfather went deaf over a period of years and at the end was profoundly deaf. Maybe it's skipped a generation? Mind you, I haven't helped myself over the years. For over ten years, 2003 – 2013, once a week, I rehearsed in a tiny rehearsal room with up to six musicians in there, for three hours each week. Some of these musicians thought it was great to play at gig volume. We never used ear protection. One guitarist claimed he turned up because I turned up as I couldn't hear myself. The reason I turned up was because of their volume. It went on like this for years, like a game of sonic tennis until the volume knob could turn no more. The result has dulled my higher frequencies. Thanks. Good job I play bass. Since realising the issues and owning up to the fact that I was dulling my sense of hearing, or as my audiologist said; you're not going deaf, just missing a few frequencies, these top end of the range digital hearing aids will replace them. Please make the four-figure cheque out to . . . They sure have made a difference. Just before I got them, I was starting to miss the odd cue, well, I never heard that frequency, so that was my excuse. The spoken word in a room with other voices, other sounds, music especially, was becoming hard to understand. I could hear the voice, but not a great idea of what was being talked about. With the aids this has improved no end. Of late, as, I presume, the age deterioration is kicking in, I have had to learn to lip read, as it helps to discern between similar sounding words. Strangely enough music has remained pretty much untouched, overall. With the missing frequencies replaced the aids have let me hear familiar and new music with a fresh insight. Yes, the term 'Listening with Fresh Ears' is very relevant. Tambourines in recorded music had been hidden from me for many years until advent of the hearing aids. I did have a shock though, a big one, and very recently too, in July 2022. For forty-eight hours I completely lost all my hearing, I've never been so shocked and distraught for these two days. I'd convinced myself that this was what it was going to be like for the rest of my life. Call it an epiphany, call it an aural epiphany. Luckily, I had an appointment booked with, at the suggestion of my audiologist, a specialist who deals with such issues caused by hardening of the natural ear lubrication, i.e., wax. I'll spare you the details but the better ear, had, over time, become completely blocked, with the not so good ear (the deaf one) heading the same way. The fully blocked one was solid, even Pink Floyd couldn't knock down this wall. So, one sunny Saturday afternoon, in a split second, I had looked over the edge of complete and utter profound deafness to being dragged back to a bright and shiny noisier world. Call it what you like but the words 'experiencing a religious aberration' is close. I've seen and had a small taste of what the world would be like and now hold the deaf in even higher esteem. No more 'pardon', or 'half past two' jokes. The symptoms I'd experienced were exacerbated by a lasting bout of Covid a week or so before, so not personally and completely to blame. Hearing is the only essential tool in a musician's kit bag. Same applies to those that only listen, but to one that makes music, in any shape or form, hearing is the one tool that is imperative. With a growing awareness, over the past decade or so, of those who have had their hearing restricted, it's even more important for the musician today to care for their hearing. Noise limiters, noise filters are in use more and more, as there's no further taboo. The cost, and technology, of In-Ear monitoring is also reducing, becoming more affordable to the masses. In the age that I grew up, late sixties and especially throughout the seventies, it was almost a badge of honour if you didn't come out of certain rock gigs without a ringing in your ears, even better if you woke up the following morning with the same, or similar symptoms. This would now be frowned upon. There's a whole generation of musicians from this era (anagram of the word 'ear' not intended) who's hearing has become blighted with hearing issues, full scale deafness, some with the odd application of tinnitus.

Whilst on this topic, back in 1996, it was 8th May, I went to see Scottish percussionist Evelyn Glennie (now Dame) at the Queen Elizabeth Hall, London as part of her then solo tour. From the age of eight she had started to lose her hearing, becoming profoundly deaf by twelve. It has always fascinated me in how she 'hears' music. She often plays barefoot, feeling the sounds, the rhythm, through her body. Whilst at the time of writing my hearing hasn't reached the level of hers (yet) despite the 48-hour period of shock I experienced when my hearing became distant and totally void, I still find her an inspiration, not only to all of those around her, but on a personal level. I draw on the fact that music can still be enjoyed regardless. I saw her again the following year (9th December 1997), this time at The Barbican Centre, London. That evening I went prepared, secretly hiding a copy of her paperback autobiography 'Good Vibrations' in my jacket pocket. I don't know who was more surprised Evelyn, or my wife, when I presented the autobiography to Evelyn at the 'meet & greet' after-show. On all occasions she has graciously signed my programmes and the book with a smile and a few chosen words. The first time I met her I made the mistake of talking to her loudly and slowly. I felt such a fool when she stopped me and said "I'm quite good at lip reading, you know. Plenty of practice." She smiled; I just wanted the earth to open! As I teeter on the edge of her audible world, I hold her in even more high esteem. Back then I had no idea as to my own impending issues.

Apart from Evelyn, over the years there have been many other memorable and (my) personal instances of close, or not so close encounters, with the more well-known of this world. Kathy Etchingham was another, an encounter

Sky Trails & Pie Tales . . .

with a distance of 10,500 miles between us. Always one to make things difficult, that's me. Kathy was Jimi Hendrix's UK girlfriend. They met on the day he first arrived in the UK, and she was to remain close for the next three years. They both shared the London Mayfair flat, number twenty-three Brook Street to be exact, to which both my wife and I went to visit shortly after it opened its doors to the public in February 2016. It was very much a fledging exhibition, minimal, but enough to catch the spark of the time and the muse of when they both lived there. The museum shop was pretty much sparse of purchasable and relatable items. However, they'd just taken a limited stock of the paperback version of Kathy's book 'Through Gypsy Eyes'. That day I was told it was selling at a great rate of knots, good sales pitch. I was also told that she was there close to the day Brook Street opened to the public, "so, only a few weeks, or so ago then" was my response. I bought a copy of the paperback, had to, before it was gone. I read it. I contacted Kathy. It wasn't too hard to find her on the Social and said what an enjoyable read it was. I never expected a response and to be honest I wasn't looking for one, just passing on my thoughts of her book and to stand in the same room as Jimi was good enough. "Hello Trev, you must be one of the first to buy the new book. They only put it on sale that day. Hope you enjoy it." were the words in my In-Box the following day. I thought what a shame I couldn't have had the opportunity to put this book, Kathy and my purchase all in the same spot at the same time. Then a few weeks later, at her cost, I received a little note, and a signed postcard of the book's cover in the post from Kathy, all the way from Moorabbin, near Melbourne, Australia. Bowled over was I, to say the least. I never saw Jimi Hendrix in the actual flesh, but this little memento from Kathy will do and be the closest I get. Generosity knows no bounds.

Sky Trails & Pie Tales . . .

Returning to future predications, and mine in particular, I have no insight and great knowledge. My version of George Orwell's vision of 1984, now probably 2084, is far beyond the mist in my personal crystal ball. However, since Lockdown in 2020/21 I do feel that live music is changing, as is the 'UK Blues' fraternity in which I mostly circulated during 2010 – 2020. Faces have disappeared, mostly retired and replaced with one's unfamiliar. The close-knit UK wide community seems to have fractured into many smaller, even closer knit, factions, cliques, families, call them what you like. For any new musician trying to impress, make a mark etc, it must be difficult as to educate oneself and decide on which 'family' to join. Each seem to have different values and areas they cover. The Venn Diagram of UK Blues seems to be shifting and receding. Some of these factions are very protective of their own patch and the personal roster they have forged. Gone has the day when the record company was king. I've felt that ever since day-one the artist, the musician, has never been dominant, only but a few have been successful after much soul bearing and probable investment. There always appears to be someone, some enterprise, leeching off the talented, whether it's for financial gain, or for a lack in their own self esteem. Today is no different, but it's fractured into a myriad of pieces. In this century I feel the venue owner; the promoter, is king. I've seen some make an artiste, as well as destroy an artiste, with a few chosen words, an e-mail or two, circulated within their faction. I grew up in what I would call the 'Golden Years' of music making. It will never return. When you have one or two so called amateurs, with a wide remit, with a tepid musical background, it concerns me as to what the future will bring. One cannot attend a two-day course in Music Management and be the next Don Arden, the next Harvey Goldsmith, the following day. During my few years as part of the Music Managers Forum I merely skimmed the surface of knowledge and experience, nothing to warrant becoming a manager, or a promoter. I didn't want too either. With all of this, as I entered 2022, and also with the formation of the Random Earth Project, I made the decision to withdraw, put some distance in, from this so-called UK Blues Fraternity. I'd been a full member of the UK Blues Federation for many years, paying my financial dues each year and having a very small amount of influence on the sterling work they do. I decided the time was right to jump ship and take my support elsewhere. So, I did. If you're looking for one single reason, there was a board change in late 2021 which drove this decision. This decision was more for my piece of mind and disassociation of what I perceived was coming, together with some real foresight from some previous correspondence of individual views and attitudes to back it up which made this decision easy. When my presence within the UK Blues Federation had been removed overnight, whilst I was still a member, without a word said, it rang a bell. It's been ringing ever since. I'm sure all will be well, but my gossamer link was tested, and the market has changed drastically. The same applies to the UK Blues Press, new faces and new policies. For my own sanity and musical stability, it was the right thing to do. I've not been proven wrong so far. I will watch with great interest in how UK Blues will progress over the coming years; good luck. However, the Blues, in general, has been good to me, but now there must be a time of change and a new voice, a young voice, to take this forward, otherwise the genre will die along with all the aging musicians and aging audience and listeners, who champion the cause. Maybe UK Blues needs to have an injection of youth, from the top down? Us old ones cannot, and should not, carry the flame any longer. My wife and I went to the 2022 Chicago Blues festival, the world's biggest free blues festival. This year was peppered with old established names, some on their last legs, literally, with the blues being kept alive from the oxygen cylinder discretely placed behind their chair. Sure, they're some fine blues players making progress up the ranks, but there's a distinct concern as to the outcome once these and this aging generation of players and audience dwindle over the next couple of decades. Maybe the draw, the legacy, will remain but be on a smaller scale. Sadly, I won't, and many others won't be around to see the future. Over the last five years, prior to 2022, time and the Lockdown has eroded the stage count and size at Chicago. The main pavilion stage and the side tented stage remained, but the other two, or three, so called alternative stages have disappeared. The blues is willing, is strong and is as bright as ever, but I feel there's a seismic shift coming. Let's think this is for the good of the lauded and the gentry.

As for live music itself this will continue. I can already see the seeds of those up-and-coming acts and artistes that will rise above the general homegrown cottage industry and hopefully forge some degree of sustainable career. For most, in the music business, the day job is a necessary evil to life sustainability. The world has changed and the value and the earning factor of music in general has become very much transient, sometimes a throw away commodity. The digital world we all now live in has pretty much destroyed the physical. With the event of on-line digital platforms and how we digest our music is only going to expand and become even more dominant. As the generation of album (proper vinyl) collectors and the like disappear then I'm sure we'll enter yet another phase of (alternative?) music digestion. I'm still of the mindset to covet the physical. This was the reason why I only made 'Cherish Ever' available on CD. Once a copy enters the digital world then I might as well have given free copies out to everyone. It doesn't stop someone from doing this, but my conscience is clean. The days of the twelve-inch album cover, and its content are themselves cherishable. For some, the artwork is more memorable than the music. I still like CD's, yet I sense their life and position in the music business of the future are likely to be

Sky Trails & Pie Tales . . .

limited, or short lived. My record collection is a physical thing, albeit mostly CD's and vinyl. The box set is currently king. Flaunting your digital 'ethernet' collection, in my view, is not to be encouraged. Plus, even with a CD, there's still a chance to read the liner notes, the who's who. Part of the vinyl experience was, and still is, taking out the vulnerable plastic disc, placing the needle down carefully, then reverently listening, whilst reading the cover and taking in the artwork and anything else that came with your purchase. Can't do that with a digital file. The listening bit you can, but then the age of the short attention span beckons, the 'skip' button is engaged. Next! With so much new music being generated and uploaded on a daily basis it's impossible to keep up, yet alone listen to the old music and the new music on repetition. I'm just one of many millions of musicians who now have their own, affordable, home studio too. I can sit here in my own studio and craft something of similar quality that the big studios of old used to do. With the event of technology, the quality is probably better, quicker and is often easier to craft something perfect. Good old digital editing. Record one verse, one chorus and a middle eight, if needed, then cut/copy and paste and the job's done, all before tea break. It's already started happening around the world. The old recording studios are closing down, selling up, pocketing any profit and going home to their own abodes and studios. Digital music file sharing around the world is rife. As for the live arena, I have no inkling here. I must admit it worries me that the seeds of the holographic live music show may become more dominant. For me this detracts from playing live in the first place. Each show, each night, is the same. The notes, the timing, the visuals. It's not for me, I might as well stay at home and watch it on the screen. Same applies to 'Tribute Bands' and artistes. Sure, there's a market, but if I'm going to watch and listen to a perfect rendition of what's on my CD/Vinyl, then again, not for me. Like my playing, I like my live music to be in the moment, a special unique event. Yes, do play the material within the boundary of the structure, but it's those moments of straying, of improvisation, verging off the beaten track that delight and make each gig unique. King Crimson has often quoted in its PR that their recorded material is a 'Calling Card', something to pick up time and time again, but the live gig is a 'Hot Date', a unique one off one-night stand to embrace, to bathe in and cement in the memory for ever. Is this how, and why, when we all hear a certain piece of music it can transport the listener back instantaneously to the exact time they first heard it? Sometimes combined with a heightened sense of smell, colour, and visual recollection. Live music will continue long after I've gone from this earth, but sometimes it just would be nice to pop back once in a while to see how things are. I can only dream. I just hope after the Lockdown and Covid constraints the public and their confidence will return to pre-Viral gig going commitments. It's taken a knock and ticket pre-sales need to rise rather than rely on 'on the night door' entry availability. In the past I too have booked rooms and promoted the event so know what's involved and what the risks are. As with all these things there's a certain amount of up-front investment required and presales of tickets help lesson the blow and give an indication of event success. All too often I'm now seeing gigs being cancelled due to poor ticket sales. What's the solution? Down to all of us to support each other. Make it a 'Hot Date'.

As I've said my future has been musically fuelled by a re-embracing of a return to the genre that started it all in the first place for me, Prog Rock. Apart from the music and its virtuosity, there's a general feeling of camaraderie and mutual respect; something I've not felt for many years. There also seems to be a general lack of competitiveness, we all work within the genre, the music is king, not the person, not the player. Music is not really a competition. Getting the most gold stars, the best reviews, the most awards has become, for me, tedious and overshadows what every musician strives to achieve in the first place. In order to progress musically, to be 'different', one has to take risks, exceed the boundaries, the line-in-the-sand. Taking risks is hard to categorise. With this in mind, trying to gauge, to compare, to judge and to rate who's 'best' is difficult if the musical boundaries are blurred, or at worse not encouraged to be different, to forge ahead. With Prog Rock I'm having a bit of a musical epiphany and loving every minute. That's where my future lies, and the Random Earth Project is perfect.

At this point I hope I've covered everything I wanted and needed to say; put pen to paper so to speak. Looking back, from when I first picked up the bass, it's been memorable, mostly for all the right reasons. Sure, there have been times when I've got close to giving it all up, but there's something inside all of us that decide to walk this path that says, "You can't give up, you have to keep on keeping on." It's ingrained. Applies to us all, no matter how well known, or insignificant. No matter how rich, or poor. No matter of what level of talent. Music makes the world go round. I for one wouldn't change a thing of what's happened, even at my lowly level. I've more than achieved the aim I set out at the very beginning and created some wonderful music over the years. It's still happening. Some of it has been cast to the wind, some of it is very much more permanent. At the end of the day we all strive for a bit more respect, more money, more fame, but then that's human nature, isn't it? As for the sex, drugs and rock n' roll stories, I'll take them to the grave with me, only because my wife and kids will be reading this book, and I need them to look after me when I can't do that myself. Fifty odd 'musical' years. It's been memorable. I've left some music behind. Imbibe. I've also left my so-called legacy; you've just read it.

Sky Trails & Pie Tales . . .

Just one more thing, please ensure that my bass guitars are not sold for what I eluded as to their cost, or are not planted in the garden, or made into a nice bonfire on a fifthly night (musical joke). As for guitar planting, this is a true story. One particular company I worked at we employed a cleaner, a rather confident woman, very much a musician's wife/partner/girlfriend, and she was. One day, she regaled this story. Many years ago, they had a rather large row, a bust up no less. When he came home at night he asked where all his guitars were? She gesticulated in the direction of the garden. "Oh right" was the nonchalant reply. He thought nothing of it, it was dark, he went to bed. The following morning, he went downstairs and opened the living room curtains, as they'd been forgotten the night before. In the bright morning sunshine, the sun glinted off six sets of machine heads and necks as they grew, proud and vertical, next to the tulips and general flora & fauna! Musicians, beware, it does happen and can happen.

It's been a blast, I can't say here's to the next fifty, so I won't. Thanks, and goodnight.

Don't forget to put the cat out . . .

Acknowledgements

Most books have a section like this at the end, here's mine.

The easiest entry would be to say thanks to all the folks that put up with me over the years. Job done.

As with most, I start with those that are nearest and dearest, so thanks and big love to Jill, my wife; for everything really. Keeping me sane and making sure I don't turn into my mother, it's been hard at times, I know, I don't think I've achieved it. Thanks for putting up with and coming along and listening to the same music gig after gig. You never did like that Enid gig! Thanks for all the evenings you sat and watched television whilst I wrote this book, my love knows no bounds. Thanks for all the proofreading too. Love and cherish-ness to my kids, James and Victoria. James can play McCartney's 'Blackbird' and I shall forever hate him for that, I can't. He has a good ear for music. I'm often seeking his wise words on new material and his view for most things crafted. He's been invaluable in the gestation of my demos for the Random Earth Project, thanks. Vicki has given me some invaluable 'Life-Tips', guidance and advice along the way, especially as regards Event Management, as it's her real job and bringing me back to earth when needed. I can't go through the rest of my family as most have either passed or are unaware. This is not meant to be sour grapes but thanks to my parents for no encouragement whatsoever as regards anything musical I've done, or got involved in, or even listened to. Thanks for even going out of your way to make it even more difficult at the odd time. Ever since the day I can cast my mind back far enough I've used this lack of encouragement in a positive light. In fact, it's possibly been the driving force behind it all, as I had a point to make, to prove, so thanks, appreciated. Over the years I have also wondered how this story would have turned out if I'd have garnered your support, your love, your encouragement. Might not have been half as interesting, I'll never know. I have no desire to find out, not now. I'm proud and pleased in the way it's turned out. However, for those that have come to see me play and bought the music, or even this book you know who you are, and I thank you. Same applies to my friends as well. The real friends are those that have just read the previous sentence, thanks. Indebted.

As for all the musicians, including the non-musicians, I've played with and had the temerity to work with and alongside of you, ever since from that very first day, I thank you with all my heart, as I couldn't have done any of this without you. I'd be here all day trying to name each and every one of you, then I'd get into trouble by missing someone out. Bit of a get out clause I know, but, like the friends one, the real important ones are those that have just read this paragraph and know who you are. Some I've mentioned along the way in the chapters that precede.

I do have to mention one, one musician, one good friend, and that is Larry Homer. Larry was there at the serious beginning of my so-called musical trek. We lost touch, then over the years reclaimed the link, only to end up working again with each other in the Random Earth Project. Both of us are still creating some wonderful music that spans the fifty odd years. If I had to name just one 'best mate' it would be him. We can be viciously obscene to each other, we can be truthful and then forget about it, even if one doesn't like what the other said. I can ask his advice and feel if there was a time of need, I can call. Plus, we can still laugh out long and loud about the most stupid of things and I always end up regretting the morning after, after accepting one drink too many when we occasionally meet up. It'll be the death of us one day. I alluded to the sex, drugs and rock n' roll stories earlier in this book. Larry has one of the keys to this safe. He may have conveniently lost it, the key as well. Bless ya mate.

Huge thanks to PJ Crook for the art and the consent to use, you are blessed with kindness and a God given talent. I have also added, where known, credited no less, who took the picture in the colour plate section, and I thank you immensely. For those I am missing, I apologise. Lost to time, my lack of memory and my poor booking keeping.

Thanks to many others involved in getting this book to print. Geoff Tristram for his invaluable advice. Nick Redfern for his razor-sharp proofreading. Dom at 4edge printers. Then there's Michaela Cutler, with no musical link at all to my story. For a brief period, she was my secretary back in the eighties and has often hinted, many times, "Am I mentioned?", so for that reason and that reason alone she appears here. A most efficient employee indeed and this request being a very fine example of that persistence does reap benefits, just like in the music business.

This now completes 'Sky Trails and Pie Tales', but I've said it many times none of this would have been possible without you, for the love and the support along the way, giving the music the immortality it deserves. I thank you. Give yourselves a round of applause.

Thanks, Trev . . .

London – August 2022

Sky Trails & Pie Tales . . .